"Edmund White, a master of the erotic confession, is our most accomplished triathlete of prose—a novelist, biographer, *and* memoirist. Truly, no other American writer of my generation manages to be all three with such personal passion and veracity.

The fiercely defiant *A Boy's Own Story* remains the coming-of-age novel that has the deepest resonance for me—notwithstanding that it's about a gay boy coming of age, and I'm straight. (No one who honestly remembers being a sensitive young man can fail to identify with the universal longing, or the frustration and the anger, underlying this semiautobiographical novel.) And White's recent biography of the mercurial and much misunderstood Rimbaud is fittingly devastating and succinct—'fittingly,' because the outcast poet's life was tragic and brief. Now comes a bold, penetrating companion to White's *My Lives*—an earlier, bittersweet memoir.

In *City Boy*, the memoirist examines his life in New York in the 1960s and '70s; not only were these vital years for White's own gay liberation, but *City Boy* is also the story of White's literary emergence—his struggles and ambitions as a writer. There is the bracing sexual candor and explicitness White is justly famous for; as he says, 'What we desire is crucial to who we are.' But what is most unforgettable are the piercing self-portraits of the young writer who describes himself as 'desperate for recognition,' and the overwhelming panoply of older, often legendary writers White meets along the way. ('I longed for literary celebrity even as I saw with my own eyes how little happiness it brought.')

This splendid book is at once fascinating social history and sublimely detailed gossip. Young gay readers who don't know what it was like to be gay in New York in the '60s and '70s should devour it; those straight readers who are somehow still unfriendly to homosexuality must open their eyes and read every word of *City Boy*, too. As for those of us, gay and straight, who have long admired Edmund White, this memoir is a wise and humane treatise on the delicate differences between love and friendship—indeed, between lovers and friends. Most deservedly, White has had his share of both, and he writes about them with an irreproachable kindness and affection."

—John Irving

# City Boy

*Forgetting Elena: A Novel*
*The Joy of Gay Sex* (coauthored)
*Nocturnes for the King of Naples: A Novel*
*States of Desire: Travels in Gay America*
*A Boy's Own Story: A Novel*
*The Beautiful Room Is Empty: A Novel*
*Caracole: A Novel*
*The Darker Proof: Stories from a Crisis*
*Genet: A Biography*
*The Burning Library: Essays*
*Our Paris: Sketches from Memory*
*Skinned Alive: Stories*
*The Farewell Symphony: A Novel*
*Marcel Proust: A Life*
*The Married Man: A Novel*
*The Flâneur: A Stroll Through the Paradoxes of Paris*
*Fanny: A Fiction*
*Arts and Letters: Essays*
*My Lives: A Memoir*
*Chaos: A Novella and Stories*
*Hotel de Dream: A New York Novel*
*Rimbaud: The Double Life of a Rebel*

# City Boy

*My Life in New York
During the 1960s and 1970s*

## Edmund White

BLOOMSBURY

LONDON · BERLIN · NEW YORK

To Claude and Ivan Nabokov

Bloomsbury Publishing Plc
36 Soho Square
London W1D 3QY

www.bloomsbury.com

Bloomsbury Publishing, London, New York and Berlin

A CIP catalogue record for this book is available from the British Library

Hardback edition ISBN 978 0 7475 9213 6
Trade paperback edition ISBN 978 1 4088 0443 8

10 9 8 7 6 5 4 3 2

Typeset by Hewer Text UK Ltd, Edinburgh
Printed in Great Britain by Clays Limited, St Ives plc

# Chapter 1

In the 1970s in New York everyone slept till noon.

It was a grungy, dangerous, bankrupt city without normal services most of the time. The garbage piled up and stank during long strikes of the sanitation workers. A major blackout led to days and days of looting. We gay guys wore whistles around our necks so we could summon help from other gay men when we were attacked on the streets by gangs living in the projects between Greenwich Village and the West Side leather bars.

The upside was that the city was inexpensive, and Manhattan, especially the part of it below Fourteenth Street, was full of young actors-singers-dancers-waiters who made enough money working their restaurant shifts three nights a week to pay for their acting lessons and their cheap rents. Unlike our hometowns back in the Midwest, where the sidewalk was rolled up at six P.M., the delis and coffee shops were open all night and the bars till four in the morning. That whole army of actor-waiters saw their restaurant jobs as just another opportunity for "scene study" ("Who am I tonight? An Austrian aristocrat who's fallen on bad times? A runaway from an incestuous family in the Tennessee Hills? A Swedish gymnast?"). No matter how big their tips were, they managed to drink them away in a bar after the restaurants closed as they talked excitedly about their art and their loves. Everyone smoked all the time, and when you French-kissed someone, it was like rubbing one ashtray against another.

New York seemed either frightening or risible to the rest of the nation. To us, however, it represented the only free port on the entire continent. Only in New York could we walk hand in hand with a member of the same sex. Only in New York could we ignore a rat galloping across our path and head out for a midnight play reading. Artists on the Lower East Side were recycling the most primitive and worthless materials—junk, really.

But there was also a mandarin New York, a place where painters and choreographers and novelists and poets strove to produce serious art of the highest order. This was an elite group of people, scattered throughout the Village and the emerging neighborhood of Chelsea and the comfortable, kicked-out Upper West Side; in this mandarinate artists and intellectuals still felt connected to the supreme artists of the past, still thought that their work would be the latest installment in a quasi-divine legacy.

I had constant daydreams of meeting Susan Sontag and Paul Goodman. I don't know why I focused on them—maybe because they were so often mentioned in the *Village Voice* and the *Partisan Review* but even by *Time*. He'd written *Growing Up Absurd*, the bible of the sixties, now largely forgotten (I never read it in any event). How could I have worshipped a man whose work I didn't know? I guess because I'd heard that he was bisexual, that he was a brilliant therapist, and that he was somehow for the young and the liberated. I read his astonishing journal, *Five Years*, published in 1966, a groundbreaking book in which he openly discussed paying men for sex and enjoying anonymous sex in the meatpacking district. Today that would seem unremarkable, perhaps, but for a husband and a father back then to be so confiding, so shameless, was unprecedented, especially since the sex passages were mixed in with remarks on culture and poetry and a hundred other subjects.

Sontag was someone I read more faithfully, especially *Against Interpretation* and even individual essays as they were published.

New York, in short, in the seventies was a junkyard with serious artistic aspirations. I remember that one of our friends, the poet Brad Gooch, wanted to introduce us to his lover, who'd become an up-and-coming Hollywood director, but Brad begged him not to tell us that he worked as a director since Hollywood had such low prestige among us. That sort of reticence would be unthinkable today in a New York that has become enslaved by wealth and glitz, but back then people still embraced Ezra Pound's motto, "Beauty is difficult."

We kept asking in 1972 and 1973 when the seventies were going to begin . . .

Then again we had to admit the sixties hadn't really begun until the Beatles came over to the States in 1964, but after that the decade took on a real, definite personality—protest movements, long hair, love, drugs, a euphoria that turned sour only toward the end of 1969. Of course for Leftists the decade began with the *Brown v. Board of Education* decision and ended with Nixon's resignation in 1974.

I suppose people hadn't really thought each decade should have its own character and be different from the others till the 1920s, although I remember in a nineteenth-century Russian novel someone remarked that a character was a typical man of the 1830s—progressive and an atheist. But at that time it seemed more a question of generations—one belonged to the generation of "superfluous men," for instance, or one was a frivolous, self-indulgent product of the Belle Époque. But certainly in the 1920s, as the idea of the modern became current, every amateur sociologist began to seek out the personality of the dawning decade.

In retrospect we could see that the 1950s had been a reactionary period in America of Eisenhower blandness, of virulent anticommunism, of the Feminine Mystique. I lived through the fifties in the Midwest when everything that was happening—the repression of homosexuality, for instance, the demonization of the Left, the giggly, soporific ordinariness of adolescence, the stone deafness to the social injustice all around us—seemed not only unobjectionable but also nonexistent. Somehow we'd all been led to think that the order of things in the fifties was "natural," eternal and unchanging. The cult books of that epoch were *The Lonely Crowd* and *The Man in the Gray Flannel Suit.*

The great triumph of the sixties was to dramatize just how arbitrary and constructed the seeming normality of the fifties had been. We rose up from our maple-wood twin beds and fell onto the great squishy, heated water bed of the sixties.

At the end of the 1970s I wrote, "There was no style for the decade, no flair, no slogans. The mistake we made was that we were all looking for something as startling as the Beatles, acid, Pop Art, hippies and radical politics. What actually set in was a painful and unexpected working out of the terms the Sixties had so blithely tossed off."

# Chapter 2

I had majored in Chinese at the University of Michigan and I'd been accepted at Harvard to do a Ph.D. in the language. But then I'd pursued a boy I was in love with, Stan, to New York instead. Stan was a junior but had been lured to New York with dreams of becoming an actor. I arrived on July 19, 1962.

I wasn't really suited for any kind of work except journalism. I'd edited the campus literary magazine at the University of Michigan and thought that somehow I could turn that experience into a job. I had no connections in New York. I had no money beyond the two hundred dollars I'd earned during the month of June delivering eggs and fruit juice in Des Plaines, a desolate suburb of Chicago. On July 19, Stan's birthday, I decided I had to fly to New York to join him. My sister and mother always later claimed that I'd flown to New York first-class, but that was just more family mythmaking.

I stayed at the Sixty-third Street YMCA, which in those days was pretty much a fairy palace, full of transient and permanent gay residents. It was (and is) a mock-Moorish fantasy of tile work and low ceilings, as well as a giant swimming pool where Tennessee Williams was often sighted. The residential floors were really like a giant sauna. Every time I'd emerge from my room to take a shower, even if it was at two A.M. on a stifling night, a grizzled, potbellied resident would come hobbling out and be standing within seconds under the adjoining spray, soaping himself up and staring at me fixedly, as if the secret to success in cruising were simply transmitting a strong enough signal, the more blatant the better.

Stan wasn't especially happy to see me. The night I arrived, his birthday, I sat on his doorstep till dawn but he never came home. The next night he met me, but somewhat reluctantly. He was living with two other actors, one of them a hot older man of thirty named Paul Giovanni, who was playing The Boy in the original production of *The Fantasticks*, which became the longest-running musical in off-Broadway history. Stan was besotted with the cool, ironic Paul, but he did let me take him out to a gay restaurant. Of course I knew about gay bars, but the idea that gays might want to socialize and feed with one another—and in public!—seemed a fascinating new possibility. Gay liberation would not take off until 1969, but when it did, it seemed to be the final piece to a puzzle that we'd all been toying with for five or six years and slowly assembling. Maybe because visible gays were becoming more and more numerous, we were finally reaching a critical density.

Throngs of gay men were in the streets of the West Village (and a few women were visible at bars such as Kookie's and later the Duchess on Sheridan Square). The unisex look of the sixties, though it didn't represent a serious change in attitudes, nevertheless made it easier to sneak in a dangling bracelet on a man's wrist or a big turquoise brooch on a striped red velvet vest (it wasn't an era known for its good taste). During the fifties it had been illegal in many communities for a woman to wear more than two items of male clothing—jeans, sweatshirt, and a cowboy belt could get a woman arrested; now they could wear T-shirts or boots if they wanted. Though interracial marriage was still illegal in many states, the Village was full of mixed couples (mostly "Negro" men, as we said then, and white "chicks"). Even the idea of a hippie counterculture—of a counter-anything—gave us an exciting new model of contemporary dissonance.

Two months later, in September 1962, Stan agreed to live with me in the little, dingy apartment I'd rented on MacDougal Street, and we stayed together for the next five years. He'd overstayed his welcome with Paul, but he'd decided not to go back to Michigan for his senior year. He wanted to try his luck as an actor. In that era, before there was any degree of widespread gay self-acceptance, it was extremely rare to find a gay couple who lived together openly as lovers, who'd acknowledged their homosexuality to their parents and friends and colleagues, who had a sense that they constituted a real romantic pair capable of being faithful to one another or if not sexually exclusive at least committed in some sense for the long haul.

I knew just three gay couples, all former students from the University of Michigan who'd moved to the big city and were trying on for size the novel experiment of living as a gay pair. I didn't know—or even know of—any older gay couples. Stan and I took our "affair" so lightly that we had no idea of fidelity, though we didn't discuss the rules of our relationship. We had no idea of growing old together. We never spoke to outsiders of our "partner" (the term didn't exist then). Another gay friend might ask, "Are you and Stan lovers?" to which I'd respond, "Sort of." It was all pretty murky, even to us. We seldom had sex with each other—and often it happened in the middle of the night, one of us wordlessly awakening the other out of need. Because we were gay, we routinely referred to ourselves as "sick," which was only half a joke. We both saw shrinks, off and on.

Even our infidelities were comical. Tom Eyen, a young but already well-known playwright, picked me up one night (eventually Tom wrote *Dreamgirls*). After we had sex, he said, "You have the same carry-on in bed as this other guy I fucked yesterday—Stan.

His name was Stan." I couldn't wait to get home to tease Stanley, and I wondered privately what our shared "carry-on" might consist of.

Of course we were still so young that our parents and fellow workers might think we were just roommates. Lots of people our age had roommates, in fact most of them, though it wasn't that way elsewhere. (When I later moved to Rome in 1970, the only translation for *roommate* was *il ragazzo con cui divido l'appartamento*). Most of our gay friends were careful to maintain separate bedrooms, although Stan and I slept on a foldout couch that made into a double bed. We didn't have many visitors, though Stan would sometimes rehearse in our tiny living room with other actors from his class. If anyone asked, he said he slept on the single bed in the spare room.

We eventually discovered that we weren't really compatible sexually. But I truly loved Stan. At first because he was so beautiful and I was an idolator of beauty. I didn't like the way I looked and I was proud to be seen with him. Nor was my admiration of his looks a subjective thing; his beauty was classic and "famous," or at least generally acknowledged. Two straight male friends of his fell for him; for both he was their only gay experiment. Once one of the best-known dress designers in America stopped Stan on the street and offered to take him to Egypt on a holiday. The man wanted to hand him a plane ticket on the spot. He and Stan hadn't exchanged a word; for the designer it was "impulse buying."

But I loved Stan not just as a trophy but because I really cared for him. He was studious and hardworking. At first when he wanted to be an actor, he took acting classes at the Herbert Berghof studio. Then he went back to school and got a master's degree in English. He enrolled in a course in Henry James from the great James biographer Leon Edel. I paid the rent and I enjoyed having this slight hold over Stan. He needed me, at least for shelter. Of course he was also attached to me but was terribly moody and given to deep depressions.

I had found my first job at Time-Life Books on the thirty-second floor of the Time-Life Building on Sixth Avenue and Fiftieth Street. Every day I'd put on a coat and tie and head uptown from our Village apartment, usually in a taxi I could ill afford. Officially we worked from ten to six but I could never get in until eleven and I kept expecting to be reprimanded or even fired, but nothing ever happened. In fact we had little work, and a whole week's worth could be dashed off during a panicky Friday afternoon. Our weekly assignment might be to write four picture captions of two lines each, a trivial workload that seemed momentous only because we had so much time to think about it. The editors above us always demanded rewrites since they, too, were underemployed.

I spent the whole day wasting time. A two-hour lunch. Endless coffee breaks with other writers and researchers. A weird man who came by to shine our shoes once told me that for two hundred dollars he could have anyone I wanted bumped off. At noon I'd pay a visit to an art gallery on Fifty-seventh Street or to the Museum of Modern Art around the corner. In those years I saw the first Pop Art works at the Sidney Janis Gallery—a ghostly life-size plaster man by George Segal standing on a ladder changing the letters on a movie marquee, or Roy Lichtenstein's benday-dot comic-strip panels ("Oh, Brad"). Or I'd go to the Gotham Book Mart down on Forty-seventh, where I'd slump to the floor and read the books that were too expensive for me to buy.

The Gotham was the ideal bookstore with dozens of literary magazines stacked on the counter up close to the front door beside the cash register and, halfway back on the right, a big table full of the newest books of poetry. On the walls were pictures of all the greats who'd read at the Gotham, including Marianne Moore and Cocteau and Dylan Thomas, some of them perched high up on a library ladder, posing above the elegant Frances Steloff (who died at 101 in 1989). Although she sold the "shop," as she called it, to Andreas Brown in 1967, she was always prowling around, sometimes urging customers to buy. She liked Oriental religions in a slightly creepy "period" way that went along with table-tapping and ectoplasmic photos, and an extensive section on Krishnamurti and the *Bhagavad Gita* was in an alcove just beyond the poetry table. Steloff, from a poor family, was self-educated. On her own, she'd turned the Gotham into a major intellectual center. I'm sure plenty of famous writers were lurking about during the hours and hours I spent there, but I didn't recognize them. Of course when you're an uninitiated kid, you're not likely to recognize literary celebrities on the hoof. You're like the Yale undergrad who (according to an anecdote of the period) saw Auden aboard the club car of the train to New Haven and passed him a note via the waiter asking, "Are you Robert Frost?" Auden wrote back, "You've spoiled Mother's day."

The Gotham was one of the great bookstores of my life. At the very rear of the store was a huge fiction department, where I would dip into dozens of books. It was there that I bought Robert Stone's *Hall of Mirrors* and Joyce Carol Oates's *them* and Pynchon's *V.*, though of all my Gotham finds my favorite was Hugh Kenner's *The Pound Era*. The store was an oasis from the philistine world all around it. To be sure, there were other great bookstores in those days, especially the Eighth Street down in the Village, with its many floors and its sullen, unhelpful clerks. By the end of the 1970s there was the Three Lives bookstore, then on Sheridan Square.

I remember one afternoon as I browsed at the back of the Gotham hearing Andy Brown talking on the phone with someone I figured out must be a rather desperate Jack Kerouac, who wanted to sell an old manuscript to finance his move to Florida with his mother (Kerouac died in 1969 in St. Petersburg). I didn't really hear what sort of deal they struck, if any, but I suppose what was most exciting was the idea that literature was still alive, that it was going on all around me, and that some of the legendary figures I'd read about (and even read) were still alive and struggling. Kerouac, for instance, was a sad drunk, which a later biography corroborated but which Andy's patient tone already half suggested, talking to Kerouac as if he were a child incapable of understanding.

This idea that literature was somewhere nearby made it only more tantalizingly distant. I remember thinking how strange it was that all the writers of the past seemed to know each other but that "we" didn't. I supposed that the writers of the future were already living and working in New York, but where to find them?

I felt professionally isolated—worse, becalmed. Nothing is more tedious than working in a big corporation. We had such a narrow range of activity and our tasks were so silly and infantile that we felt degraded.

Part of my isolation, no doubt, was due to my being attracted only to men my own age or younger. I wasn't meeting older people who were accomplishing things. At Time-Life Books there was only one exception, an editor, Ezra Bowen, a tough guy with rolled-up sleeves, a wiry frame, and a punched-in nose who kept a photo on the wall of a father lion licking his cubs. Ezra was the son of Catherine Drinker Bowen, the celebrated biographer (Tchaikovsky, John Adams, Ben Franklin), and he had literary— well, not ambitions but rather manners. He'd been married to a novelist, Joan Williams, who before that had been one of Faulkner's personal favorites, his protégée. When they'd met, Faulkner was in his fifties and already a Nobel Prize winner and Joan Williams was just a redheaded college girl from Memphis. They were briefly lovers and even collaborated on a play, but she'd ended their affair because he wasn't free to marry her (he already had a wife) and he was thirty-some years older. By the time she married Ezra Bowen in the early fifties, Faulkner was in love with the even younger (and more receptive) Jean Stein, but he remained friendly with Joan Williams and wrote her hundreds of letters. She and Ezra had two sons and divorced in 1970. She fictionalized her relationship with Faulkner in a novel called *The Wintering*. People around the office said that Ezra had taken a year off from Time-Life to write his own novel, but had wasted the time constructing a study for himself in a shed in the garden—and that Joan, saddled with the children, the housework, and a part-time job, had turned out a successful novel in the same period. She wrote five highly regarded novels in all, and Ezra only did a few Time-Life books on such things as skiing, Native Americans, the wheel.

I was afraid of ending up like Ezra. I forced myself to write plays and novels during the evenings after work—anything creative as a break from the torpor of an imagination-killing office job.

# Chapter 3

I was making four hundred dollars a month. Stan's and my apartment cost just a hundred. It was on MacDougal between Bleecker and Houston, in the heart of the old Greenwich Village, right around the corner from the Little Red School House, a bastion of progressive education, and directly across the street from Bob Dylan's apartment, though I never once glimpsed him and didn't quite see the fuss over a man whose singing sounded whiny to me. On the corner was the San Remo, which had until recently been a famous gay bar but was now straight. Here, in the men's toilet, Terry Southern in his novel *Candy* had set an abortion scene. Frank O'Hara, the New York poet, had hung out there. I pictured thin gay men in Brooks Brothers suits, smoking, drinking martinis, their pale faces covered with light hangover sweat, their teeth brown from cigarettes, their bluish white hands shaking.

There was also a coffee shop across MacDougal called the Hip Bagel. *Hip* was for a while crossed out, then later reinstated, as the word itself was condemned for being square, then rescued through a second degree of irony. It had black walls and individual spotlights trained down on booths. In a back booth on the left I would sometimes drink espresso with an oversize girl who swore she was going to be a famous pop singer someday. I'd never heard of a fat singer off the grand opera stage, so I just nodded politely, though I was impressed to hear that she'd already appeared in *The Music Man*. A few years later she emerged as Mama Cass in the Mamas and the Papas, which meant little to me since except for the times it would provide the sound track for my romances I didn't care for pop. By now I've loosened up a little more and have over the years learned, through repetition perhaps, to appreciate and even enjoy some of the popular music boyfriends have pressed upon me or played for me.

Another place where I'd sit and nurse a beer was the Bleecker Street Tavern, a barny old bar with many tables and few customers and a kindly waitress with a man's face and dyed hair. Little did I know that this had been the first gay bar in New York, the Slide; in the nineteenth century all these tables had been crowded with transvestite prostitutes in crinolines and their top-hatted customers. In the basement were little rooms where the whores had taken their johns, and though the rooms are still there the place is now a heavy-metal hangout called Kenny's Castaways.

The beatnik/hippie revolution was swirling all around me. After work I'd take the subway down and get off at the West Fourth Street stop and walk to our tiny, dirty, roach-trap apartment on MacDougal. On a warm evening my street was so crowded with kids with long hair and burgundy velvet jeans and mirrored vests and filmy shirts with puffy pirate sleeves that few cars would venture down it. It was still an old Italian neighborhood with little cheap pasta joints down two or three steps from street level (Monte's was our favorite), cafés serving espresso such as the Caffè Reggio, and funeral homes with alabaster urns lit from within by electric bulbs, the stained-glass windows shrouded by closed beige curtains that were never opened. Our neighbors were Italian and spoke to each other every morning in, I guess, a Neapolitan dialect. Out our scrap of back window we could see old Italian wives cranking laundry across the air shaft on pulley-operated lines. We were far from our Midwestern suburban roots. Over that bedrock of the Italian Village was scattered the more recent topsoil of stores offering hookahs and shabby finery and light boxes and paintings that one could make oneself by splashing acrylics on a revolving potter's wheel—the centrifugal force threw the shiny colors out in crazed patterns. The smell of incense and patchouli filled the air.

As I came home in my suit and tie, weaving my way through the motley throngs, skinny kids in fringed leather coats would growl at me, "Go back to the suburbs." Which made me indignant, since I knew they were probably living with their parents in the suburbs and had to sneak out of the house with a paper bag full of their trendy new clothes. They'd change in the back of an unlit bus, leave behind their bourgeois togs in a bus station locker, and traipse down to the Village in their beads and bangles. They were the "plastic hippies," not I!

Through Raymond Sokolov, one of my high school friends, I did some freelance reviewing for *Newsweek*, which would have landed me in trouble at Time-Life if anyone had noticed. I reviewed Malraux's *Anti-Memoirs* (published in 1967 in America) and Solzhenitsyn's *The First Circle* (1968) and disliked them both. Malraux was obviously a fake, a bore, and a liar, though Americans were still impressed with his name and *Man's Fate* was still considered a "classic," much like that other Communist classic, Mikhail Sholokhov's *And Quiet Flows the Don*—which won its author the Nobel Prize in 1965 though most critics now believe it was largely plagiarized and written by a committee.

*The First Circle*, though a novel that protested Stalin's regime, seemed to me proof of the sad consequences of Soviet censorship, since it could easily have been written in the nineteenth century. I told my editor at *Newsweek* that the publication of the book should serve as the pretext for a cover story on the samizdat press (clandestine self-published manuscripts that had been censored by the Soviet state), but my advice was ignored and every other publication in the States declared the book a masterpiece. One wonders how many people read either book today. I wasn't given any more books since my reviews put me out of step with everyone else in the country.

I went on to review a few books for the *New Republic*, but those pieces, too, were mostly nasty—and in 1978 I wrote a negative if respectful review of Edward Said's *Orientalism*, one of the most influential books of our day. I suppose I was so underpublished and resentful in those days that it was hard for me to write a positive review of anything by anyone. Said, unfortunately, remembered my bad review, and it took years for me to repair the damage, which I very much wanted to do because upon reflection I came to admire him so much. In the end, in the early 1990s we became friends and continued to be so until he died.

I suppose that just as art was still meant to be difficult at the beginning of the sixties and only gradually became just another form of mass entertainment through the high jinks of Pop Art, in the same way politics were austere and Marxist in 1960 but had become "fun" by 1970, turning into the psychodrama of the New Left.

In fact, everything in the America I knew after 1965 was warming up, becoming more subjective and democratic and amusing and accessible. Although in my own way I, too, was moving toward the personal through my writing, I was never entirely convinced it was the right way. I still idolized difficult modernist poets such as Ezra Pound and Wallace Stevens, and I listened with solemn but uncomprehending seriousness to the music of Schoenberg. Later I would learn to pick and choose my idiosyncratic way through the ranks of canonical writers, composers, artists, and filmmakers, but in my twenties I still had an unquestioning admiration for the Great—who were Great precisely because they were Great. Only later would I begin to see the selling of high art as just one more form of commercialism. In my twenties if even a tenth reading of Mallarmé failed to yield up its treasures, the fault was mine, not his. If my eyes swooned shut while I read *The Sweet Cheat Gone*, Proust's pacing was never called into question, just my intelligence and dedication and sensitivity. And I still entertain these sacralizing preconceptions about high art. I still admire what is difficult, though now I recognize it's a "period" taste and that my generation was the last to give a damn. Though we were atheists, we were, strangely enough, preparing ourselves for God's great Quiz Show; we had to know everything because we were convinced we would be tested on it—in our next life.

In the late sixties I was a living contradiction. I was still a self-hating gay man going to a straight psychotherapist with the intention of being cured and getting married. I had an almost Catholic awe before the whole institution of marriage, which I mocked at the same time. My parents were both Texans, and in one small corner of my mind I silently objected to the way Yankee intellectuals dismissed all Southerners as rednecks. Most of my new friends in New York scoffed at Lyndon Johnson because of his accent, ignoring the value of his Great Society reforms. At Time-Life I would read through Johnson's off-the-record remarks to journalists in the presidential plane; he'd talk about "niggers" but at the same time he was determined to help black Americans get a good education. Because he used the N-word I believed him.

I was a nerd and an egghead but I was also going three times a week to the Sheridan Square gym and building up my body. I'd never liked sports and I'd been bad at them in school, but now I was spending hours every week pumping iron. When other men stared at my newly muscular body with lust, I could scarcely breathe. Their attention frightened me, though I sought it.

As a socialist I longed for the Revolution, but in the meantime I held on to my nine-to-five (or eleven-to-six) office job. And felt bad about it. We "socialists" were so naïve that we thought no one with progressive politics should drive an expensive car or live in a big house; if he did, we accused him of hypocrisy, not realizing that an individual's personal wealth has no relevance to his politics once he's freed himself of self-serving arguments. At the same time, ironically, we were so uniformly and unconsciously sexist that we saw nothing strange in that all writers at Time-Life were male and all researchers female.

One day a top editor, a real New England patrician named Maitland Edey, overheard me and my researcher—and great friend to this day—Sigrid talking about feminism. Edey was genuinely curious about what rights women might still be demanding, and he invited Sigrid and me to a pleasant lunch at the top of the Time-Life Building in a private dining room. Faced with this kindly but starchy and highly skeptical aristocrat, we couldn't come up with much. I'm sure he was disappointed by our fuzzy, halfhearted observations and was probably convinced by the end of the meal that this new, only half-formulated version of feminism was nothing but empty complaint.

I thought I wanted to be a serious novelist but I consecrated my days to journalism (for some reason I could never use my empty hours of time on the job for my own writing). My nights I gave to playwriting. I'd go out for dinner and then come back to the office and write plays until ten or eleven before heading home. I had written a play at the University of Michigan that had won a prize and was eventually staged in New York, where it received mixed reviews and closed after a month. It was about angry black servants in a white household and was out of step with the conciliatory civil rights era. The content may have been ahead of the times, but the style was passé, since it was inspired by Ionesco's theater of the absurd and the baroque, menacing mockery of Genet's *The Blacks*.

Now that I had an agent and *The Blue Boy in Black* had had a production, I felt I must go on writing plays. I knew almost no one in the theater aside from the actors who'd starred in my play, Cicely Tyson and Billy Dee Williams. And I scarcely knew them; not till years after the fact did I read Cicely had married Miles Davis. She was totally mysterious as a person—I didn't even know where she'd been born or if she had a boyfriend.

I read the "News of the Rialto," about showbiz, every day faithfully in the *New York Post*. I immersed myself in the gossip-column tittle-tattle of who might be replacing whom in a certain production and whether the new Murray Schisgal comedy might or might not be in trouble on the road.

In those days, before Xerox copiers, faxes, and computers, the chief problem facing a poor playwright was making copies of his work. I swore that if ever I became rich I'd endow a free script-copying foundation for the indigent young. Sometimes I would compose plays directly onto mimeographing stencils. I'd make my agent, Sylvia Herscher at William Morris, read my scripts off the stencils. If she didn't like them, I wouldn't waste the money having copies run off.

She never liked my plays after that first one, which she'd ushered onto off-Broadway. She disliked *Mrs. Morrigan*, my play about a divorced woman slowly going crazy who turns into what used to be called a nymphomaniac. Much of the play was devoted to my protagonist's anguished exchanges with the grotesque imaginary figures who haunted and hectored her. Nor did Sylvia like my ritualistic play about a violent, incestuous family who sacrifice one of their own members to appease a dark god or exorcise the curse of some ancient tribal crime (I can't really remember the plot). I rewrote that play several times, but Sylvia remained unconvinced. Nor did she like my comedy of manners *Madame Steiner*, nor my gender-switching one-act *Trios*, which I would eventually present in a staged reading to a few friends, who were polite. I had a weeklong affair on Fire Island with Mart Crowley, who'd just written the hilarious *Boys in the Band*. I made him read *Trios*; when he finished it, he looked up and asked, "Is this supposed to be funny?"

It never occurred to me to seek out a new agent, even though Sylvia was actually more famous for the musicals she worked on for fifty years as producer, publisher, and agent. Nor did I think I should give my plays to one of the casual little cabarets springing up off-off-Broadway, despite the fact that my lover, Stan, sometimes performed at the Caffè Cino. The owner, Joe Cino, would stand at the back of the theater manning the rumbling, hissing espresso machine while a drag queen emoted about the horrors of aging in Lanford Wilson's *Madness of Lady Bright*. The stage was just eight feet by eight feet and there were fewer than twenty tables, most of them empty. A hat was passed by the actors at the end of each performance. I remember seeing Warhol actress Mary Woronov cracking a whip onstage and growling sadistic curses. I remember an incestuous brother and sister calling mournfully for each other in *Home Free!*—another Wilson one-act. Leonard Melfi, a scruffy heterosexual who sweated and shook and laughed painfully while making constant frightening little jokes about his funny looks, wrote cabaret comedies until he was whisked away by the producer Carlo Ponti to Rome, where he wrote the one-page idea for *Mortadella*, a vehicle for Sophia Loren. In the movie Loren tries to smuggle a huge Italian sausage through American customs.

In 1970, when I met Carlo Ponti, who was Loren's husband, he pushed my hundred-page film script aside and asked why I couldn't be brief and to the point like the great Melfi. He didn't like my scenario because it satirized Italian men. Americans like me were so used to self-satire in the style of Mort Sahl and Elaine May and Mike Nichols that it astonished me when smaller, prouder nations didn't welcome satire at all, especially if written by foreigners. A comedy was fine, such as *Divorce, Italian Style*, but a satire about Italy by an American was most unwelcome.

# Chapter 4

I admired a theater director called Joe Chaikin and would attend the rehearsals of his company, though not often. I did nothing often. As though I knew how compulsive I could be, I was almost afraid of developing habits. And as a writer I defended myself against—and this will sound even crazier—immersing myself in my own period.

I suppose my reasoning went something like this: A writer must be eternal and universal; if he falls prey to the fads and fancies of his own period, he'll disappear when his epoch ends. Therefore he should discreetly sample it but make all the great writers and thinkers of the past and of every culture his true contemporaries. I belonged to no clubs and could not be labeled with any sticker except *gay* and *WASP*. Still, at that time *gay* was a secret designation and *WASP* was so general as to be meaningless. Only later did Jewish comedians make the idea of a WASP (and a Jew) funny.

I felt I had this admirable surfeit of negative capability precisely because I wasn't a Harvard man or an aristocrat. I had no visible markings. I considered myself lucky to be invisible. I was a free agent. No one owned my soul. If anyone asked, I'd say that a Midwestern intellectual had nothing glib about him. It didn't occur to him that he could social-climb through making references to Flaubert or Baudelaire. If an Ohioan read *Flowers of Evil*, I argued, he did so because he liked the poetry. No one back home would ever be impressed by his knowledge of any topic, especially not a cultural one—which he'd do well to conceal if he didn't want to be considered a ridiculous egghead. Does anyone think this way now? In the age of the Internet, of fifteen-minute fame and above all such local fame ("I'm famous to the fifteen people who read my blog"), in a time when cultural space is so segmented and time so speeded up, does it still make sense to worry over how to construct a lasting reputation? Will any reputations last?

I took fiction so seriously (which I thought of as art) that I wanted my prose to be un-American, not of any era, unidentifiable because it was original. Of course I didn't do much to realize these preposterous ambitions. I was too busy writing unproduceable plays and meeting new people and killing time at work.

Joe Chaikin had a lover, the playwright Jean-Claude van Itallie, but apparently Joe and I had a brief affair. At least in the early 1990s, when I was writing a biography of Jean Genet and asked the librarian at Kent State for copies of Jean Genet's letters, the librarian wrote back, "Perhaps you'd also like copies of your own love letters to Joe Chaikin." I couldn't recall ever having been in love with Joe. I can picture only one hot summer night with him in his little apartment, his body covered with curly hairs, his face and back lightly filmed in sweat. There was something unhealthy about him, I thought—and soon enough he had to have open-heart surgery, which left him partially paralyzed and unable to speak normally. He incorporated that disability into his work; earlier for no apparent personal reasons he had learned sign language and worked with the deaf on the stage. He had a great sweetness and intelligence about him—an intelligence of the senses and of the instincts.

I thought he should stage my play *Mrs. Morrigan*, but he was far more attracted to plays he and his company would piece together during months and months of improvisation, though the final text might be set down and polished and shaped by van Itallie. *America Hurrah*, a trilogy of plays produced in 1966, was a watershed anti–Vietnam War protest, one with expressionist elements (puppets designed by Robert Wilson) and dialogue that sometimes sounded like Beckett and sometimes like Ionesco. Chaikin directed only one of the three plays. Another play that van Itallie developed with Chaikin was *The Serpent*, performed in 1969, which toured all over the world in the following years.

Chaikin had worked out a kind of theater that would suddenly lurch without transition into enactments of repressed feelings. A man picking up his dry cleaning would suddenly click into a slow-motion rapturous embrace with the woman working in the shop.

One of the participants in the Open Theater, as the troupe was called, was an actor who in those days had a caveman virility and a brooding, almost scary presence—Gerome Ragni. He had been a member of the Open Theater since its founding in 1962 and starred in its production of Megan Terry's 1966 play, *Viet Rock*, perhaps the first theater event to protest the war in Vietnam. Ragni then went on to write the words and lyrics for *Hair*, which also used Chaikin's stage techniques. Later, after the success of *Hair*, Ragni lost his manly good looks and became a sort of clown, with a white man's Afro and gaudy, flowing tie-dyed clothes. He was always stoned and talking and baring his teeth. His script for his next musical, the short-lived *Dude*, was originally two thousand pages long. His apartment had a narrow, plush birth canal as its entryway. Everyone laughed at him.

Joe, too, was swept up in the Vietnam protest movement. He told me that he'd never do anything ever again in the theater that wasn't in opposition to the war. I didn't care about the war. During my army physical I'd checked the box saying I had homosexual tendencies, which got me out of having to serve. Some people frowned on me, as if I were deliberately avoiding my patriotic duty, but I argued that to have lied in answering the questionnaire would have been illegal. I was being honest—and honesty in this case saved my life. Of course most of the men I knew personally never went to Vietnam; they stayed in grad school for years and years getting academic deferments. Or they fled the country to Canada. Or they checked the box.

Not that concepts like "patriotism" meant anything to me. As a gay man I didn't think that I was American or that I belonged to a society worth defending. Of course I wouldn't have said such a thing out loud; I didn't want to sound disgruntled. But truthfully I felt powerless to affect national policy, and I also knew that any policy that might be devised by any government present or future would contain a clause condemning me as a homosexual. There was no "gay pride" back then—there was only gay fear and gay isolation and gay distrust and gay self-hatred.

I didn't even feel part of "homosexual society"—we didn't think like that back then. The term would have made us laugh: "Homosexual society? My dear, I'm not even a queer deb." I didn't follow politics nor did I ever vote in elections. Kennedy's death saddened me but less so than Marilyn Monroe's. Stan went to Washington and marched with Martin Luther King, but I didn't. I can still picture Stan in his short-sleeved white shirt, carefully pressed, and his pegged black pants as he headed off for Washington in a bus. I never gave a penny to any political cause—or wrote a word on behalf of any movement.

If I'd thought about it, I might have said I was too "radical" to vote or that "revolutionaries" like me saw no need to reinforce the "system" by participating in it. I'd learned to talk that way at the University of Michigan, where my friends and classmates Tom Hayden (later married to Jane Fonda) and Carl Oglesby had written the *Port Huron Statement* and had been among the first members of the Students for a Democratic Society. This was the beginning of the New Left. In the *Port Huron Statement*, which was completed on June 15, 1962, the Vietnam War was still so minor that it rated only a brief mention. The rights of Negroes were the primary concern. No thought was given to women. "Man" and his future were endlessly discussed. Nevertheless, it was a sensible and inspirational document, though of course from the perspective of the early twenty-first century it appears naïve. For instance, it calls for the United States to help third-world countries to industrialize; ecological worries are never voiced. Competition in the economy must be replaced by cooperation. The Cold War must give way to nuclear disarmament; the Bomb weighed on everyone's mind.

Though I knew how to talk the Leftist talk, those high-flown demurrals would have been dishonest. I wasn't a dissenter; no, I was disaffected. When I was fourteen, a plainclothes cop had entrapped me at the urinal of a movie theater and threatened to arrest me. At last he'd let me go, but I had grasped the lesson—gay desire was illegal. The most fundamental thing about me—my desire to sleep with other males—was loathsome to society, even to other gay men, as much as pedophilia would be today. Many of the gay men I picked up made it clear that what we were doing was dangerous. If I could have stopped my "acting out," as my various psychiatrists called it, I would have.

I was an individualist in the sense that I responded in no way to the appeal of clannishness. I didn't belong to a clan. I didn't know any published novelists except one friend at my office, George Constable, who brought out three novels in the sixties. I had a few college friends in New York, but we'd gone to the University of Michigan, a huge state school that didn't instill the same pride or command the same loyalty as Harvard or Yale or Princeton. I was a Midwesterner living in New York, but even in Ohio and Illinois my parents had been displaced Texans. My mother made spicy Tex-Mex food that was distasteful to the few kids from school I invited home. I had no regional allegiances. I had friends now at work but all but one of them were straight and would have felt intensely ill at ease or even repulsed had I discussed with them my sexuality. My one gay friend at work was in the closet. Two or three of the girls at Time-Life might have guessed I was gay, but that recognition was never articulated and would have called for no possible response beyond melancholy compassion for my "sad" affliction.

Perhaps if I'd gone to Harvard or Princeton (I'd been accepted to both) I'd have benefited from those connections after graduation. As it was, I had no contacts with the rich or even the prosperous or the influential in New York. I'd obtained my job with no help from anyone. My parents, now that I'd graduated, never gave me a penny. I loved New York, but not because it had showered its favors on me. The people I worked with were all Ivy Leaguers, but I seldom hung out with them after work.

I didn't feel an affiliation with anyone. I had a few friends but I don't think at that age I'd yet learned what friendship was, what it would eventually come to mean to me. I knew how to be interested in the people around me and how to say warm things that would attach them to me, and I was so grateful to anyone who seemed to like me that I would pursue him or her tirelessly. But that was exactly the problem. I hadn't stopped to wonder what was in it for me. Perhaps my self-esteem was so low that I was mainly eager to placate people, to amass allies in what I perceived to be a hostile world. I had a character that anticipated disaster, and with that eventuality in mind I was accumulating friends. For me friendship was nothing but an entente cordiale; I didn't know how to confide. I never shared my doubts with anyone. I'd mastered a fetching way of confessing shocking, colorful details of my life to the initiated, but I never mentioned to anyone any of my serious doubts or fears or hopes. Nor any of my ideas, which I knew would bore them; as a result, those ideas remained half-formed because never articulated. Maybe because I spent my forties and fifties in Paris, I later came to embrace the importance of the "milieu." I could see that our American brand of Romantic individualism didn't really amount to much; one was only as good as one's circle, and a superior, stimulating milieu could raise the general level of conversation, of sophistication, even of moral discrimination and esthetic refinement, certainly of ambition and accomplishment.

In my twenties and thirties, before I left New York for Paris, I might have confided in friends if I'd have thought that would make them like me more, but I was so cynical that I assumed everyone around me was entirely self-absorbed. I'd deflect a question with a question of my own. Like a girl who's been to a Southern charm school, I knew that one could always count on the other person's inexhaustible egotism and that no one had any possible motive for unmasking a flatterer. One of my favorite writers of the time was the eighteenth-century cynic Lord Chesterfield, who in his letters to his illegitimate son taught him the amoral arts of the courtier (how to curry favor, how to coerce others to yield up their secrets while remaining discreet oneself, how to make oneself amusing and indispensable to the powerful). I remember one particularly repulsive passage in which Chesterfield's poor witless illegitimate son is counseled to endear himself to a French hostess by stamping his foot prettily and insisting that some onerous task is his duty and his alone and that he refuses to share it with any of her other *cavaliers servants*. Chesterfield thought this kind of pretend petulance was particularly charming and attractive.

I knew several girls at work and two from Ann Arbor who'd moved to New York at the same time. Stan knew two or three girls with whom he rehearsed for the Berghof scene-study classes. Otherwise after work we lived in an entirely male world. It wasn't that we were misogynists, though we were probably a bit scared of women and felt some lingering, irrational guilt around them since we had silently, surreptitiously excluded ourselves from the ranks of their potential suitors. I didn't think of women as horny but as needy. I attributed to all women the loneliness and desperation of my divorced mother. In college I'd dated two or three girls. They were there partly for therapeutic reasons, since I hoped to go straight (slowly) and to get married (eventually), but they were also in my life because they were good bohemian women, physically generous, cozy pot-smokers, artistic—and above all tolerant.

The one woman who spanned all these years, from 1956 when I met her till now, more than half a century later, was Marilyn Schaefer, whom I've written about again and again (often under the name of Maria) from my first published story ("Goldfish and Olives" in 1962, published in *New Campus Writing*). She was six or seven years older than me, which now means nothing (she looks much younger than I do), but at the time was of some consequence. I'd met her when I was at Cranbrook, a boy's boarding school outside Detroit, Michigan. She was a painting student next door at the art academy, one of the five schools that made up the Cranbrook complex at that time.

She was so far from any of my received ideas about women that I found her to be at once disconcerting and reassuring. Unlike Marilyn, most women in the fifties devoted considerable energy and ingenuity to dramatizing gender differences. That was the era of crinolines puffing up skirts, of carefully coiffed hair, of subtle pink lipsticks and painted-on all-over Pan-Cake makeup, of tightly cinched-in waists and stupid poodle decals in felt blazoned across the front of a skirt. Women simpered and blushed and pouted; as in Orwell's discussion of working-class penny dreadfuls, they went directly from being a Honeymooner (all curves and ditsy innocence) to being Mom (prettily outraged fists planted on ample hips under a tailored skirt below a perfectly pressed blouse). From soprano to contralto. The older version of womanhood was best enacted by Lucille Ball, the mindless, eye-batting redhead, always adorably confused by the world's complexities and endlessly hatching another harebrained scheme.

Marilyn had pretty, small features and was slim and nearly flat-chested. She had a tiny wen on the lower lid of her right eye, which gave her gaze an intriguing asymmetry, as if it were an artfully placed beauty patch. She never wore makeup at all and had a well-scrubbed look, a bit like the actress Nicole Stéphane, the sister in Cocteau's (and Melville's) *Les Enfants Terribles*. Marilyn's parents were German-Americans who'd been born in the reclusive Iowa religious colony of Amana. They'd moved away from the colony when they were young soon after they were married, but they'd imparted to their children an idea of the possibility of being different from other people. Marilyn's older brother Dick had studied philosophy in Vienna, become a communist and a West Coast longshoreman before ending up a conservative, pious Catholic. Marilyn's next older brother, Carol (named after King Carol of Romania), ran the family construction business and became a gentle, cultured, kindly Midwestern businessman. Marilyn was, and remains, a militant atheist and has always been left-leaning, though eventually her activities as a feminist displaced her sympathies for the Soviet Union, Red China, and Castro's Cuba. Her younger sister became a Catholic convert who worked an office job in New York but devoted most of her spare time to absorbing the wisdom of her intellectual guru. The youngest brother lived in Chicago and was in finance.

All of the Schaefers, somewhat surprisingly, had a terrific sense of humor, dry and self-deflating. They were all devoted to their mother but had a more difficult rapport with their father, a big lovable man who'd tear up when he'd had a few schnapps, who still had a German accent though he had been born in Iowa—and who had an unfortunate habit of defending anything Germany did, including the election of Hitler as chancellor. He was what the French call a *négationiste*, someone who denies that the Holocaust took place (a crime in Europe that can result in prison time). Back in the religious colony he'd been trained as a youngster to be a carpenter. After joining "the world" he became a successful real estate developer and builder. At first a union man and progressive in politics, he soon drifted to the right.

Marilyn loved her father but found his politics infuriating and his assumption of traditional gender roles even more maddening. Old Mr. Schaefer would, no doubt, have had no idea what she was talking about, though he had learned to cool it in public with his views on the Führer. She grudgingly admired his interest in history, though she regretted he was always deep into the latest worshipful biography of Bismarck or Hindenburg. When her family went to Europe, it was to head directly for the Fatherland; even a change of planes in France or England they thought of as sullying them.

I learned (and remembered) all of this about her family because I idolized Marilyn, coaxing stories about Amana and its strange rites and regulations out of her. For instance, I knew that if a young Amana couple wanted to get married, it became a cause for regret, since the elders thought it was tragic to bring more children into the world. Accordingly, the betrothed pair were first separated for a long time to see if they would still want to persist in their folly.

Marilyn had retained none of these beliefs, but her zeal in defending her brand of socialism (and later feminism) struck me as extreme. Now she'd say that I was exaggerating the violence of her opinions of that period. Although Marilyn liked the "sophisticated" side of New York (the songs of Bobby Short and Mabel Mercer, the chic black singers at the Café Carlyle), she was less susceptible than I to the rush toward celebrity, the push to be famous in the arts that dominated New York life in that period. I was obsessed with being famous—not rich, which held no interest for me, but famous among the top echelons of the cultural elite. Marilyn found my ambition incomprehensible—and laughable. She was "down-to-earth," to use a favorite American phrase that always puzzles my European friends. I have never stopped being influenced by her sensible, de-dramatizing way of looking at the world, though by nature I am overwrought and desperate for recognition.

She was enamored of passionate Puccini arias, and she and I would listen over and over to *Manon Lescaut*. She was esepcially fond of the great passionate Swedish tenor Jussi Björling and, after seeing him at the Chicago Lyric, reported back that he was short and corseted and elderly—a real dumpling. She liked that his youthful heartrending voice didn't go with his looks at all. She was also a big fan of the Italian soprano Renata Tebaldi. In those days everyone was either for Tebaldi or Maria Callas (as so often happens, the runner-up, Tebaldi, is less often mentioned now).

In college I got it into my head that I should marry Marilyn. I felt that she'd be understanding about my struggle against homosexuality. I told her I loved her and wanted to spend the rest of my life with her. She responded with long, passionate kisses. I was thrilled and frightened, as though I was about to spoil a wonderful friendship or get myself into water far deeper than I could navigate. But then again, I thought I'd been saved. I'd been so afraid of spending the rest of my life as that frightening hippogriff, a homosexual. Now I'd been transformed into an ordinary male, and yet with Marilyn nothing would be banal or conventional. We'd be normal, a happily married couple, but we'd be artists, enraptured by our Puccini.

She drove us everywhere. I could drive, but not well—I preferred her behind the wheel. When she said she never wanted to marry, I took it with a whole box of salt; I knew about women, about their biological drive to marry and procreate. The urge was stronger than they were. Nothing could stop their need to nest and hatch. Though I must say we never spoke of children and I felt no need, not even the slightest passing twinge of desire, to have offspring, to see little Eddies and Marilyns looking up at us with trusting or resentful eyes.

I could scarcely acknowledge to anyone, not even to myself, how relieved I was to be straight. I'd so feared spending my life as a freak, of watching myself become more and more effeminate under my mop of dyed blond curls stiff from a permanent, imprisoned behind a pair of frightened, frozen eyes under painted-brown eyebrows. I'd seen swishy men in their forties and fifties working as waiters in Chicago at little gay restaurants along Rush Street, alternating between icy efficiency and campy self-dramatization, their red-and-white-checked shirt collars turned up over a red silk knotted scarf, the raised collar lightly grazing their peroxided duck's-ass hairdo.

I was so proud of my escape from this fate that I even bragged to my father that I wanted to marry Marilyn. He didn't know her, but when he discovered that she was seven years older than me, he advised me against such an unpromising union. "An older girl might look good to you now, Ed, but women don't age well. If you don't watch it, you'll be stuck with an old bag. Better to marry someone seven years younger." I was offended at his butcher's way of sizing up a side of beef. But I was amazed that after worrying himself sick over the shameful reality of my homosexuality, he didn't rejoice in any approximation of heterosexuality I might come up with. The bourgeoisie! I thought indignantly. They don't really care about the happiness of their children, only about respectability in the eyes of others.

Although Marilyn and I were planning to spend a summer together (after my junior year) in Chicago—she painting, I writing—I was so worried about the consequences of my declaration of love that I went inert. I played dead. I didn't call her. I didn't write her. She wrote me two or three letters to which I did not respond. I kept intending to write her a really long, ardent letter, but with every passing day I became more panicked and immobilized. At last she sent me a curt little note saying, "Yours is not like any love I ever heard of. Let's just skip it and be friends. Anyway, I've decided I prefer girls. I'm spending the summer with Miranda."

I felt as if I'd somehow missed a crucial beat. Girls? Miranda? I remembered there'd been a beautiful, butchy Texan by that name at Cranbrook, a rich girl from Fort Worth who laughed at all of Marilyn's jokes. But hadn't there also been a bearded Jewish painter named Jay from Brooklyn?

Three years went by, Stan and I had moved to New York, then one day I got a call from Marilyn, who was in tears. She'd just had her heart broken by a wild, fast-driving, heavy-drinking Southern girl named Megan who looked like Anthony Quinn. Marilyn was distraught—what could she do?

"Move to New York," I said. "Move in with us. We have a spare room with a little single bed."

"Really?"

"Really," I said. Stan was nodding on the couch. Later he would claim that I hadn't warned him Marilyn was bringing her cat along.

A few days later Marilyn arrived with a single suitcase, her 1911 edition of the *Encyclopaedia Britannica*, and her black cat, Booboo. We were all three very happy, three Midwesterners in the Big City. Of course Stan was moody and suffered over his acting, his future, his strange family, his insecurities. He would take an hour getting dressed to walk to the corner. He'd try on one outfit after another. "Does this blue sweater make my ass look too big?" "Should I roll up these sleeves—or are my arms too hairless?" "Is this pimple on my nose grotesque—should I stay home today?" Marilyn still cried a lot over Megan. But she found a job at the Encyclopedia Americana and an apartment on the Upper West Side. After two or three months with us she moved out and was living on her own. Stan and I spent all our holidays with her and many weekends. She and I would sit up late over a bottle of wine and argue about politics. She was coldly dismissive of America's achievements and invariably enthusiastic about what the Soviet Union had accomplished. The motto "From each according to his ability, to each according to his need" made perfect sense to her (and to me). A redistribution of property and an equalization of income seemed only fair to us. If I vaunted American civil liberties, Marilyn insisted that so-called freedoms that were not backed up by economic equality were empty. And anyway, how could we be sure what was going on within Russia? Our only source of news was the hysterical American press, blind with its prejudices and fear.

Our longest and most recurring discussions were about the role of the arts in an ideal socialist state. If I criticized the well-known censorship practiced in the Soviet Union, Marilyn would say that if she could save a single human life by destroying the *Mona Lisa*, she would do so. Although she was a painter, art meant little to Marilyn. She saw it as some sort of bourgeois religion, a milder but no less absurd substitute for the deadlier original forms of piety. She admitted that she was inordinately fond of art herself, but at the same time considered her interest to be something like a regrettable hobby—certainly nothing that mattered to the people. She remembered that when she was working with the socialist newspaper in Iowa, they had tried to introduce sketches instead of photographs as illustrations, and that the few genuine workers who actually read the paper hated the drawings. She admitted with a laugh that she was in the uncomfortable position of being an abstract expressionist who knew that her ideal public, the proletariat, disliked her chosen form of art. She felt that until the revolution came along, she could continue to doodle with oils on canvas, but knew that her paintings were of no lasting significance. Not to History. Not to the People.

This austere self-abnegation appealed to me. Her beliefs in no way served her personal goals. During those Cold War years we seriously believed that one side might triumph over the other, and we felt communism had a fighting chance of winning. Of course we were for communism because it was fair. I suppose that if we'd been in France or Italy, where the Communist Party was strong and where people lived in constant dread of a Soviet invasion, we would have had to face up to the consequences of our beliefs. But in America what was called the Left was so weak and so centrist that a revolution seemed both totally unreal and theoretically possible. We were free to build our communes in the sky. The American Communist Party had been all but hounded out of existence.

Marilyn found the putative equality of men and women in the Soviet Union especially appealing. She would draw my attention to the number of women engineers and doctors and scientists in Russia, just as she would refer to the prevalence of free love in the early days after the Bolshevik Revolution. If I mentioned the show trials, the mass murders of kulaks, the anti-Semitism, she'd say that I'd merely fallen victim to CIA propaganda.

I spent a lot of time thinking about the status of art, not just from a political point of view. In those days we still believed in the avant-garde—a belief that was in fact the opposite of the socialist realism promulgated by the Soviet Union. In the States in the late sixties and early seventies, the cutting edge in literature was metafiction, the sort of storytelling that is hyperconscious of its status as an artifact and that constantly draws attention to its own devices. I proposed to Farrar, Straus and Giroux a book of essays and interviews devoted to the leading metafictionists—John Barth, Robert Coover, Rudolph

Wurlitzer, and Donald Barthelme. Although I was crushed at the time, I'm now glad that the book was rejected. I'm still fond of individual works by these various authors today, but as a movement it no longer intrigues me, or anyone else.

In the late sixties and early seventies, however, everyone who was "serious" about the arts believed that the avant-garde still existed and always would—and that the only problem was how to divine the direction in which art was moving at any moment. Today, by contrast, art is moving in dozens of directions and nothing seems inevitable or imperative.

Back then we'd ask things such as "Is Pop Art just a temporary diversion or is it the next swing in the dialectic after abstract expressionism, a cool, ironic way of reintroducing the figurative without returning to realism?" There could only be one "advanced" trend, and it would necessarily point the way toward the next and the next development and the one after that. Was op art a way of raising the stakes of Pop—or was it a dead end? And what about conceptual art—was it a return to Duchamp's mind games? Was Duchamp the true father of contemporary art (not Picasso, as we'd so long imagined)? Ironically, only in retrospect could anyone be sure what the true path had been.

The evolution in fiction was less obvious, though it did seem that the novel was steadily moving away from realism and that the most vital new novels were inventing new forms, new language, new strategies. We were all bewitched by Donald Barthelme's bejeweled word collages in which nothing was predictable, everything was surprising to the point of headiness.

I was so convinced of these notions that in some of my first book reviews I haughtily dismissed any novel that struck me as old-fashioned—until I was asked to review a collection of stories by Isaac Bashevis Singer. His way of narrating a story, his love of strange and telling details, his humanity (joined unexpectedly with a bracing lack of sentimentality), all bewitched me. This stuff wasn't new formally, I conceded, but it was obviously good. I decided to put aside my art-historical preconceptions and to embrace what was inarguably great.

Because of Singer I became interested (through an illogical and strictly private set of associations) in the Great Russians—Tolstoy and Chekhov, Turgenev and Gogol and, as best as I could make him out in translation, Pushkin. For two years I immersed myself during every free moment in these authors. I'd put behind the avant-garde tricksters I'd so recently admired, who now struck me as nothing but classy jugglers. Their cleverness shrank into insignificance next to the pathos and clear-eyed universalism of Tolstoy and Chekhov. I was in my late twenties and early thirties and at that point still had an excellent memory, an entirely involuntary and untrained gift, like good eyesight. My living guide to these writers was Nabokov, whose lectures on literature had not yet been published but whose interviews had been collected in *Strong Opinions*. Like Nabokov I dismissed Dostoyevsky, just as Nabokov convinced me to skip over Conrad and Faulkner in English. At about this time the great Russian scholar Simon Karlinsky published in *TriQuarterly* an essay called "The Other Tradition," which rejected the "radical utilitarianism" prevalent in Russia in the nineteenth and twentieth centuries (all that social uplift, which anticipated socialist realism) in favor of a more purely artistic tradition: Pushkin, Gogol, Chekhov and Nabokov. I read Chekhov's letters to Gorky in which he instructed him not to try to be inventive in his descriptions of nature. He told him to stick to expressions such as "the sun set" or "the snow began to fall." Simon Karlinsky's and Michael Henry Heim's annotations to Chekhov's letters constituted the best biography of the short-story master that existed—and one of the most fascinating books about literature published at that time. My immersion in Russian literature was so

total that when I met Karlinsky, he told me that I could easily pass
the Ph.D. orals in Russian—except for the inconvenient fact that I
knew not a word of the language.

It is difficult to convey the intensity and confusion in our minds
back then in the sixties and early seventies as we tried to reconcile
two incompatible tendencies—a dandified belief in the avant-
garde with a utopian New Left dedication to social justice, both
of which in my case could be overruled by an admiration of the
simple humanity of the Great Russians or Singer. Looking back
now, I'd say that because we were Americans emerging from the
stultifying 1950s, we were extraordinarily naïve about both politics
and esthetics—humorless, unseasoned, dogmatic because untested.
What was shared by these two doctrines—the continuing (and
endless) avant-garde and radical politics—was an opposition to the
society around us, which we judged to be both philistine and selfish.
America had changed in seismic ways in the decades that preceded
us, but we knew little or nothing about these forgotten changes.
The twenties had seen mass migrations of African-Americans
from the South to the industrial cities of the North. In the thirties
much of the country had been unemployed, poor, and spoiling for
a fight. The fight came unexpectedly in the forties in the form of a
world war; domestically the war had meant women went to work
in offices and factories as young men were killing and dying in the
trenches. The fifties—the period of my adolescence—had put all
these rebellious impulses to sleep; it had functioned as a soporific to
the spirit. I'd belonged to the Eisenhower Club at the YMCA, and
General MacArthur's farewell tour (after he was fired by President
Truman for his excessive martial zeal in Korea) was one of the
significant events of my youth—he came to our town! I saw him!
The arts were actually flourishing during the 1950s in America,
but almost secretly. The museums were empty, the concert halls
were dedicated to no one more adventurous than the three B's—

Bach, Beethoven, and Brahms. People read and discussed the same ten "serious" novels every season. During the student shows at the Cranbrook Art Academy, the Detroit public came to scoff at the messy, scary abstract paintings—and the students stayed to scoff at the scoffers.

Marilyn seldom applied her theoretical acumen to her own development as a painter. I can't recall her ever discussing the art-historical underpinnings of her work—or the changes in her work. She admired Richard Diebenkorn, the California painter, because he'd returned to figurative art when everyone on the East Coast was still resolutely nonrepresentational. She liked the way he painted those California excesses of sunlight and their blue, accumulating shadows. She loved Bonnard, whom the New York critics could never quite place in the first rank. She was an improbable kind of Midwestern German sensualist. Not that she surrendered to the appeal of luxury or decadence, but rather she followed her nose and her eyes and her sense of touch and taste toward what intrigued her in some direct, unmediated way.

Perhaps because I lived in a world made of words, I half envied Marilyn her wide-open senses. She was alert to the beauty of the everyday, even the banal. She'd go into raptures over something anyone else would have considered ugly, but not out of perversity or an inverse snobbery. She would suddenly be struck by some purely visual aspect of something—a wonderful passage of brickwork or a slice of Tiepolo-blue sky above a windowless wedge of black buildings or the weave of metal in a manhole cover, the dissolving steam exhaled by a subway grate, or a kitschy but carefully done memorial wall hanging of John F. Kennedy in a Puerto Rican beauty shop on Columbus Avenue.

The New York School poets (John Ashbery, Kenneth Koch, James Schuyler) were hymning the city in the same casual, shrugging, but secretly precise terms. In "An East Window on Elizabeth Street,"

Schuyler writes, "I don't know how/it can look so miraculous and alive/an organic skin for the stacked cubes of air." Later he writes:

> Mutable, delicate, expendable, ugly, mysterious
> (seven stories of just bathroom windows)
> packed: a man asleep, a woman slicing garlic thinly into oil
> (what a stink, what a wonderful smell)
> burgeoning with stacks, pipes, ventilators, tensile antennae—
> that gristling gray bit is a part of a bridge,
> that mesh hangar on a roof is to play games under.
> But why should a metal ladder climb, straight
> and sky aspiring, five rungs above a stairway hood
> up into nothing?

Marilyn had a two-room apartment on the West Side between Riverside and West End that she was endlessly decorating, then stripping and filling up again. Bits of savage finery, a blue feather on a bone, would hang on the burlap wall above a massive bedouin bracelet with its brass welts and multiple locks, like some horrible chastity device. She had a kneehole round table that her father had made her of good pale oak and, in another corner, a drawing board covered with pastels of "famous" lesbians. She liked lace curtains worthy of a concierge from the Pas-de-Calais and a strength-sapping sofa heavy with bolsters and pillows.

I was surely a strange, edgy, difficult friend—excessively polite and docile, patient and indifferent, but then rebellious, on the lam, a master of the disappearing act. Chain-smoking and filling the air with my noxious clouds. Some of my primitive fears of women, based on my dread of my stifling mother, attached to Marilyn—except she was herself elusive, quick to cancel appointments, horrified by the idea of marriage. She made a cult of friendship but scorned the family, though she was wonderfully kind to her own mother and siblings. More than two evenings out in a row spent even in our unintimidating, undemanding society would give her a splitting headache. She loved solitude and needed it as a plant needs light. Marilyn certainly was as full of contradictions as I was—she was a sensualist who loved baths and delicious little meals, but at the same time she was virtually a Stalinist in her politics, as far as I could tell, though at other moments she alternated between a superrational, unforgiving Aristotelianism she'd acquired during years of study at the University of Chicago and a highly Romantic love of lush, swooning verismo operas.

I've forgotten to say how funny and affectionate she always was, how much warmth she radiated, what good humor she brought to every occasion, how much interest she lavished on her friends, how forgiving and tolerant she could be. She loved turning her back courtyard into a little vernal paradise in the summer, where she'd serve cold Riesling and warm potato salad.

In the summer we'd fill the tub with ice and thirty bottles of white wine (a bottle per guest) and run about with old friends from the Midwest and a few new ones from the East Coast, men and women, and it seemed those exciting days of youth and independence and exaltation would never end.

# Chapter 5

In 1964 Stan and I moved to West Seventy-first Street, to a spacious apartment that cost $175 a month. We each had a bedroom and we shared a living room and a dining room. We furnished it at Goodwill with big, heavy oak pieces that were ugly but that looked solid and respectable to us. The neighborhood itself was run-down. Puerto Ricans would throw beer bottles from the window. On the corner was a big Cuban restaurant that reeked of black beans and slabs of roast pork. Next door to us was a bodega where black-magic candles were sold, poured into glass jars and smelling of bubble gum; they were for everything from placing a curse on an enemy to winning back an errant husband. Our neighborhood was so dangerous at the time that it was called Needle Park. A *Life* reporter wrote a nonfiction book, *The Panic in Needle Park*, that was adapted into a violent movie about the heroin trade, from a screenplay by Joan Didion and John Gregory Dunne. One winter night, walking home from Marilyn's at two in the morning, swaying a bit drunkenly, I saw a man in an overcoat and a fedora brandish a gun and shoot another man under the marquee of a shabby hotel. A woman in high heels threw herself on the body and shouted, "*¡Ay, Dios!*" It seemed like a bad sequence in a film noir, something that would need to be reshot. I hurried home, undressed, went to bed, and only the next morning over breakfast did it occur to me to tell

Stan what I'd witnessed. I decided not to report it—no one had much of a sense of civic responsibility in that wild city back then, least of all me.

We knew which blocks were safe and which were dangerous—it really went according to a block-by-block pattern. We'd say to out-of-town relatives and friends, "Oh, don't go down Eighty-fifth Street between Columbus and Amsterdam, though Eighty-sixth is perfectly safe." Our apartment was robbed once, despite all the gates on the windows and the police lock (a stout metal standard that fitted into a socket on the floor and braced the door against intruders). Everyone we knew had had his or her apartment burgled. We would just shrug and say gallantly, "Oh, well, private property is a crime anyway." One evening at six o'clock my friend Stephen Orgel and I were robbed at gunpoint on Christopher Street while other people streamed around us. The thief had torn the inner pocket out of his overcoat and was able to point the pistol inconspicuously at us, the gun shielded from view by the bulk of his coat. Not that anyone would have helped us in any event, even if he or she had seen the weapon. The man told us to give him our wallets and to walk to the end of Weehawken Street without looking back; if we called out or looked back, he'd kill us. Once we were out of sight and around the corner, we saw a cop car and told the policeman what had happened; the cop just laughed and shrugged and asked with a weary chuckle, "Wanna file a complaint?" We didn't.

When I moved to Rome in 1970, I suggested to an Italian friend that we switch sides of the street to avoid confronting three teenagers coming toward us. "Why?" she asked, astonished. In New York we paid the cabdriver to wait at the curb till we were safely inside past the locked front door. We were always aware of everyone within our immediate vicinity. You never lost yourself in conversation on the street, but had to be alert at all times. We made sure we had at least twenty dollars with us every time we left home so that a robber wouldn't shoot us in frustration, but were also careful not to carry more—nor to be too well-dressed. Whenever we went out in the evening, we always left the radio and a light on to discourage thieves. As we approached our apartment building we prepared our key in our pocketed hand so that we wouldn't fumble at the door a second longer than necessary. We walked in straight lines down the sidewalk and only at the last moment did we veer off toward our door, not wanting to signal our intentions or our vulnerability to a watching mischief-maker. On the subway we didn't look at other passengers.

Stan and I discovered Puerto Rico for holidays. So many Puerto Ricans traveled back and forth to San Juan that the plane was virtually a commuter flight. The round-trip cost $140. In San Juan we'd stay at the YMCA in the Old Town and take the Number 10 bus out to luxurious Condado Beach, where we met a beautiful local teenager so proud to be pale he belonged to the Castilian Club, restricted to the descendants of Spanish settlers. The girl who sold ice cream on the beach was so dark that the other local teens called her King Kong. They laughed; she didn't. The boys we pursued all lived at home but would slow-dance with us in clubs late into the night and smelled of achiote powder. They were romantic and would make love to us in public parks, since we couldn't sneak them past the vigilant desk clerk into the Y. When we'd get on a bus, an old man would sneeze theatrically. I asked my Puerto Rican friend why he sneezed. "The word for *gay* is *pato*, 'duck,' and he's sneezing because one of our feathers got in his nose."

The streets were lined with blue cobblestones that had been brought over centuries before in Spanish galleons as ballast. Because it was a hot tropical country, the cooler nights stretched almost to dawn. Even at three A.M. you could always find someone sipping a tall rum drink in a dimly lit courtyard bar behind a locked grill while a guitar rambled on to itself. The only Spanish word I knew was *corazón*, but luckily it featured in nearly every song being wailed out of the jukeboxes.

We met boys who soon joined us in New York for a vacation of a week or two. Stan's was called Pepito, and although he'd been manly and "Castilian" back in San Juan, in New York he evidenced a disturbing propensity for drag. He wanted us to call him Pepita and encouraged us to think of him as a great lady, as a great Hollywood star. Suddenly Stan was completely turned off. Mine was less imaginative, a stolid *macho* named Angel who didn't have the wit to want to be a woman. Though less handsome than Pepito, he turned out to be better value.

New York in the summer was itself tropical with people sitting on their stoops and drinking beer from the bottle and listening to the salsa station on the boom box. Men strode around in sleeveless, collarless T-shirts, the kind called wifebeaters. They sat side by side on stoops and talked without looking at each other. They sometimes listened to deafening Spanish-language broadcasts of the baseball games.

After Pepito returned to San Juan, Stan took up with a sexy New York Puerto Rican named Jimmy, who was a student at New York University and read everything and knew everything about the history of cinema but worked hard to maintain his Latin identity. He was sweet but macho. He and a friend practiced Latin dances every afternoon. I'd always envied those twirls and syncopated steps on the dance floor, the sudden dips and unfurlings and unexpected recouplings—and stupidly assumed they came "naturally," as if a genetic code inscribed in Puerto Rican infants facilitated salsa. Now I saw that they worked it out, segment by segment, over long hours of careful rehearsal, punctuated by a sudden cry of insight or a groan of confusion as they got tangled up and bumped into each other. Stan and I were besotted with these tan-skinned, uncircumcised young dancers with their "Aztec" faces and slim, rotating hips inside pegged trousers and thin black lizard-skin belts, their rapid talk that derailed quickly from English into Spanish, these boys who lived on "Christians and Moors" (rice and black beans) and wore crucifixes or white enamel medals dedicated to the Virgen del Carmen dangling from a thin gold chain. Their combination of sweetness in bed (Angel would kiss my closed eyelids while fucking me) with their street-smart switchblade reflexes excited the Midwestern nerds in us. Stan and I had both grown up watching westerns in which the only men we ever saw in loincloths were Indians (in reality, Italian-Americans). Now we had our own Cheyennes between our legs, their cold religious medals grazing our mouths; or we could overhear them in the next room endlessly rehearsing tonight's salsa as they lost count, made a false step, got caught up in an elaborate body pretzel, and broke down in a sudden gust of laughter.

# Chapter 6

My shrink, Frances Alexander, convinced me that I'd never get "better"—go straight—unless I moved away from Stan. I took the plunge and got an apartment of my own on West Thirteenth Street just off Eighth Avenue. As I left, Stan looked stunned and sat around listening to a 45 called "Seven Rooms of Gloom." I loved him so much but back then no one could defend a homosexual relationship; it was by definition "sick," spiritually impoverishing, infantile, doomed to repeat itself in a horrid circle of compulsiveness. To the degree that someone was "intellectual" like me, one was au courant with Freudian theories and knew how to torment oneself with extra zeal. At that time I read a book about the Salem witch trials in which the author pointed out that it was precisely the Puritan "intellectuals" who believed in witchcraft. They had the subtlety and instruction needed to detect the presence of the devil in the loony actions of eccentric old ladies and the hysteria of teenage girls. I resented my shrink for pushing me in this direction. Yes, I agreed that homosexuality was second best. But what if I never found a woman as kind and funny and loving as Stan?

I'd never lived alone before. When I'd come home from work to my new solitary apartment, my heart would start to beat harder as I approached the door. I bought Julia Child's *Mastering the Art of French Cooking* and began to prepare elaborate meals, recipes that would sometimes take two days to execute—*veau Prince Orloff* or *boeuf à la cuillère* (in which a big square of beef was boiled, cooled, hollowed out, the minced meat then mixed with sautéed mushrooms and shallots and combined with a sauce, then reinserted into the beef shell and covered with Gruyère and heated up under the grill—or something like that; I can't remember, I only did it once, and it was pretty dry). I realized that despite my therapist I probably wasn't going to get married, and that I should start giving dinner parties to fill up my lonely evenings.

Much of my spare time was devoted to sex—finding it and then doing it. In those days before online hookups and backroom bars and outdoor sex, when there weren't even very many gay bars, we had to seek out most of our men on the hoof. Back then people glanced back over their shoulders, though few do it now (or do I say that only because now I'm old and uncruisable?). Then we had to look back or we'd spend the night alone. The whole city was awash with desire and opportunities to satisfy it. Now people can afford to be arrogant and to scurry past one another haughtily, knowing they can always go online later, but then they were driven to tarry and gawk. Typically we'd walk up and down Greenwich Avenue and Christopher Street—not with friends, which might be amusing but was entirely counterproductive. No, only the lone hawk got the tasty rabbit.

If you looked back and he looked back as well, you'd pretend to scan the contents of a shop window. He'd do the same thing twenty yards down. You'd keep exchanging reciprocated glances at an ever-increasing rate. Then you might just smile simply and stroll toward him and he'd pull away from his window and the two of you would form your little conversational duo. If you were still afraid of being rejected or arrested or beat up, you might ask him the time or for a light. It was considered especially cheeky to ask for a light while you were already smoking. Usually you'd just say, "Do you live around here?"

If he was willing, you'd invite him back to your apartment, which in your mind you'd refer to as your trick pad, since he was the trick you'd just scored. Sometimes you'd trick more than once in an evening ("Oh, God, last night I was a real nympho, I tricked three times in a row, my cooze was oozing, must have been the full moon"). The way you could tell the difference between your friends and your lovers is that you never camped with a trick. When discussing him the next day, you might refer to him as "she," but never to his face ("I thought she was so butch, but within seconds she had her legs in the air!"). As one of my friends said, "If God had wanted men to be fucked, he would've put a hole in their ass."

We tried to trick every night, if we could do it efficiently, but we reserved the weekends for our serious hunting sorties. I'd clean my apartment carefully, change the sheets and towels, put a hand towel under the pillow (the "trick towel" for mopping up the come) along with the tube of lubricant (usually water-soluble K-Y). You might even "douche out"—sometimes, if you were a real "senior girl," with a stainless-steel insertable nozzle attached to the shower. You'd buy eggs and bacon and jam and bread for toast, if you wanted to prove the next morning that you were "marriage material." You'd place an ashtray, cigarettes, and a lighter on the bedside table. You'd lower the lights and stack the record player with suitable mood music (Peggy Lee, not the Stones) before you headed out on the prowl. All this to prove you were "civilized," not just one more voracious two-bit whore. Once you'd landed a man, there was no way to know what he liked to do in bed. No frank discussions about who was a top and who was a bottom. Not yet any color-coded hankies in back jeans pockets or keys on the left or right. You usually walked home with the minimum of small talk, sometimes in total silence. Everyone knew that you could lose a trick if you were too mouthy; a sibilant *s* could make an erection wilt in a second. Only once you had him back home behind closed doors and curtains did you serve him a drink and then begin to kiss. If you had to say something, you'd keep your monosyllables in the baritone register. You could tell his intentions pretty quickly by whether he felt for your ass or your cock—but even that wasn't done instantly. A slight pretense of romance was still required, some closed-eyed necking and French-kissing before his hand would drift down into the exciting zone. With any luck he'd claw your clothes off and shed his own in one quick shrug ("My dear, you could hear the Velcro ripping!"). If he folded his trousers neatly and looked around for a hanger, you knew he'd be a bore ("She turned out to be an accountant, of course. I could see that by the way she fussed over that pleated skirt of hers. Betty Bookkeeper . . .").

From the time of the World's Fair in 1964 to the beginning of gay liberation, the Stonewall uprising in 1969, the city was repeatedly being cleaned up. Subway toilets were always being locked shut. Bars were constantly raided. I remember one, the Blue Bunny, up in the Times Square area near the bar where they first danced the twist. There was a tiny dance floor at the back. If a suspicious-looking plainclothesman came in (supposedly you could tell them by their big, clunky shoes), the doorman would turn on little white Christmas lights strung along the ceiling in back, and we'd break apart and stop dancing while the music roared on. I can remember a two-story bar over near the Hudson on a side street south of Christopher that was only open a week or two. When the cops rushed in, we all jumped out the second-story window onto a low, adjoining graveled roof and then down a flight of stairs and onto the street. I used to go to the Everard Baths at 28 West Twenty-eighth Street near Broadway. It was filthy and everyone said it was owned by the police. It didn't have the proper exits or fire extinguishers, just a deep, foul-smelling pool in the basement that looked infected. When the building caught fire in 1977, several customers died. There was no sprinkler system. It was a summer weekend.

On Fire Island it was scarcely better in those days. Of course the Suffolk County police couldn't control what went on in the dunes or along the shore at night, but in discos in both Cherry Grove and the Pines, every group of dancing men had to include at least one woman. A disco employee sat on top of a ladder and beamed a flashlight at a group of guys who weren't observing the rule. At a dance club over in the Hamptons, I recall, the men line-danced and did the hully-gully, but always with at least one woman in the line.

Then everything changed with the Stonewall uprising toward the end of June 1969. And it wasn't all those crewnecked white boys in the Hamptons and the Pines who changed things, but the black kids and Puerto Rican transvestites who came down to the Village on the subway (the "A-trainers"), and who were jumpy because of the extreme heat and who'd imagined the police persecutions of the preceding years had finally wound down. The new attacks made them feel angry and betrayed. They were also worked up because Judy Garland had just died of an overdose and was lying in state at the Frank F. Campbell funeral chapel. At the end of Christopher Street, just two blocks away, rose the imposing bulk of the Jefferson Market women's prison (now demolished to make way for a park). At that time, tough women would stand on the sidewalk down below and call up to their girlfriends, "I love you, baby. If you give it up to that big black bitch Shareefa, I cut you up, I'm telling you, baby, I cut you good." Inside the Stonewall the dance floor had been taken over by the long-legged, fierce-eyed antics of the S.T.A.R. members (Street Transvestite Action Revolutionaries). Angry lesbians, angrier drag queens, excessive mourning, staggering heat, racial tensions, the examples of civil disobedience set by the women's movement, the antiwar protesters, the Black Panthers—all the elements were present and only a single flame was needed to ignite the bonfire.

\*     \*     \*

The Stonewall wasn't really a disco. It had a jukebox, a good one, and two big, long rooms where you could dance. Bars were open till four in the morning in New York; gay guys would come home from work, eat, go to bed having set the alarm for midnight, and stay out till four. Of course there were no Internet sites, but also no telephone dating lines, no backrooms, and up till then no trucks or wharves open to sex.

There was a lot of street cruising and a lot of bar cruising. We had to have cool pickup lines. We were all thin from amphetamines; my diet doctor was always prescribing "speed" for me, and I'd still be up at six in the morning reading the yellow pages with great and compulsive fascination. We had long, dirty hair and untrimmed sideburns and hip-huggers and funny black boots that zipped up the side and denim cowboy shirts with pearlescent pressure-pop buttons. We had bell-bottoms. We all smoked all the time (I was up to three packs a day). We didn't have big showboat muscles or lots of attitude. Our shoulders were as narrow as our hips. We didn't look hale, but we were healthy—this was twelve years before AIDS was first heard of and all we got was the clap. We had that a lot, maybe once a month, since no one but paranoid married men used condoms. I dated my clap doctor, who spent most of his free time copying van Gogh sunflowers.

I would go to the Stonewall and drink three or four vodka tonics to get up the nerve to ask John Stipanela, a high school principal, to dance. I had a huge crush on him but he wasn't interested in bedding me, though we did become friends. One night there I picked up an ultra-WASP boy working in his family business of import-export, but I found him a bit too passive—until I discovered he was the guy my office-mate at work was obsessively in love with and had been mooning over for months. I felt bad about cock-blocking my office-mate ("bird-dogging," as we said then) and sort of impressed with myself that I'd scored where he, a much better looking man, had failed.

Then there was the raid, the whimper heard round the world, the fall of our gay Bastille. On June 28, 1969, the bar was raided, and for the first time gays resisted. The Bureau of Alcohol, Tobacco, and Firearms staged the raid, since they'd discovered the liquor bottles in the bar were bootlegged and that the local police precinct was in cahoots with the Mafia owners. As the patrons and workers were being led out of the bar and pushed into a paddy wagon, the angry crowd that had gathered outside began to boo. Then some of the queens inside the van began to fight back—and a few escaped. The crowd was energized by the violence.

Everyone was so pissed off over that particular police raid because once the World's Fair was over, the cops seemed to forget about us and lots of new bars had opened. There were raids, but only once a month and usually early in the evening, so as not to spoil the later, serious hours of cruising and dancing and flirting and drinking. Now we had a new, handsome mayor, John Lindsay. But he only looked better. He was in constant conflict with the unions, with antiwar protesters, with student radicals who took over Columbia—and with the gay community.

Before the Stonewall uprising there hadn't really been much of a gay community, just guys cruising Greenwich Avenue and Christopher Street. But when the police raided Stonewall and gay men feared their bars were going to be closed once again, all hell broke loose. I was there, just by chance, and I remember thinking it would be the first funny revolution. We were calling ourselves the Pink Panthers and doubling back behind the cops and coming out behind them on Gay Street and Christopher Street and kicking in a chorus line. We were shouting "Gay is good" in imitation of the slogan "Black is beautiful."

Up till that moment we had all thought that homosexuality was a medical term. Suddenly we saw that we could be a minority group—with rights, a culture, an agenda. June 28, 1969, was a big date in gay history.

GLBT leaders like to criticize young gays for not taking the movement seriously, but don't listen to them. Just remember that at Stonewall we were defending our right to have fun, to meet each other, and to have sex.

A Black Maria had carted off half the staff and a few kicking, writhing drag queens, while the rest of the policemen waited inside with the others. I'd been walking past with a friend and now joined in, though resistance to authority made me nervous. I thought we shouldn't create a fuss. This was bad for our image. I said out loud, "Oh, come on, guys."

Yet even I got excited when the crowd started battering down the barricaded door with a ripped-up parking meter and when someone tossed lit garbage into the bar. No matter that we were defending a Mafia club. The Stonewall was a symbol, just as the leveling of the Bastille had been. No matter that only six prisoners had been in the Bastille and one of those was Sade, who clearly deserved being locked up. No one chooses the right symbolic occasion; one takes what's available.

The next day I wrote a letter about the event to Alfred and Ann Corn, a young married couple I'd only recently met and who were away for the summer on the West Coast. I obviously had no idea how serious the uprising was or would prove to be, how it would usher in a whole new era of gay consciousness. It would turn out to be as epoch-making as the 1934 Nazi raid on and destruction of Magnus Hirschfeld's Institute for Sexual Science in Berlin, which ended the first gay liberation movement in history. In the late 1980s I concluded a novel, *The Beautiful Room Is Empty*, with a lengthy description of the event.

# Chapter 7

About this time I met Richard Howard, the poet, critic, and translator. A guy I'd been dating named Frank had started chatting with Richard at a West Village gay bar. Frank told Richard that he had a friend (me) who'd written a "brilliant" novel no one would buy. (In truth, Frank hadn't read it.) Richard scrawled out his phone number on a trick card provided by the bar and kept close to the entrance and told Frank to have me call him.

As Frank said, "I think he's the only established writer who goes to the bars." Certainly no one I knew had ever met a real writer, though strangely enough one of the first things Richard said to me was "When we were young, the older writers were all very remote and regal, but now we are completely available to the young."

I called Mr. Howard and he laughed a bit insultingly (or was it just nervously?) and said in a brisk, possibly peremptory tone, "Stand on the corner of Thirteenth Street and Eighth Avenue exactly at two o'clock today and I'll come hurrying past on the way to my shrink and effect a manuscript-lift."

A bit stunned, I repeated the details just to make sure I'd—but Mr. Howard interrupted me and laughed and said, "Yes, that's what I just said." And he hung up.

At the appointed time I was standing on the corner (half a block from my new apartment) with the manuscript in hand. I was wearing sawed-off blue-jean shorts and a maroon T-shirt. My hair was freshly washed and combed, but I wished I'd slept better and didn't have such dark circles under my eyes. Suddenly I saw him whirling up the street at a fast clip in a cape, his bald head gleaming. He sized me up with a head-to-toe survey and a cocked eyebrow. I had no idea what sort of impression I made. I had already been going to the gym for three years by that point, long before most other gay men, and my body was certainly revealed by my tight clothes.

"Have you included your phone number on your manuscript?"

"Yes," I said. "It's on the top page."

"Now I have lots of things on my desk at the moment to clear up, but I can assure you I'll have some sort of word for you about your work at the weekend." Then he was off. A bit stupefied, I watched him rush uptown, my manuscript in his hand.

My novel was called *Forgetting Elena* and became my first published book, thanks to Richard (the only blurb on the back was written by Richard as well). It was (and is) mysterious, experimental, original. I'd become so frustrated writing plays and novels I thought would please other people that I'd finally decided to write something I would want to read. I thought, if I'm always going to be rejected, I might as well like my hated "child." It was obvious, by perusing *Forgetting Elena* (which at that point was called *Something Valentine*), that I'd been reading Kafka and Beckett, though it wasn't a pastiche of either of those great writers. I was fascinated by court ritual and had immersed myself in books by and about courtiers in Heian Japan—*The Tale of Genji* and *The Pillow Book of Sei Shonagon* in particular. I'd read and reread Ivan Morris's *World of the Shining Prince*, about Genji. I was also fascinated by Versailles under Louis XIV, and I loved W. H. Lewis's book about it, *The Splendid Century*.

My book, however, wasn't a historical novel. I'd written several chapters of it while vacationing on Fire Island in the Pines. The rituals of gay men there—the afternoon swimsuit "tea dances" at the Botel next to the harbor, late dinners together at a cottage (the whole house propped up by stilts on the dunes) that a group of six or eight had rented together, the men's return to the harbor at midnight for more stoned dancing till dawn—rhymed in my imagination with the rituals of medieval Japan or Versailles. In Japan sudden, sometimes brutal sexual encounters in the dark would erupt, just as on Fire Island the communal living would be punctuated by quick, thrilling fucks in the dunes at the "Meat Rack." After the disco finally closed shop at dawn, beautiful, sweaty men would stagger off into the scrub brush between communities to have group sex. At Versailles no titles were used in conversation, though everyone was conscious of exact gradations in rank; in the same way on Fire Island penniless beauties and millionaire lawyers all laughed and made love together, all dressed in the same swim trunks or jeans and sandals. With no cars on Fire Island, everyone was reduced to hauling home his groceries in a kid's red metal wagon over the raised, bumpy boardwalks.

As if this blend of court ritual and Fire Island communal living weren't hard enough to grasp, I'd decided to have my first-person narrator be an amnesiac who's afraid to admit he has no idea who he or anyone else is. Since he remembers nothing, the whole book is told in the present tense. The narrator is constantly building up and revising suppositions about what's going on around him and where he fits in. I thought this was what we were all doing all the time: modeling our behavior on the expectations of those around us and the cues we were being fed. The self was a social self; at our core lay a reciprocity. Admittedly I was an extreme example of this adaptability. I was inspired by Erving Goffman's idea that the self is defined through reciprocal role-playing—that life is theater.

Richard met with me a week later. He'd gone over the entire manuscript and corrected many errors in taste and diction. I had inserted footnotes here and there, which he thought (correctly, I'm now convinced) drew too much attention to the text as a text and added an unattractively coy note. It provided the reader with an escape route out of the labyrinth of the book. Richard argued that the whole book couldn't be called *Something Valentine* since, in fact, the narrator is wrong—he's not one of the Valentines. Richard said the book was too short. I needed to add another long chapter of thirty or so pages, since a novel shorter than two hundred pages was impossible to sell.

I worked on the book for several months. My heart sank at the prospect of adding new pages since I'd composed the novel by instinct alone. It was as if I had tuned my dials to a certain frequency; once my mind started emitting the right hum, I knew I could proceed. I was convinced I'd written a wonderful book—but I wasn't exactly sure how I'd done it. Richard didn't overpraise me but in a businesslike way let me know that he thought it was worth rescuing. His practical manner gave me the courage to revise.

Once I'd finished the revisions he did no more than glance at them. I gave the revised, much longer novel to my agent, who submitted it to Robert Gottlieb, who was then head of Knopf. He took months and months considering it (which, I was later told, was quite uncharacteristic of him). Finally he rejected it, though at one point he'd seemed on the verge of buying it. He wrote, "I like high-class junk and junky junk—but this book isn't junky at all." I was confused. By that time I was living in Rome. I remember walking back from the American Express office beside the Spanish Steps, where I received my mail, and thinking that I wanted to commit suicide. I sobbed and said aloud to myself as I walked along, "I can't speak! They won't let me speak!" I sat down on a bench looking out over the ruins of the forum and thought that if God didn't send me a sign, I'd just kill myself. At that point a handsome blond Roman came up and asked me if I was all right. I decided to live at least long enough to have sex with him—he was obviously an angel.

Maybe my book was bad, I conceded, or too weird, but hundreds and hundreds of bad books were published every year. Anyway, it wasn't bad. It was good. I felt that all I'd ever wanted was to be a published writer. Now I was thirty and nothing was working out. I felt humiliated. Gottlieb went on to edit the *New Yorker* and to write with lyricism and insight about Balanchine. In the late 1980s, in Paris, I was introduced to him several times, and mutual friends told me I was all wrong about him, he was a great defender of the arts, poor man—he'd suffered for his exquisite taste. Now that I've become someone to whom other people submit manuscripts, I know there must be at least a dozen young writers out there who detest me for not helping them enough. One of them has started savaging my books in print. He wrote, "Edmund White is the fattest, ugliest writer in America, rivaled only by Harold Bloom." He asserted that all my books were failures, including my biography of Jean Genet—a subject, he said, I'd spoiled for a whole generation.

Richard Howard, back then when I first met him in 1969, suggested my book be sent to Anne Freedgood at Random House, even though that publisher had already rejected it once (as had twenty-some other publishers). Richard called Anne and told her she must accept it. She did, but only after waiting many more months. I'd finished and revised *Forgetting Elena* by 1969 after three years' work; it was published in 1973—seven years from start to finish for a book of two hundred pages. When I was back in New York, and Mrs. Freedgood and I had lunch to discuss revisions (more revisions!), it suddenly dawned on me that my agent had submitted the old manuscript to her, not the one I'd rewritten under Richard Howard's direction. I asked to look at it; yes, it was the old dog-eared text. I realized the agent had been sending out the wrong version all along.

Anne liked the revised text when she finally received it a few days later, but she still insisted that the book couldn't end so vaguely. I, who'd been so impressed by the abstract expressionist painters at Cranbrook, had wanted to create a verbal equivalent to those nonrepresentational paintings. Or rather, I knew that language (unlike strokes of paint) was symbolic and that nonsense syllables or strings of meaningless words à la Gertrude Stein would be tiresome to read. The trick, I thought, would be to write real sentences and to seem to be heading somewhere but to have the action keep canceling itself out—something I soon realized John Ashbery was doing in poetry. But Anne Freedgood said that in my novel I was entering into a contract with the reader; I was promising a mystery and I must deliver the payoff at the end. In the end, the book was widely reviewed as a mystery. How frustrating for true devotees of the genre!

But I'm getting ahead of my story. Before I went to Rome and before the book was accepted, Richard and I had become inseparable. He was always affected and pedantic and arrogant, but somehow these qualities, so tiresome in other people, were delightful and refreshing in him. He generated a kind of constant brio, as if he possessed many motors and they were all fed by the highest-octane fuel. Every moment with him had a sense of occasion. I felt that I was leading my usual backwater life when suddenly a pleasure boat would roar into view, its decks brilliant with guests in evening clothes. Except there was no way not to notice Richard. Richard wasn't putting on the prevailing upper-class manner or the American version of a donnish style; he was inventing a whole new way of talking and moving and laughing. He spoke in a high, nasal voice with an elegant stutter, yet he was groping not for words but for rhetorical effect—for emphasis, surprise. He didn't have an English accent, nor the "mid-Atlantic" one so popular in New York in those days, but rather something that seemed to correspond to his idea of how Henry James might have talked—with elaborate grammar, odd word choices, sudden boutades, and an eerie emphasis on ordinary, everydayish words. He had a stylized way of throwing his head back, of holding a hand frozen in the air like Jupiter hurling a thunderbolt. He could cock an eye to devastating effect and raise an eyebrow in lofty disdain. His laugh was warm and encouraging, but theatrically so. Then once in a great while he'd have a little, humble smile, as if he'd caught himself being such a camp.

He was a great source of information on the eccentricities of his friends and acquaintances (he had a well-stocked memory, and if it ever failed him, he would strike his forehead lightly with his fist, as if to startle the mechanism back into functioning). But whereas Henry James wanted to be a gentleman and worried about any irregularities in the lives of those around him, Richard gloried in the strange, both in himself and others. He wore a red cape and many of his clothes were flashy or funny. It wasn't that he was unaware of the effect he was making—he just wanted to be making one.

Richard could be harshly impatient if one "failed" him in some way—if one hadn't read George Meredith's *Diana of the Crossways* or if one said one didn't "get" Gerard Manley Hopkins. He would roll his eyes, looking for help, possibly divine intervention. He'd whisper, "Oh, darling, how can you say such a thing?" For him the pantheon of great artists and writers and composers included almost everyone I'd ever heard of, past or present. No friend was allowed to have blind spots or preferences (though later he wrote a book of poems called *Preferences*). He was finishing in those days *Alone with America*, his thousand-page tribute to forty-one living American poets; I'd heard of only five or six of them (though later I came, through Richard's good offices, to read and even meet many of them). He admired his forty-one "immortals" extravagantly, but he could treat them with a strangely sadistic edge. I remember when he introduced the bibulous Alan Dugan at the venerable YMHA (where T. S. Eliot and Dylan Thomas had read). Dugan has largely been forgotten, but he had won the Yale Younger Poets award and later the Pulitzer and the National Book Award for slim volumes austerely named *Poems I*, *Poems II*, *Poems III*, and so on. Richard said, "Alan Dugan is a souse, in the original sense of the word as 'salt,' 'source,' 'spring.' " For several years Richard had been a lexicographer, and these bizarre, sometimes shaming verbal associations would crop up in his writing and conversation.

At the same time that he was writing these admiring if edgy essays, he was constructing his own poems. When I first met him, he was working on *Untitled Subjects*, a collection of dramatic monologues à la Browning about Victorians. The best one was "said" by Mrs. William Morris as in old age she went through a box of memorabilia: "These are mine. Save them. / I have nothing save them" were the solemnly beautiful last lines. He would recite these poems at full volume and with great hamminess to Marilyn and Stanley and me. He overarticulated, spun on his heel to stare at us, banged on a table, sank into a long dramatic pause, tilted his head back and closed his eyes and whispered something prophetic before expiring on the chair behind him. The three of us, sitting in my little living room in my new, chic apartment on West Thirteenth Street, were terrified we'd surrender to torrents of weeping laughter, though I'm sure Richard would have interpreted our *fou rire* as exactly the response he'd been angling for. Richard confided that Sandy, his lover, had carefully rehearsed him and taught him his reading style. Privately we wondered if Sandy's wasn't a poisoned gift.

Of course I was terribly proud to be Richard's friend, not only because he was celebrated and knew so many distinguished people, but also because he was so lively and amusing, such tremendous great fun. He was an electrifying presence.

As Midwesterners, Marilyn, Stan, and I were embarrassed by his theatrics, especially at such close quarters, yet we all admired the poems and his chutzpah. And anyway, Richard was a Midwesterner, too—from Cleveland, just like Hart Crane, as he always mentioned. He'd just returned from a reading in Cleveland where an ancient aunt of his, a former Ziegfeld Follies girl, came up to him afterward. Richard was proud of his bald head, which he polished, and he was equally proud of his fearlessness in displaying it. But all his old aunt could mutter as she moved up to him in the reception line was "Get a rug."

He won the Pulitzer Prize for the poems and seemed delighted by the recognition. He had something about him of the bar mitzvah boy who thinks it's perfectly natural that a roomful of adults should be beaming at him with affection and pride. Since he was no fool, he knew all about envy and cattiness, but his wariness of others was an acquired response. His first instinct was to think everyone liked him and was happy for him.

Like me he'd gone to progressive schools—he in Cleveland, I in Evanston, Illinois—and these schools had discouraged competition. He even wrote a poem, "From Beyoglü," for an old classmate, Anne Hollander (who would go on to write *Seeing Through Clothes* and other fascinating works about costume and how it makes us look at the body). Richard's poem referred to "the year we were Vikings" and related how in progressive public grade school, in accordance with Dewey's principles, the children would explore other cultures (that of the Norse in this case) by dressing up and impersonating them in a safe, grade-free, noncompetitive environment. As a result, both Richard and I expected our friends to share in our successes. In our world there was no rivalry.

He was indefatigable, and wonderfully faithful. In the course of a day he might visit a friend in the hospital, sit in on another friend's rehearsal, see his shrink, have lunch with Jackson Pollock's widow,

Lee Krasner, read two first books of poems and blurb them both, teach a class at Columbia, attend a board meeting of the Society of Poets, then have dinner with his lover. The lover was Sanford Friedman, the author of *Totempole*, an early gay novel that involved the love affair between an American soldier and a young Korean man. Sandy and Richard lived together in a spacious apartment in the West Village, where Richard and I would have to tiptoe through the darkened room in which Sanford was prostrate on the couch, afflicted with depression or migraine, I never knew which. We'd head back for Richard's cozy, brilliantly lit study, packed from floor to ceiling with books, everything brass and green glass and red upholstery. We'd close the door and try to keep our voices down. When Sandy's father died, I wrote him a complicated, overly literary, neurotic condolence letter, which Sandy responded to by writing back, "I appreciate the gesture if not the sentiment."

Richard loved literature with a magnanimous, all-encompassing, energetic love. Whereas many established poets or novelists read only the talismanic texts that had impressed and shaped them in their youths over and over or, with a mixture of disdain, curiosity, and distrust, skimmed the latest books by friends and rivals, Richard had nothing but friends and no rivals and he liked everything. He had translated more than 150 books from the French, and if the authors were alive, he usually knew them—Robbe-Grillet, Claude Simon, Roland Barthes, the pessimistic Romanian aphorist E. M. Cioran. Later in the seventies Richard would introduce the poet James Merrill and the critic David Kalstone to Cioran in Paris, and they were astonished that the invariably gloomy writer did nothing all evening but crack jokes, drink wine, and consume hundreds of periwinkles, fishing them with a straight pin out of their tiny black shells.

Richard had even translated Charles de Gaulle and had a story about being invited to an official lunch at the Élysée Palace.

Academicians, admirals, and actresses were at the lunch, and de Gaulle posed a question to each. When de Gaulle got to Richard, he asked where he'd learned such good French. Richard replied, "In a car between Ohio and Florida, *mon général*." When Richard was a child, an uncle had started teaching him French while they were driving down to Miami. After the lunch de Gaulle took Richard aside and asked him what had been his model for his style while translating the de Gaulle memoirs. Richard said, "Tacitus." Which was just the right response.

Richard was only ten years older than I but he treated me as if I were a child—an intelligent, well-mannered child who was eminently *sortable*, but a child nonetheless. He'd call me up and say, "I have a little surprise for you. Meet me in half an hour at the Riv on Sheridan Square."

I'd drop whatever I was doing and rush to join him. He'd take me off to meet one of his eminent friends. Through Richard I met Howard Moss, the poetry editor of the *New Yorker*, who had a dry sense of humor and looked like Mr. Magoo, the nearsighted cartoon character with poached eyes and folds in his face. Howard lived on Tenth Street off Fifth Avenue in an apartment in a brownstone with a bright red door. He said he was "allergic" to cigarettes. In fact, he probably just didn't like the smell of smoke, but in those days the smoker had such unquestioned rights that people who objected had to invent a medical excuse. Howard had stopped smoking two years earlier but still sucked a plastic cigarette all the time, a sort of pacifier. I, who smoked three packs a day, would become so desperate that I'd have to lean out his window—and pull the guillotine-style sash down to my knees, so that no smoke would leak back into his rooms. Even on freezing nights at midnight I'd be hanging out his window; now smokers would have to go down to the street.

Howard was a New Yorker born and bred and seemed a holdover from the 1950s. I never saw him out of a coat and tie, but not the sumptuous Italian suits men wear now. No, he always had on those pinched, buttoned-up, pin-striped Brooks Brothers "sack suits" writers and profs wore in the fifties with the skinny rep ties. He had a creased, unhappy face with a crooked smile on his lips and a little baritone, muted chuckle. He'd say something funny and despairing and chuckle and pull a long face. He had the famous New York humor that someone once defined as mordant Jewish wit strained through a martini. He was a Jew but never mentioned that. Howard actually drank martinis, which had largely been replaced by white wine by the time I came along. They didn't seem to affect him any more than a glass of water would affect me.

He was always a bit unhappy and joked a lot about it in his dry way. He was unhappy that his poetry wasn't more widely recognized; he blamed this on his position as the poetry editor of the *New Yorker*, which made him the most powerful arbiter of poetry in the country. Howard thought that all those people he'd rejected hated him, and that the ones he'd accepted didn't want to appear to their fellow poets as if they were paying him back or currying his favor. So no one wrote reviews of his books, he said, and few editors solicited his poems. He complained so much that I wrote a glowing review of his poems in *Poetry* magazine. I was happy to acknowledge that he'd written one of the great comic poems of our day, "Ménage à trois," which ends with the unforgettable line "It's old, inadequate and flourishing."

He also wrote verse plays, one based on King Midas and another that borrowed Giacometti's title—for a sculpture that belonged to the Museum of Modern Art—*The Palace at 4 A.M.*

At the *New Yorker* he worked regularly with James Merrill and Elizabeth Bishop, not to mention dozens of others of the most celebrated poets in English. He was especially close to the great Anglo-Irish novelist Elizabeth Bowen, who'd lived and taught briefly at Princeton in the 1950s. I'd been reading her since college days, and once I gave up my determination to be "experimental," her influence became palpable in my work. Probably no one would notice the connection (people seem almost blind to quite obvious influences), but her technique of making neat, short moral observations about her characters was something I started shoplifting in my autobiographical novels from *A Boy's Own Story* on. What E. M. Forster was for most writers of my generation, Bowen was for me; I never took to Forster's combination of closetedness, snobbishness, and blending of fable and Edwardian morality, whereas Bowen's quiet passion and sense of the tragic appealed to me. For me she was genuinely tragic in the sense that in *The Death of the Heart* or *The House in Paris*, her best books, the protagonists face a dilemma and either choice they might make is bad—very bad. She didn't have an affected prose style like Virginia Woolf nor did she overestimate the importance of "moments of being." She had no religious preconceptions like Graham Greene (though Greene I'd rank as a novelist right after her). Her ethics were all subtle and situational. I heard Ian McEwan say recently that modernists such as Joyce and Woolf have cornered so much critical attention that they've eclipsed all of the (superior, to his mind) realists such as Bowen and Rosamond Lehman. I should mention here that my lifelong love has been Henry Green and that his novel *Nothing* is the only book I've read ten times. His stylishness and his ear for dialogue are celebrated, but one should also include his appreciation for the sensuality of women, the comedy of adultery, the absurdities of class. I think of Henry Green as my opposite— my blessed, enriching opposite.

Howard kept wanting me to fix him up with someone, though one day a sexy Puerto Rican was hanging around and later Howard said he'd been "seeing" that man for years and years. But I guess he wasn't enough somehow, maybe not blond or educated or presentable enough.

*Edmund White*

Howard was being psychoanalyzed by a Freudian shrink. He'd
been going to this man for years, and Howard spoke of Freudianism
as if it were a perfectly ordinary and respectable branch of medicine,
like orthopedic surgery. In the true Freudian style Howard lay
down on a couch and duly reported his dreams. The shrink, he said,
seldom spoke, or rather, seldom "made interpretations." Also in the
Freudian tradition, Howard knew nothing about him except that he
treated several other writers—that was his "specialty." Howard talked
about childhood and sexual fantasies and realities—and about his
"transference" (in this case, of his feelings toward the doctor). The net
effect, I thought, was to make him even gloomier, even more fatalistic.

It was always evening in Howard's mind, but in the midst of
these lengthening shadows ran his jaunty humor, which really was
adorable and improbable as a puppy, a golden retriever, say. He was
an addict of the wisecrack, an aficionado of the parting shot. No
matter how sad his creased face might look, he could always, at some
unexpected moment, wedge it open with a little smile. Or more
often his eyes would become the crudest of stars (one horizontal
line and one vertical), and he'd avert his gaze, turn his mouth down
in a circumflex, nurse his invisible prop cigarette, then laugh at
his own expense. I remember he told of a French television team
that called him and said they'd been impressed with his short book
on Proust and wanted to film him for a French literary program.
"Sure," Howard said, "you bet. But I don't speak French." "Oh,
you're too modest! A great scholar like you? We'll be over at three."
"Sure, but I don't speak French." When the whole team had set up
the lights and the sound equipment and the camera and Howard
had been made up and powdered, the interviewer posed the first
question—in French. Howard looked blank and said, "But I don't
speak French." The interviewer laughed and started over again.
Once more a blank. Within seconds the whole team had cleared
out, left the premises, muttering resentfully.

One day, four years before *Forgetting Elena* was published, Howard said to me, "I'm terribly embarrassed, but I've never read any of your books. Where should I start?"

I said, "But that's because I've written several but not one of them has ever been published."

He looked at me with compassion and said, "That must be terribly painful for you."

I felt wonderfully understood and I nodded.

He'd understood how brave I was going out into the world and meeting Richard Howard's writer friends even though I wasn't armed with a single publication. Yes, it was great meeting all these literati who might someday blurb me or review me or just pass along the word that I was bright and funny and attractive (in those days, especially given the low standards of pulchritude in the literary world, I was considered handsome). But it was a trial explaining that even though I'd reached the great age of twenty-nine and even though I'd already been writing for fifteen of those years, I had nothing in print beyond a story and a few articles. My problem was especially acute because it seems to me that people published younger in those days, just as they married and had children and careers much younger. Of course, I could have added to all these solicitous writer-friends that Richard Howard had taken me under his wing. That remark would no doubt have set off a storm of exchanged looks since it would have been assumed I was his latest catamite.

I turned thirty on January 13, 1970, and at the same time decided to move to Rome. I was sick of killing time at the office, of feeling stale and trapped, of waiting for my life to begin. I knew my destiny lay with New York, but I welcomed a chance to wipe the slate clean. I'd only visited Rome once for a week two years earlier with Stan. The dollar was still strong in those days and we'd stayed in a hotel on the Corso that had once been the palace of the Queen of Sweden (Garbo!). On the same trip we'd stayed in the Casa Annalena pensione in Florence for four dollars a night, breakfast and one other meal included, and the Palazzo Gritti in Venice in what was known as "the Elizabeth Taylor suite," since she and Richard Burton had stayed there not long before. The room looked down on the Grand Canal and across to the Salute. Though we could never have afforded a dinner at the Plaza Hotel, say, back in New York, the exchange rate made it possible for us to stay in the most luxurious places in Europe. We'd liked Italy, and like many happy tourists we'd dreamed of living there. I might have preferred Paris, but it intimidated me.

So at the beginning of the new decade I took Italian lessons in New York for a month and I quit my job—the only real office job I'd ever had and that I'd obtained only after two months of interviews. Maitland Edey, the same New England mandarin who'd asked Sigrid and me about feminism, now said to me that I was foolish to give up my job with Time-Life Books with all its benefits and job security and four- and even five- and six-week vacations thanks to our union, the Writers Guild. But I was determined, if frightened. I withdrew my seven thousand dollars in profit sharing and converted it to traveler's checks, which the bank officer thought was also rash.

Just before I left, Richard introduced me to a person in New York who would become my best friend: David Kalstone. He was living not far from Howard Moss in a sublet. He was a professor (he'd written a book on Sir Philip Sidney) at Rutgers, but I gathered he was in a state of change—wintering in New York City, summering in Venice, being outfitted with contact lenses and more up-to-date clothes, even writing about contemporary poets such as Bishop and James Merrill.

None of that struck me at the time. What impressed me right away was how subtle and gentle and observant he was, though he was almost legally blind. He had a sweet, wise smile, eyes that blinked into the indistinct void around him, hands that made wonderful rounded gestures. Richard Howard treated him a bit as if he were a distinguished but dim cousin, but I felt right away that he could be a . . . playmate. Although Richard liked all of us to sit up straight and present to the world our best face and to say right off our cleverest remarks and to speak of our serious reading or our life-transforming experiences (the ballet, Angkor Wat, the Sistine Chapel), David would never jump through that hoop. He was completely obliging, but a slightly goofy sense of humor played over everything he touched. He didn't write as much as his friends expected, or so I gathered, but I guessed that was partly because he spent a lot of time at friendship. He was a generous, amused man and he liked me a lot, I could see, maybe because in a sense we were both newcomers. Although he was ten years older than I, he'd devoted less time than I had to being a New Yorker, which in those days was something like a religious vocation, full of obvious penances and rarefied rewards.

My time in Rome is not part of this story. I stayed from January to June and ran through all of my savings inviting Italian and American acquaintances out to dinner. We'd sit at long trestle tables in the Piazza Navona and look out at the spotlit lavishness of Bernini's fountain of the continents (Is that a camel there? A palm tree? A Negro?). We'd eat plates of spaghetti and clams and drink liter after liter of sour white wine poured from those official transparent receptacles that had the exact liter level legally scratched into the glass—which made no sense since the wine could always be watered to bring it up to the right level. I took an Italian lesson nearly every day in a modern brick apartment block near the Vatican. My original apartment building in Trastevere was gutted by a fire after I'd been there for one unhappy month. The English girl Lulu, the agent who'd rented me the apartment, had been sacked for other reasons but we'd stayed friends. Now she told me of Phillip, an acquaintance who needed a roommate and who lived on the Largo Argentina.

I moved in with Phillip and soon met all his friends and played his piano and walked his dog and learned his ways. His two-room apartment had a terrace planted with azaleas and a view of the traffic below and a constant free-flowing source of water that the neighbor lady told me must come from an ancient Roman aqueduct. We led a useless Roman life compounded of worries about money, two mild hangovers a day (lunch and dinner), and lots of empty talk and not much sex. The long-aproned ten-year-old boy who worked in the café downstairs would take our order over the phone and climb the six flights to our apartment at ten or eleven in the morning with our caffe lattes and our round, dry buns or *cornetti*. Sometimes he'd come back two or three times a day, always cheerful and uncomplaining, and take away our empties with a professional smile and a snappy gesture. In this city everyone seemed to be stylish; Phillip told me that people would eat nothing but bread for dinner under bare lightbulbs but step out into the square in a bespoke suit swinging Maserati keys that lacked Maseratis. The white-gloved policeman directing the traffic in front of the Victor Emmanuel monument was exactly that—a symphony director. We might cook some sauceless spaghetti for ourselves and the half-wild cats—until I became convinced that they were missing some essential minerals found only in proper cat food and persuaded Phillip to let me serve it to the animals, and they both died in horrible agonies.

Phillip had no money. Once in a great while he'd be an extra in a movie. His mother was a rich American and his father an Austrian nobleman. Phillip had been raised in Mexico, where he'd been valedictorian of his high school class, though now, just ten years later, his excellent, idiomatic Italian had entirely supplanted his once-fluent Spanish. He spoke American with an accent similar to mine but would grope after even some of the most common English words.

I paid his back bills and bought him meals and paid all the rent. I suppose I was a little bit in love with him, though he didn't fancy me. His queeny ex-lover, a small, skinny Sardinian, pitied me for being "double-bodied." I asked my Italian teacher what "double-bodied" in Italian meant. She said that Italians were still so close to their peasant backgrounds that they prized an aristocratic leanness that showed they'd never done any physical labor. American-style muscles, in their eyes, were a shameful reminder of rural origins. I stopped lifting weights but I did go to an exercise class at the Roma Sporting Center near the Piazza Barberini where everyone followed the *professore*'s instructions, and where jumping jacks were called *farfalle*, or "butterflies." Every ten minutes the *professore* sprayed the air with cologne to disguise the shocking smell of sweat.

The gay scene in Rome at that time was pathetic. A few married men sat in a particular movie theater just off the Corso at a certain hour with their raincoats in their laps and might let you jerk them off. A few foreigners, mostly Romanian refugees, would meet at midnight in the Colosseum. I'd get drunk during those endless dinners in the Piazza Navona and go out cruising; usually I'd end up with another American, a big, handsome black man named Ron. Our racial differences would have kept us apart back home (it was the era of the Black Panthers), but in Rome our shared horniness and nationality united us.

I wrote Richard Howard about all of my shoddy adventures. He admonished me, "Here you are in the central city of Western culture and you've managed to turn it into some sort of kicky version of Scranton."

I thought that the most that could be said was that in Rome I'd re-created my life in New York but in an inferior version. Like a marble statue copied in lard. I'd written a screenplay that no one wanted. I'd seen historic monuments only when other Americans visited me. I'd met Farley Granger through my Italian teacher and written my screenplay for him. I'd invested endless hours in courting Phillip but had slept with him only during one drunken weekend when we had emptied several bottles of vodka and rolled around like animals. I'd killed his two cats. I'd learned to speak a halting, broken Italian. I'd drunk hundreds of liters of white wine, many of them with Diana Artom, a painter and poet who was in love with me even though I kept telling her I was gay. I'd say, *"Sono froscio,"* which I guess was the rough equivalent of saying "I'm a fag" in English. She was horrified and said it wasn't a good word, only my faulty Italian would allow me to say such a thing. I tried to tell her about our habit back home of embracing the insult but she just shook her head vigorously. She also told me that because of my unfamiliarity with Italian society I'd fallen in with some dreadful types, Phillip and his friends. They were nothing but *ladri*, "thieves."

# Chapter 8

And then I was back in New York and the 1970s had finally begun. Stan met me at the airport, popped something fun in my mouth, and took me on a tour of all the discos and backroom bars that had opened since Stonewall and my departure. After six or seven months in Italy, starved for sex, I couldn't believe how unleashed New York had become.

For the first time I realized how much New York gay life had gradually been changing all along. Now it seemed as if ten times more gays than ever before were on the streets. With ten times as many gay bars. After the furtiveness of feeling up married men in the Roman cinemas, here were go-go boys dancing under spotlights and hordes of attractive young men crowding into small backrooms and abandoning themselves to each other's mouths and arms and penises. Although people still talked about quick sex as "disgusting" and "filthy," I thought of it as romantic. The idea that I could spot a pair of broad shoulders above narrow hips and mounted below a perfect column of a strong neck crowned by black hair and follow this prodigy into a dark room and within seconds be feeling his muscular, hot arms around me and his tongue in my mouth—that I could taste him and instantaneously know him—struck me as a miraculous but strangely easy transition. The intimacy that one would before have had to work for during months of courtship was now available for a whistle and a wink and a ten-step walk into the shadows.

I kept buzzing around a couple who were obviously looking for a third man to go home with them. They weren't interested in me till I happened to see a Roman friend and started to talk to him in Italian. The two men came up to me and asked me, respectfully and somewhat timidly, if I spoke English.

"A lee-tle beet," I said.

They asked me to go home with them, and for the entire evening I impersonated what I thought was their idea of an Italian.

The Gay Activists Alliance held a dance every Saturday in an old firehouse they'd taken over. Here the clothes and bodies were more varied, perhaps less ideal, than in the discos, but the sense of camaraderie was stronger. Men and women danced together. The middle-aged and the pudgy dared to show their faces. People who purported to be gay farmers or gay nurses put in appearances. Blacks, who had trouble gaining entry in the usual gay venues, came to the Firehouse with their black or white lovers and friends.

Not only had the number of visible lesbians and gays increased exponentially, they were also more fearless and affectionate on the street than ever before. They were loud and flirty or grim and sex-crazed, giddy or pompous—the whole gamut. I knew that it was only on the island of Manhattan that this visibility and variety existed. When I went to my mother's summer place in Michigan, I walked aimlessly along Lake Michigan through whole vast armies of sunbathers and not once did I see anything that resembled a gay man. Not one eye strayed toward me or gave me that shutter-click of recognition I was so eager to detect in them.

In New York I attended a meeting of the Gay Academic Union; perhaps no more than fifty women and men were in the audience, young professors for the most part, though some were independent scholars, and they were talking about gay history and gay culture and the intersection of feminism and the lesbian struggle—or they were asking, was Thoreau gay? Whitman? Melville? Just to see all those earnest faces tilted up toward the speaker, not cracking jokes, not looking around for ironic grins of confirmation, made me realize how quickly everything was evolving.

But the sexual abundance and opportunity struck me the most. Even though I was only thirty, I felt too old, too late to enjoy the new dispensations. Yet when I entered a backroom or the back of a truck parked under the piers beside the Hudson, or went into the abandoned piers themselves, I didn't worry about my age or psychic readiness. At first we didn't get into the holds of trucks but rather the gay boys crouched under one truck and the "straight" teens from Jersey stood in the narrow space between two trucks and got sucked off. The brackish smell of the cold water flowing nearby and the dance of New Jersey lights on the small, faceted waves in the wake of a passing barge filled me with a cool romantic ardor. This was the chase, the adventure. We heard of bodies discovered floating down the river, of horrible mutilations, of drive-by murders, but nothing could make us abandon the prowl.

In one of the old piers there'd be no lights at all beyond the occasional flare of a match seeking a cigarette, a sudden phosphorus flash revealing that what you thought was an embracing couple was actually a thick stump of wood with a rusting chain wrapped around it, or what you saw as a gull's wing was really someone's shirttail. Ramps led up to rooms with missing doors and floorboards, to a seething Laocoön entwined by snakes or by arms as he held fast to his sons or lovers . . .

I had a joyful, drunken reunion with Richard Howard and in my sentimental excitement about seeing him sent him a wrong signal. He said, "Oh, darling, I was hoping you'd feel that way someday," and I was too polite to clarify the point. Richard spirited me away for a bucolic weekend at the country house of Coburn Britton, a rich poet from Cleveland who was publishing a little magazine called *Prose*. Coby had an old apple farm in northern New Jersey. We all went over to visit Glenway Wescott, the novelist in his seventies who had been a beauty back in Paris in the 1920s and who'd written one classic, *The Pilgrim Hawk*. Now he no longer wrote anything beyond his journals but devoted most of his time to being a member of the American Academy of Arts and Letters. I thought that was a terrible fate—and now that I'm in my late sixties I, too, am serving on the awards committee of the academy.

After my all-too-apparent physiological lack of interest in him, Richard politely withdrew and never said a word about it. He was tactful and worldly in the best sense.

For a few weeks I lived with Marilyn. I'd grown my hair long and I'd come back from Rome with a blue velvet jacket and a white suit. I was skinny and not healthy looking. I'd drunk so much white wine and eaten so many olives and so much bad bread that I looked jaundiced. Italian words kept flitting through my head; I was translating everything I thought into Italian, but badly. In Italy a man could not be seen carrying laundry or groceries; he had to put everything in a suitcase as though headed for the train station. I went along with that. He dared not step outside even to go to the corner without wearing a coat and tie; I went along with that. The last day I was in Rome was a steaming day in July. I went in shorts to pick up my laundry and the laundress complained, "I work day and night to make you look well dressed and here you are disgracing me."

In New York no one south of Fourteenth Street ever wore a tie or anything but a ripped T-shirt and dirty jeans and sneakers or cowboy boots. Gay men held cologne and jewelry in abhorrence. Some of the bars posted rules forbidding cologne, hair spray, dress slacks, cuff links, and even underpants. For New Yorkers the streets were considered "backstage," and even beautifully dressed women wore gym shoes on the street and put their heels on only when they arrived at the office, a dinner party, or the theater. For Romans the street was the stage. In returning to New York, I felt as if I'd boarded a forward-flying time machine.

Now in New York a friend of a friend offered me a job as a stock boy in his shop on Madison Avenue selling clear plastic furniture. But I was hoping to find something better. I tried to get a job in publishing. Tom Congdon, the editor who would nurse *Jaws* toward bestsellerdom in 1974, interviewed me. My seat for this encounter was a low child's chair and his a high executive throne (in fact, there was a book out at the time about how to intimidate others, and this tactic of relative chair size and positioning was one of the key strategies). I also was interviewed by Matthew J. Bruccoli, the biographer and scholar of F. Scott Fitzgerald and others. Then there was someone at Atheneum. They all told me that it was unheard of for a writer to be a book editor. In England, perhaps, that might work, but in America it would be a clear conflict of interest.

I found some freelance writing work and a one-room apartment on Horatio Street in the West Village, not far from the Hudson River, for a hundred dollars a month. There were a few scraps of furniture—a kitchen table, a pretty desk, two chairs, a single mattress on the floor. There was a closet and a small, dirty bathroom. The windows were covered with heavy metal gates, but through the bars you could see big green ailanthus trees. As soon as I turned on the light, cockroaches scurried off into hiding.

I never met any of my neighbors but most of them were young. I could hear them running up and down the stairs all the time, all through the night—not a heavy tread, just a light scampering. They, too, were roaches, fleet of foot and light-phobic. On the corner of Horatio and Greenwich Street there was a laundry run by a sweet old couple who had concentration-camp tattoos on their arms and were always smiling and spoke almost no English. Unlike my lady in Rome, they were indifferent to how their customers looked. On one side of Horatio were elegant brownstones from the middle of the ninteenth century. On my side were tenement buildings, shabby structures from the beginning of the twentieth century meant to be temporary housing for immigrants.

From my aerie I would swoop down on men of all ages and shapes, usually late at night. Not that there was much happiness in a life of pleasure. Once I was in the backs of trucks or in the ruined piers along the Hudson, I simply couldn't make myself go home. Even after a satisfying encounter with one man or ten I still wanted to hang around to see what the next ten minutes would bring. What it brought was the morning light, the sudden explosion of expensively shod feet on pavement as well-dressed men and women, pale from too much work and too many late nights and too little sleep, rushed out of their apartment buildings and hurried off to their jobs and I, in need of a shave and a bath, slunk home in semen-stiff jeans and a T-shirt that stank, my spirits depressed, my body thoroughly reamed.

I mentioned that I sometimes felt I was too old for all this.

But gay men—like straight women—always feel they're too old. I remember that my twenty-sixth birthday was the most difficult one, since suddenly I thought I was no longer a student who could get away with being sloppy and unfocused and riddled with bad habits. Having no longer any chance to be a prodigy, I now had to content myself with being a late bloomer, if I was going to bloom at all. I would do isometric exercises for my face (a new fad at the time), trying to avoid age lines and saggy pouches. I was on a lifelong diet (in three months I once lost fifty pounds with the help of amphetamines and a regime of steak, salad, and white wine). I who took no pleasure in sports was launched into a lifelong program of exercise. I who hated shopping and was too poor to buy new clothes would do whatever was possible within my means to obtain the latest "hot" look. I had my hair "relaxed" to resemble a surfer. I remember in the sixties glancing at the first gay men to sport mustaches and saying to a friend, "I could never kiss that!" Within three months I had my own mustache. Just as ten years later I shaved mine as soon as everyone else did. Long hair, straightened hair, crew cuts, long sideburns—I followed almost every fad.

I felt I'd come down in the world. Before Italy I was living in the nicest apartment I'd ever had, I was wearing suits, and I'd had a retirement plan. Now I was thirty and unemployed and living in a roach trap. But at last I'd become the long-haired hippie in dirty jeans and torn T-shirt, even if the era for hippies was gradually passing. I wasn't sure if I preferred the living death of respectability linked to a dull job or the peril of living on the economic edge, free to keep my own hours—and to fill them up with tedious, ill-paid freelance work.

Richard, with a complete lack of resentment and a nearly unique generosity linked to his natural ebullience, fixed me up with not one but two different young men, one after another. There was a bright, skinny writer, impotent from heroin; we spent an uncomfortable New Year's Eve together. There was a dark young doctor who was always depressed, whom I was half in love with. He lived in another city and spent weekends with me in my pitiful apartment. I didn't see how bad it was, nor did I ever think of myself as poor. Broke, perhaps, but not "poor." Maybe because my father had been rich, maybe because I'd had a well-paying job I hated, maybe because I thought of my life as enviable, maybe because it all felt like gleeful slumming, and anyway an average tidy studio apartment in a doorman building would have seemed like even a bigger comedown after my father's house—better the gutter than the curb.

New York was a broken city, literally on the verge of bankruptcy. A woman I knew bought a brownstone in the Village for thirty thousand dollars and said to me, "I know I'll never get my money out, but I'm sentimental about the city." Uncollected garbage piled up along the curb. The sidewalks were cracked and tilted by tree roots. Streetlights burned out and weren't replaced. The crime rate was high. My little apartment was broken into, despite the metal gates on the windows, and my radio and typewriter were stolen. I hired a burglar-proofer who, he assured me, was a convicted thief himself and therefore knew "all their tricks." He lined the front door, which had painted glass panels, with sheet metal. Into the window frames he put long metal pegs that had to be extracted before the windows could be opened. As the man said, "They only have two or three minutes from the time they break the glass and the time they have to hop in and clear the place out. If the window is too complicated, they won't bother. But of course they could always get into the apartment downstairs and bore their way through." Heroin addicts, everyone said, were responsible for the thefts. Burglaries were so common that no one paid much attention to them except the victims. I was haunted by memories of New York when I'd first moved there in 1962 and lived in the Y and had to borrow money from friends just to eat. Now, just less than a decade later, I was back down to five hundred dollars again. I'd blown my profit-sharing money inviting everyone out to dinner in Rome, though I didn't regret it.

I began to see David Kalstone all the time. He'd moved up to Twenty-second Street between Eighth and Ninth avenues, the block where I live now. He lived in a floor-through of a brownstone in a lovely disorder of half-filled teacups and freshly opened "little" magazines, of ballet programs and long telephone cords, of cast-aside Missoni sweater vests and extra pairs of reading glasses, of a big silver bowl full of freesias as fresh and unbent as spring onions still in the ground. He loved Maria Callas and I pretended I did, too (worshipping her was an article of faith among gay men in those days). To my ears, she sounded shrill and flat, though I was prepared to believe she'd been a great actress, never mind the screeching.

David never had much money because he was always saving up from his salary, and the extra income he earned as one of the several editors of the Norton anthology of English literature, for his extravagant summers in Venice, where he would rent a whole floor in a palazzo. Chelsea in those days was mostly Puerto Rican and the rents were low. Men in T-shirts sat on their stoops listening to Latin music and drinking beer. David took the subway everywhere in the city, never a cab except late at night, and commuted to his job at Rutgers University by bus rather than train because it was fractionally cheaper. Despite his budget, we'd go out to dinner, dutch—usually to Duff's on Christopher Street, where we'd sit in a booth and eat our rare sirloin steaks and green beans and drink white wine and bid the waiter, "Take the bread away—we're dieting!" After a few weeks we'd see the waiter, smiling a mild acknowledgment at us, turning away the busboy carrying the bread basket.

I adored David but he represented the adult, charming, sexless world for me. Though I was thirty I wasn't quite ready to be a grown-up. I'd get restless as midnight approached. I longed to escape and to run out to the backroom bars or the trucks. I needed to leave the salon before my hands began to sprout hair and my teeth to sharpen.

David was extremely close to the poet James Merrill, and slightly in awe of him. Merrill's father, Charles Merrill, had been one of the founders of the brokerage firm Merrill Lynch. James Merrill had written a vaguely autobiographical novel, *The Seraglio*, in which the young hero feels burdened by his wealth and wants to give it away, but it turns out that a legal divestiture of that magnitude is virtually impossible. In real life, Merrill started the Ingram Merrill Foundation (Ingram was the maiden name of

Jimmy's mother), which gave small grants of five or six thousand dollars to many needy writers. Cleverly, Merrill had figured out that if he wanted to spend time with other poets rather than bankers, he needed to share the wealth without making it look like handouts. If a friend put the touch on him, Jimmy could always say, "Apply to the foundation, but remember I'm just one of the board members." Of course in reality Jimmy had the last say, but no one was supposed to know that (ostensibly he conferred with John Hollander and Irma Brandeis). If someone got money from the foundation, he or she didn't have to feel beholden to Merrill himself. Nor was it a loan that had to be paid back—or that could potentially create bad blood if, as might have been more likely, it wasn't paid back.

David arranged for me to meet Merrill over after-dinner drinks. Merrill was a bit lined from excessive dieting but from a distance he had a boyish look and manner. He was partial to purples and heathers and earth tones, to the colors that fall leaves assume on the ground after the first rain. He wore serapes and embroidered jackets and creased linen trousers and sandals, the antidote to the three-piece suits and bluchers his father must have donned. He was clearly a bohemian. Later when I visited his apartment in the fishing village of Stonington, Connecticut ("Jimmy lives in the only ugly building in Stonington," as catty friends said), I realized that the top two floors he occupied in the old Victorian house above a store and the floor between were crammed with objects he'd described in his poems: the mirror and bat-motif wallpaper and the red bohemian crystal chandelier above a round table for Ouija messages in the bay window and the widow's walk above, graced with a Roman bust. They were all magical in the eyes of the aficionado, but they didn't necessarily go together. His friends, of course, nodded sagely when they read:

Backdrop. The dining room at Stonington.
Walls of ready-mixed matte "flame" (a witty
Shade, now watermelon, now sunburn).
Overhead, a turn of the century dome
Expressing white tin wreathes and fleurs-de-lys
In palpable relief to candlelight . . .
The room breathed sheer white curtains out. In blew
Elm- and chimney-blotted shimmerings, so
Slight the tongue of land, so high the point of view.

Something about Merrill made you want to please him and fear you couldn't. He alternated between a silken, silly giggle, but one that was boyish and never girlish, and an earnest unsmiling way of nodding agreement or encouragement. He could listen to an overly long explanation of one's own (nervous, pompous) and raise his eyebrows and say, "Ah-h-h . . ." Was that an *ah* of recognition and agreement? Or was it merely a slightly weary way of marking the transition into the next, more amusing topic? He loved to make puns, usually good ones (like the "slight of tongue" in the last line above), then lower his eyes and sit forward or wrap his arms around his knees and lower his lids and purr. He never tried to sell his wit but would sit back and contemplate it with no more proprietorial sense than the newest comer. He was so afraid of protracting a point that he just sketched it in and then licked his dry lips with the sudden, darting flicker of the amphetamine dieter. He could look deeply sympathetic for a short minute, but that solemnity was built on mercury, not bedrock. A moment later his eyes were flashing humor and he was quoting something one wasn't quite sure one had recognized. When he'd been a young man, as he revealed in his memoir about the 1950s, *A Different Person*, he'd feared he was superficial and he'd felt easier with people of his own class who knew to do no more than smile and shrug in most situations. The one area in which Jimmy had never been superficial or dismissive was writing. As he'd said, "I wrote, therefore I was."

I suppose it's always strange to know in the flesh someone who is destined to be "immortal," or at least studied and analyzed long after his death. He was the American poet who possessed a grand Proustian sense of time and a Nabokovian love of language and sensuality. Comparing him to two of the best novelists of the twentieth century makes sense given that his poems always possessed a narrative sweep—and that he wrote that most readable and enduring epic poem, *The Changing Light at Sandover*. Having actually known such a person doesn't give one a special purchase on the reality. In fact familiarity can lead to slightly idiotic complacencies. The French critic Sainte-Beuve wrote that he couldn't see why everyone made such a fuss over "Beyle" (Stendhal), since good ol' Beyle would surely have been the first to laugh at his exaggerated posthumous reputation. Even so, everyone wants to hear the story just because it "really" happened, and yet in truth its reality—fragile at best and now largely mythologized into a new shape—is scarcely telling.

But there's another, more moving aspect of having really known someone destined for fame. It's that they were once young, uncertain, had a roll of fat about the waistband, one nostril bigger than the other, a shifty look that gave way to a wise stare. They existed in the present, with all its contingencies, not in the safety of the past. They were breathing, digesting animals as vulnerable to injury as the next creature, at any moment liable to have been run over or to fall ill. Their careers, which in retrospect look so triumphant and inevitable, might just as easily have come to naught. Maxime Du Camp, Flaubert's traveling companion, wrote that the great realist had an irritating way of repeating a feeble joke over and over until it became truly tiresome, and that the humor, scarcely detectable the first time around, never failed to amuse the

Master each time he repeated it. He tells us how sadistic Flaubert was in the desert when a camel fell and broke their saddlebags and completely drained their water supply, how for the next three days (until they reached an oasis) they were painfully thirsty and, just to be cruel, Flaubert kept talking about the marvelous cold lemon ices they used to get at Tortoni's in Paris. This prematurely balding man with the light eyes who refused to exercise and took almost no interest in the Middle East until they arrived in Greece—could he be the same writer the next generation of novelists would memorize (Ford Madox Ford had most of *Sentimental Education* by heart)?

James Merrill could be led reluctantly back to serious topics. Then he would stroke his throat almost as if he were easing down the lumpy but necessary nourishment. He'd make his eyes round and would say, "Ahh . . . ," but with more a sagacious than an astonished intonation. His eyes would get so wide it wasn't even certain he was still paying attention instead of miming it. If his interlocutor wasn't careful, Merrill would soon slip free of the bridle pulling him toward solemnity and dart off toward the gay and frivolous wilds. He wanted to laugh, though not in some familiar, commonplace way, but rather at his own jokes, told in his own particular way. Listening to his sudden shifts in register was a way of learning how to read his poetry with its corrugated surfaces, its way of moving from the lightest tone of social gossip to the most Dantesque invocations—a tone he'd learned from Pushkin and from Nabokov, not to mention the Byron of *Don Juan* or the Pope of *The Rape of the Lock*, but one he'd made entirely his own.

Young people (especially the uninitiated) were always astonished at Merrill's readings by how much was funny, how much everyone around them laughed. What interested me was how Jimmy made use of so much that came his way—and how deliberately reducing that flow from the indiscriminate flood of Manhattan to the mere trickle of Stonington or Key West or Athens (his three "villages") had been a central creative act of his life. He thrived on anagrams (and belonged to an anagram club in Key West) and crosswords and, of course, the Ouija board, not to mention acrostics and all disciplined forms of poetry, the sestinas and rondeaux. Sometimes I'd be reading a long poem by Merrill with all the concentration I'd naturally bring to a cliff-hanger—and suddenly I'd notice the narrative was being relayed through a string of sonnets.

Merrill loved to tease and maybe couldn't bear to do too much hand-holding, but in spite of this he was kind and sponsoring. He certainly nurtured me without ever being mindlessly affirmative. He could be harsh if the occasion required it. After reading my novel *Caracole* he voiced my worst fears, saying, "That first chapter, my dear!" and rolling his eyes.

His mother was from Georgia and his father from Florida, but Merrill had grown up on Long Island and had had foreign nannies and then had been sent off to Lawrenceville School in New Jersey. His accent was his own, drawled in a soft Southern way, but the vowels weren't twangy or yearning or eager to open up into diphthongs. No one could say his voice was irritating or off-putting, and when he gave a reading, it was a beautiful orchestration out of which many different expressions, from the silly to the oracular, could be coaxed.

That first evening I found him polite but remote. He would so obviously have preferred a good informal talk with David alone and wasn't interested in David's protégé. I suppose, being a generation younger than either, I projected a certain raw sexiness. But as I found out later, Jimmy's type was the tall, romantic youth, preferably straight and unavailable though longing to be a best friend and fellow poet; someone serious and talented who, even if much younger chronologically, would treat Jimmy as a sweet if devilish little brother. I wasn't eligible for any of those roles—and as David's beloved I was off-limits in any event.

David urged me to read Merrill the first chapter of *Forgetting Elena*. During the whole recital of fifteen terrifying minutes, Merrill's face was illegible. Jimmy didn't give a hint as to whether he was amused or struck or bored, and when it was all over, he didn't say a word but merely nodded, giving the smallest possible indication that he was still alive. I gathered up my papers and hurried the fifteen blocks home. I was so distraught, I longed to throw myself in front of the first speeding car that came along. I felt that I'd failed in my first great test. My failure was especially painful because David was so enthusiastic about my work—and would he now have the independence of spirit to remain convinced of my book's worth?

Eventually I found out that Jimmy liked Proust, sure, but he also liked to read the bestseller of the moment if it had any literary merit, just as he liked to follow fads about the interpretation of hand gestures. ("Oh, look!" he'd exclaim. "She's palming!")

Years later, when I mentioned that fatal evening to Merrill, he said, "I was drunk that night. I barely knew who you were, much less what you'd just read." Since Merrill had in the intervening years joined AA and stopped drinking (but some people said it was only to keep a new boyfriend company), I believed him. Then after Merrill died, his literary executor (and one of my closest friends), J. D. McClatchy, said, "But he didn't like *Forgetting Elena*. He didn't get it."

Through David I met many other poets and writers. John Ashbery gave *Forgetting Elena* a blurb that delighted me, just as he personally fascinated me. John lived across the street from David Kalstone in a 1960s white brick building. He would get so drunk that he'd fall down. Yet he was hilariously funny in a deadpan way that camouflaged, nearly, his perfect recall and edgy intelligence. He adored obscure "serious" music and had the most esoteric tastes.

What was distinctive about New York in the 1970s was its uncompromising high culture masquerading as slouching, grinning gee-whiz—Wallace Stevens in sneakers. John Ashbery had lived in Paris for years, where he'd been the art critic for the *Herald Tribune*, and now wrote art reviews for *Newsweek*. When he gave a reading in the austere and large auditorium at the bottom of the Guggenheim Museum, it was packed with young people in black and older, art-world people. There were German women in full-length black leather coats and hennaed hair and men in faded blue work shirts, insect-eye glasses, white stubble, and oversize porkpie hats. Ashbery was always surrounded by art-world people, which brought a whiff of money and internationalism to the usual seedy gatherings of poor poets. Like Warhol he gave the impression of never trying. His drinking seemed clear proof of his social indifference. Not that he wasn't charming and solicitous with friends. Once I was with him at one of his readings in SoHo, just when SoHo was becoming a gallery center. After the reading a young woman who was a total stranger invited us all back to her nearby loft. There we stood around drinking jug wine while she scuttled about in an adjoining room, dragging into place what turned out to be canvases and snapping on lights. Finally she led Ashbery, who was about to pass out, into her studio. In her mind, no doubt, he was supposed to discover her and arrange overnight for a one-woman show. All he did was look at the work through swimming eyes and say in his high, slurred voice, "Those are some paintings." The poor girl broke into tears. Actually, it wasn't such a put-down coming from the author of *Some Trees*.

David Kalstone liked that first book, *Some Trees*, which had been selected by W. H. Auden as the winner of the Yale Younger Poet series. Both Ashbery and Merrill revered Auden—and there all resemblance between the two junior poets ended. David dismissed Ashbery's next collection, *The Tennis Court Oath*, though

David's approval soared again with *The Double Dream of Spring* and even the all-prose *Three Poems* (published in 1972), which had somehow been inspired by Ashbery's psychoanalytic sessions. But the crowning glory of not only Ashbery's growing oeuvre but of American poetry in the 1970s was *Self-Portrait in a Convex Mirror*. The title poem was a long, sustained look at the self, at what it might and might not be in these godless days. About the soul, the poet asks, "But how far can it swim out through the eyes. / And still return safely to its nest?" The questions become more tendentious, taking a sharper, more pessimistic tone:

> But there is in that gaze a combination
> Of tenderness, amusement and regret, so powerful
> In its restraint that one cannot look for long.
> The secret is too plain. The pity of it smarts,
> Makes hot tears spurt: that the soul is not a soul,
> Has no secret, is small, and it fits
> Its hollow perfectly: its room, our moment of attention.

With this one poem Ashbery, intimate but impersonal, pinpointed the shifting uncertainty of the way we lived now. We saw him at parties (once I even went to bed with him and his boyfriend), and he was a hapless, amusing presence ("a combination / Of tenderness, amusement and regret"), but we knew that we were in the presence of genius. It was as if we were seeing Whitman on the Staten Island ferry or Emily Dickinson wrapping a cake and scribbling a poem on the paper.

# Chapter 9

A science writer from Time-Life named Frank called me up in 1971 and asked me if I wanted a "gig." He said that the two publishers, Charney and Veronis, who'd made a success out of *Psychology Today* had bought the dowdy old *Saturday Review* and didn't seem to know anyone in the arts—and besides, they wanted to "democratize" the arts. Their idea was to have stories on quilting and Adirondack ceramics and furniture made out of driftwood. They were as hostile to East Coast snobbism as a Beltway politician speaking for effect. They were even considering moving the whole operation to the West Coast. We quipped that they were irritated because no one noticed them when they entered their box at the Metropolitan Opera, that they thought they'd be big fish in the small pond of San Francisco. Little did they realize that in San Francisco they'd be just as ignored.

Some of the old-timers had been kept on at the *Saturday Review* and were darting about angrily like late-autumn bees since they'd been promised that nothing would change and they'd still be in charge of their old hives, and now obviously everything had changed. Critics with triple-barreled names and old tweeds were ignored as ambitious youngsters who knew nothing shoved past them. I was one of the barbarians. I wrote a "Letter from the Publisher" in which I made two crucial mistakes. I confused

Walker Percy's name and called him Percy Walker. And I dimly remembered Marilyn once telling me that T. E. Hulme had said that Romanticism is nothing but "spilt religion," but I'd misinterpreted his words. As a result, dozens of letters to the editor ridiculed poor Charney for being an illiterate fool—and it was all my fault. I was the fool. I was illiterate. Today an essayist would google his sources, but back then fact-checking could take up a whole day, and I was working long hours without assistants.

For some reason the new owners attributed all the malice of the letter writers to East Coast elitism and didn't chuck me. They were counseled by Peter Drucker, a celebrated business guru, who told them they should turn the weekly magazine (whose typical reader was a middle-aged Midwestern librarian) into four flashy monthly supplements: the *Saturday Review of the Arts*, the *Saturday Review of Society*, the *Saturday Review of the Sciences*, and the *Saturday Review of Education*. They wanted me to be an editor in charge of the arts, but since I wasn't experienced enough to run a magazine, they thought I should have a boss. I could interview my own boss and give him my approval or not. The person they chose was a chipper, bright-eyed, well-groomed West Coaster of about forty named John Poppy, who had been an editor of *Look* and was a surprisingly buttoned-up disciple of George Leonard, an Esalen West Coast touchy-feely leader of the "human actualization" movement. Mr. Poppy didn't look or act as if he'd ever been in a hot tub or been "rebirthed," but he did have a permanent smile on his face and a robin's way of cocking his head to one side, of beaming very deliberate alpha waves over his much more natural and native jitteriness.

None of us liked him, although he was extremely likable— polite, receptive, kind. I didn't like him because I had an allergy to all authority figures and didn't want a boss. I said I disliked him because he didn't know as much as I did, but in fact he was clever, and even if he'd been a genius, I would have wanted to undermine him. At Time-Life Books our supervising editors had been so much older than us and so remote and established that I suppose it never occurred to us as trainees to defy or question them. We complained about them, but as privates complain about generals while obeying them unquestioningly. Now I said yes, they should hire Poppy, but only because he seemed pleasant and inoffensive and also because I could tell that Charney and Veronis wanted him.

The magazine moved out to San Francisco and I went along for the ride. I hired some old friends of mine. Stan, my first lover, became the production director and stage-managed the difficult transition from East to West Coast and from one magazine to four. The printers we contracted in California had never done a big job beyond the telephone book. The idea of producing a weekly magazine with four-color illustrations staggered them. In those days before computers everything still had to be set in type and the photos had to be carefully inserted into the copy. Color correction, proofreading, binding, stapling—every process took hours upon hours and we would work late into the night.

Although I'd written book reviews for magazines, I'd never been on the staff of a weekly. I loved it because it was exciting and relentless. An idea, good or bad, was realized in just a few days. No expense was spared. In a year we spent sixteen million dollars, a fortune back then.

I lived in a charming little house behind a house on Russian Hill with Stan. By that point he'd fallen for a willful ex-marine drug addict back in New York who was obsessed with him. Jerry and Stan were on the phone every day, and Stan was always planning his frequent rendezvous with Jerry back in New York or Los Angeles or some other city.

Our house was ravishing with its little garden full of fuchsia and its Japanese interior and vast panoramic views of the bay, San Quentin prison, and Mount Tamalpais in the distance. In the mornings the bay would be cold and fogbound, but by noon the mists had burned off and the city was suddenly warm. But every neighborhood, it seemed, had its own microclimate. The hills were so steep that cars had to be parked with their wheels turned into the curb lest they start rolling away. The trolley cables were always humming hollowly under the street, like thick metallic arteries pumping and singing in a body on life support.

At the time, San Francisco was almost bucolic. The beatnik era was over, though the City Lights bookstore was still flourishing. Italian immigrants were everywhere. My watch repairman was Italian and I'd speak to him in his language. Pastry shops offered big cannoli covered with red and green sprinkles. On Telegraph Hill an old Italian restaurant had booths for ladies with doors that closed, a holdover from the period just after the earthquake. Hundreds of vagrants were in the Tenderloin, attracted by the good weather and the liberal public-welfare laws in California. San Francisco was not then a rich city, not as it would become after the start-up of the high-tech industry. Rents were cheap but salaries were correspondingly low. Educated young people with Ph.D.'s in art history were willing to work for two dollars an hour as checkout clerks at the supermarket. Of course rich retired people had moved in from all over the West because it was a beautiful and cultured metropolis with Victorian houses. It was also the financial center of the West. There was a harbor but it had missed out on the recent containerization revolution and lost business to other ports such as Seattle.

To us New Yorkers, San Francisco seemed eerily quiet, the streets empty, the lights doused after ten o'clock, the restaurants full of health food and skinny, blond hippie waiters on tranquilizers. The air seemed thin, as if we were high up instead of at sea level. The light was as delicate as a blonde's eyelids—and just as defenseless. We would wander through the Golden Gate Park and look at all the plants we couldn't name, the splendid exotic flowers that seemed too tropical for this chilly climate. We were heavy-smoking, grimy, soiled, fast-talking, and abrupt, and everyone out here seemed weirdly characterless and "nice," as if they were newly hatched. Climbing a hill would leave us winded.

The famous gay life was just starting up in the Castro, but most of it was still centered, as it had long been, around tacky Polk Street. Except it wasn't visibly "centered" anywhere but rather went on behind closed doors, in gated patios or in small, scattered neighborhood bars pulsing sadly like scattered pods promising eventual life.

We were worried that we were missing out on something by not being back in our own dirty, impossible, exciting city. As editors we complained that all the good stories originated in New York and that all the good journalists lived there. Although we tried to honor the notion of reorienting the magazine to the West Coast, we couldn't find much to write about in San Francisco. David Bourdon, our art critic, did one story (my suggestion) on Richard Diebenkorn, a genuine San Francisco artist and one respected in New York. Bourdon also wrote about the quirky, humorous ceramist Robert Arneson, who was recognized by the international art market. If we had to do something on weaving, it shouldn't be about local looms but rather about the great fiber-artist innovators, Lenore Tawney and Claire Zeisler. But the idea that we could single-handedly elevate San Francisco novelists (well, there was Herbert Gold . . .) or composers or painters (there'd been the Bay Region figurative painters of the 1950s, but who since?)—all that seemed impossible. Of course some poets of importance were in Bolinas, but our bosses weren't too keen on devoting much space to them.

We worried about our own careers. What would happen to us if and when the magazine folded, as seemed inevitable? Would we just be forgotten? Were we in danger of falling off the edge of the world? We noticed with anxiety that even natives in San Francisco referred to their city as being "out here." I'd struggled to get to New York from Illinois and Michigan and now it seemed as if I were going backward. My novel *Forgetting Elena* was about to come out, but of course I wouldn't be in New York to "promote" it, whatever that consisted of. The cover art arrived in the mail for my "approval." I disapproved of it—a color drawing of a seashell weeping a single tacky tear—but that made no difference. If I'd been in New York, would they have paid more attention to me? Probably not.

One night we walked to the foot of Russian Hill and attended a midnight performance of gender-fucking bearded drag queens, the Cockettes. The audience was in makeup and glitter and bits of finery as well. Everyone was high on LSD except us, who were sullen and drunk. They were all weeping and laughing uncontrollably and singing along and responding to tiny, nearly invisible gestures, or to inaudible words as if they were listening to the bizarrely eloquent but perfectly banal peepings of Kafka's mouse-diva, Josephine. The public devoured with delight the terrible silent-movie overacting. At certain points various actors straggled purposelessly across the stage in dirty organdy skirts and torn stockings, their eyes more mascaraed than a Kabuki actor's. The unpatterned traffic jam of personnel onstage no longer suggested coherent pictures for the audience. As at the Kabuki, a cult of personality surrounded several transvestites, in this case long-legged, terminally skinny black or white speed freaks. "Oh, Marsha!" someone would cry from the audience. "Betty, girl, we love you!" We were totally puzzled. We weren't on acid. We didn't know these people. "Amateur hour," someone in our cynical group muttered. I suppose we felt vindicated when the Cockettes bombed in New York soon afterward, though the New York critics' agreement with us, a New York audience, was merely tautological. If the Cockettes had truly been Japanese dancers and we'd had to wear interpreter's headphones and read a monograph on them, they might have had better luck and might have been just as foreign to our Broadway-trained sensibilities.

Also, it seemed to us as if everyone in San Francisco were doing yoga and reading Krishnamurti, gardening and obsessing about the presentation of his or her macrobiotic diet on an artfully misshapen, partially glazed Korean kiln-fired plate. They were turned inward, dedicated to self-cultivation, and we were turned outward in vigorous competition with other people. We didn't care what we ate or how our chakras were lining up. We were hungry for fame. We wanted to be noticed. We wanted to have high-flying careers. Out in San Francisco people spent their afternoon installing wind chimes in their trees or stretching. We didn't stretch, though we lifted weights at the gym to make a more formidable impression on potential sex partners. Nor did we integrate sex into a larger, holistic pattern. We were abysmally genital and wholly localized. Californians were squeamish about eating meat, some of them not only vegetarians but raw vegetarians. We thought that they were so overwhelmed by their lives and so inept at living them that they believed everything might work out if they could control what went into their mouths. We knew what we wanted in our mouths: steak and cock.

I think we were mostly antipathetic to the locals. For one thing our rhythms were out of sync with theirs. We wanted to score right away; we liked the idea of the one-night stand or bend-over. They were in no rush. Of course they had quick pickups, but nothing was allowed to seem rushed.

I had hired various boyfriends and part-time boyfriends of mine, which would have sounded perfectly normal to another gay man in the 1970s, but today is sufficiently strange to merit a comment. Back then we had no notion of "gay marriage," partly because so many of us were equally opposed to marriage for straight people. Among the heterosexual artists and bohemians and intellectuals I knew, few got married. Gays were more markedly and deliberately promiscuous, though we didn't like that word, which is always negative. Were we erotic adventurers because, as the Freudians said, we were too immature to maintain a committed relationship? Or was it, as the Christians said, that we were licentious and vicious and so unnatural that we submitted to no decent limitations to our lust? Or was it, as I thought, that we'd been so deprived sexually in the fifties and sixties (because we'd had so few places to meet each other and were so fearful that we had become almost invisible, even to one another) that now we were glorying in all those previously missed opportunities to couple (and triple, quadruple)? We thought that sexual freedom was the same thing as freedom. We were willing to contemplate the possibility of "gay politics" or "gay culture," but only if we'd first secured total gay sexual liberty.

Of course at that time sodomy was still illegal in most states, and in a few it was still subject to capital punishment. In New York and San Francisco gay couples walked around hand in hand, but in most other American cities (including nearby outlying districts such as the Bronx and Oakland) they would have been beat up. We ourselves still thought it was pretty strange being gay, and half the time that we were claiming our gay rights we were really whistling in the dark, trying to convince ourselves we weren't really public menaces or monsters either pitiable or frightening.

As the decade wore on, we became more and more convinced that monogamy—and even the concept of the couple—was outdated. We wanted to hook up with one another in giant molecules of adhesiveness and love and friendship, all distinctions leveled, all possibilities open. Friends of our friends became our lovers. Lovers of our lovers became our fuck buddies. In the bigger and bigger gay discos that were being constructed, we'd get high and show up at two or three in the morning and dance till late the following afternoon in a bright hot wash of tribalism. Soon after arriving, before my drugs kicked in, I'd be appalled by the touch of an unknown sweaty body; by the end of fifteen hours on the dance floor, no one was alien to me and I loved everyone. How could monogamy—mom and pop, the suburban quarter acre, and the isolated agony of long evenings in front of the television or in the basement crafts shop—possibly compete with the radiance pouring forth from all of these worked-out, tanning-booth bodies and intelligent, ironic, and seductive faces leaning in and smiling?

While I was still at *Saturday Review* in San Francisco, Nabokov's *Transparent Things* was about to be published. He was my favorite living writer along with Christopher Isherwood. Different as Nabokov and Isherwood were from each other, both inspired me with a respect bordering on reverence and an excited anticipation for each new title. Nabokov was funny and wicked, baroque and heterosexual; Isherwood was sober and good and classical and gay.

I thought that Nabokov's new novel would be a good occasion for devoting a cover story to him. Although John Poppy would have preferred something on redwood furniture or local dancers, he thought it might be wise to throw a sop to those few "literary" subscribers to the *Saturday Review of Literature* still hanging on. And I think he could see how thrilled I was at the prospect, and . . . well, he was a kind man.

I approached a number of writers—William Gass, Joyce Carol Oates, Joseph McElroy (*Women and Men*)—and asked them to write short essays about Nabokov's oeuvre. I intended to contribute something myself, especially after Mr. Poppy generously urged me to do so. He could see that I longed to write about my idol.

Who would take Nabokov's photos? People around the office suggested a true artist such as Cartier-Bresson, but I insisted (yet in truth knowing nothing) that Nabokov was more a social than artistic snob and would respond more favorably to Lord Snowdon, Princess Margaret's husband, the former Antony Armstrong-Jones. My hunch turned out to be right. Nabokov spent a week clowning around with Snowdon, chasing butterflies, of course, but even posing as Borges with a serape over his head. No matter that they weren't terribly good photos; more important for our needs, they were intimate and funny and highly original.

Of course I wanted something from Nabokov's own pen. After the relative failure of his preceding book, *Ada*, something he'd worked on for years and that recycled more autobiographical elements than any preceding book except possibly his much earlier *The Gift*, I thought he'd be open to the full treatment we were offering him. He told me over the phone (I had to get up early to reach him in Switzerland at the cocktail hour) that he'd write me a short piece on inspiration. He was genial over the phone and at that moment was having a drink with Alfred Appel Jr., the editor and commentator of *The Annotated Lolita*. Nabokov had a strong Russian accent, stronger than I'd anticipated; his voice was a high baritone. His *a*'s were long and English, his *r*'s rolled and Russian, his accent more French than anything else, at least to my untrained ears. He had an odd way of punching certain syllables, like an old-fashioned orator.

When his excellent piece came in, I decided to illustrate it with the charming and kitsch painting of Pygmalion and Galatea by the *pompier* French artist Gérôme. In the painting the white marble statue of the beautiful young woman is just beginning to turn to delicious pink flesh, shoulders first, the sculptor stepping back in delighted alarm. Nabokov wrote later that he loved the whole presentation, especially the painting.

But I had a problem. Nabokov's mini-essay had minor mistakes in punctuation and even in diction. How did one edit Nabokov? My solution was to have the essay set exactly as he'd written it, mistakes and all, then to reset it in my corrected version. I messengered both versions to him with a short but polite letter explaining what I'd done. He wired back YOUR VERSION PERFECT.

When the essays by various writers came in, they were mostly a bit bored with Nabokov, as if everyone had praised him long enough and now it was more interesting to be critical. Of course as an idolator I was scandalized by the measured tone of my contributors, and so my own page became all the more dithyrambic. I compared Norman Mailer unfavorably to Nabokov, which would today be so obvious as to seem comical, absurd, but which at that time was still a highly debatable gambit. It was as though I had preferred European dandyism to the raw nerve of America, an Old World beauty to a New World ugly. Even then still, the United States was divided between cultural elitists (supposedly located on the East Coast) and the great unwashed. Richard Howard wrote me that he and James Merrill had just been at a conference in Minnesota where the audience hissed at them for their elitist opinions. As they left the stage, Merrill said loudly, "See what happens when the Great Plains meet the Great Fancies?"

The issue came out with Nabokov glowering in black and white on the cover and the four-color illustration of Pygmalion glowing within. He was happy, he said, in a long and appreciative letter, with the entire issue and the visual elements. About then, in 1973, *Forgetting Elena* finally came out, and I sent Nabokov a copy. Some time later he mailed me a letter in which he said that this praise was not for publication but that he and his wife had liked my book, "in which everything is poised on the edge of everything." A true enough (and flattering, of course) description of my novel, though later I read the same phrase, about this unstable "everything," in a Nabokovian description of the visual experience of a passenger in a train just leaving the station.

Three years later, after my book had sold six hundred copies and the other fourteen hundred had been pulped, a man from *Time* I didn't know named Gerald Clarke called me and asked if I'd be willing to talk to him about my relationship with Nabokov. "I don't have a relationship with him," I said. "I've never met him."

"That's strange because he talks about you very fondly. In fact he said that he loved your novel *Forgetting Elena*."

Would he have loved it, I wondered, if I hadn't orchestrated a cover story on him? Clarke, later to be celebrated for his extraordinarily readable biography of Truman Capote, had gone to Montreux to do an interview with Nabokov for *Esquire* and followed the usual drill: he submitted his questions at the Montreux Palace Hotel every evening, and the answers, clever and a bit artificial, were neatly typed and placed in his box the next morning (Nabokov retaining the copyright). Clarke was an experienced journalist and felt that this author-approved method hadn't produced much, so on his last evening in Switzerland he confronted Nabokov over drinks: "So whom do you like?" Clarke asked—since the great man had so far only listed his dislikes and aversions.

"Edmund White," Nabokov responded. "He wrote *Forgetting Elena*. It's a marvelous book." He'd then gone on to list titles by John Updike and Delmore Schwartz (particularly the short story "In Dreams Begin Responsibilities"), as well as Robbe-Grillet's *Jealousy* among a few others. Clarke decided to break the rules and to publish these off-the-cuff comments.

Nothing in my life changed right away, I was astonished to discover. No marching bands appeared outside my window. But I did feel that I was being acknowledged in some extraordinary way. I thought of Baudelaire's "Les Phares," in which writers down the ages signal each other like lighthouses through the dark. (In our innermost fantasies we have the right to be pretentious.) Later Nabokov even wrote his editor at McGraw-Hill and suggested he take a look at my next novel, which I called variously *Woman Reading Pascal* and *Like People in History*, but the recommendation seemed not to count for much. Maybe the editor realized Nabokov hadn't actually read the manuscript; Nabokov merely knew that I'd written it and was looking for an editor. Later in the 1970s my shrink kept urging me to make a pilgrimage to Switzerland to meet Nabokov in person, but I was reluctant—maybe a bit frightened. Then in the mid-eighties, when I was living in Paris, I went with the French editor Gilles Barbedette to Montreux, where we had tea in the hotel lobby with the widowed Mrs. Nabokov. She had memorized a page from *Forgetting Elena* and recited it. Apparently she had a photographic memory and was able to recall anything she'd ever concentrated on. Treating a novelist to a page of his own work must be the most winning thing anyone can do. I was completely under her spell.

I loved the humor of Nabokov's fiction, his aristocratic *mépris* for morons and pedants, his lively if mocking appreciation of madmen. At the secret heart of his writing was a certain sentimentality: a doting on the couple; a belief in romantic love; a chivalric scorn for bullies and a consecrated respect for women who were as clever as they were beautiful; a hot, irrational cult of sex and of sexual passion, but not its mechanical replications. This dandified, Romantic code, so vulnerable to the world's crude scorn, he protected by ringing it round with the magic fire of his humor, his aggressive dismissal of everyone else, his satirical stabs at Freud, academics, Marx, progressive education, and crass commercialism. For Nabokov everything not coherent with his own cool, elegant style was vulgar or kitsch, a kind of *pashlost'* (his name for a special form of Russian romantic pomposity).

In his interviews, he would attack sacred cows—Thomas Mann, William Faulkner, Conrad, Dostoyevsky. Why, I thought (scandalized), Mann and Faulkner won the Nobel! Conrad was a classic, even if deciphering his books was like undoing knots in a barrel of oil. And Dostoyevsky was a moral giant—even if his scenes went on too long and after they'd reached a rapturous climax and everyone was weeping with tears of reconciliation and relief, they'd start to slide queasily off in some new, horribly disappointing, anxiety-producing direction. Jean Genet had recognized this queasiness, this disquieting anticlimax, but approved of it as being lifelike buffoonery.

Nabokov was a great hater and a rather meager lover. He liked Pushkin and Chekhov and parts of Tolstoy but not all, and nothing of Stendhal (Nabokov's father had been an unquestioning fan). He liked Biely's *St. Petersburg* and all of Khodasevich, whom he'd beautifully translated. He liked Genet but didn't understand why he didn't write about girls instead of boys. And he liked me. Was it a joke? After all, Nabokovian jokes were famous—and everyone was on the lookout for them, and afraid to be taken in by them.

In preparing the Nabokov issue I'd contacted Simon Karlinsky, a professor of Russian at Berkeley. Earlier, Simon had tracked down all of the Russian sources for *Ada* for the *New York Times Book Review*, and now I wanted him to do the same for *Transparent Things* for the *Saturday Review*. He accepted and quickly wrote a brilliant exegesis we were delighted to use. I met him and we became friends. He was friendly with Nabokov, and for me to meet an acquaintance of the Master was thrilling. I sometimes wondered if Nabokov had based *Pnin* (the otherworldly, thoroughly Russian professor so at a loss in the America where he'd settled) on Simon, but the dates didn't work out. Maybe Nabokov was making fun of his own absentmindedness.

Simon was short and maybe twelve years older than I. He had a black beard and small, pudgy hands, a bald head, and intelligent eyes that constantly roamed over the objects around us, as if there was nothing in our conversation to absorb his attention, or as if he were plotting out an escape route. Or maybe he was afraid that actual eye contact would mean he'd have to stop and consider the opinions of his interlocutor, and he wasn't disposed to do that. He had unshakable but subtle and refined opinions of his own. Usually those who hold to their ideas inflexibly don't have very interesting thoughts, but Simon was wonderfully erudite and his articles of faith were highly nuanced, full of major and minor clauses and lots of codicils, but with all the fine print set in bronze.

He'd been brought up in Mukden by Russian parents who'd fled the Revolution. His mother had a dress shop there. He remembered the deep snows of Manchurian winters and stepping over a frozen Burmese tiger in the street that had been delivered early in the morning in front of a Chinese pharmacy, which needed its whiskers for a highly prized medicine. He could also remember that when he'd met a foreign businessman's son, little Billy from Ohio, that child's origins and name had seemed to him unbelievably exotic.

From there he and his family had moved to Los Angeles, where Simon as an adolescent fell in love with contemporary music. During the war years, Los Angeles, thanks to its refugees, was the cultural center of the world—the home of Bertolt Brecht and Thomas Mann, Stravinsky, Schoenberg and Kurt Weill, Isherwood and Aldous Huxley, not to mention all the glamorous stars in exile such as Garbo and Marlene Dietrich. Simon began to attend the avant-garde concerts held on the roof of a building in Los Angeles.

When he was old enough, he was drafted and sent off to Europe during the years immediately following the war. His Russian came in handy, but he was more serious about being a composer than a spy. He entered a competition sponsored by Marie-Laure de Noailles, but her American friend and permanent houseguest Ned Rorem won. Simon felt that no one else had stood a chance against the handsome Ned, obviously the *vicomtesse*'s favorite. Then Simon was commissioned to write ballet music for a small German dance company. He was horrified when he heard the results and decided to abandon an artistic career.

He returned to California and was driving through Berkeley when his car broke down. It would take several days to be repaired, and Simon decided during that time to investigate getting a degree in Russian. Soon he was accepted and dragooned into being a language teacher; within a few years he had his doctorate in Russian and was a professor in the same department.

At the time I met him in the early 1970s Simon had two great arguments with me. He couldn't understand why we young gays would camp and call each other *she*, not realizing that that sort of old-fashioned queeniness had died out and was now so out of fashion that we thought it was funny. For him it was merely a disgusting reminder of the bad old days when gay men hadn't liked themselves, had seen themselves as pathetic stand-ins for women, and had considered their only charm to be their youth. Those of us who were one generation younger thought that we'd put all that safely behind us and that now we were free to joke about it—on the same principle, perhaps, that Richard Pryor used the word *nigger* over and over in his routines during the same period. I'm not sure that we gays were really so sure of our new identity (neither, as it turned out, were African-Americans).

The bigger bone he picked with me was over socialism. I had routinely said in print and in conversation that I was a socialist, which made me no different from millions of American Leftists of that period. Simon would say, "If you only knew how misguided you are! You're generous and worried about the sufferings of the poor and the marginalized, about what America is doing to the third world, but communism is the biggest scourge the world has ever known."

"But, Simon, I'm not a communist, I hate Stalin."

"But you think you can pick and choose, reject Stalin in favor of Lenin."

"Well, yeah . . ."

"But Lenin was just as bad. There was no good period of communism. They were thugs and built into the system is an authoritarianism that crops up everywhere—in Cuba, China, Vietnam, the most different cultures."

"I can understand how you White Russians might be bitter. After all, you lost all your wealth—"

"That's an insulting argument. It has nothing to do with my family, which was always pretty poor in any event. No, this is just a terrible blind spot in Americans of your generation. You're prepared to believe that Stalin was a tyrant, but you'll see that Mao is even worse, that Ho Chi Minh will be as bad as he can be, that Castro— well. Just take gays. Castro has been running concentration camps for gays, or 'work camps,' if you prefer. In Russia the last public display of homosexuality was the funeral for Kuzmin in 1929. After that it was too dangerous to reveal to anyone that you were gay. And gays to this day have to get married to women and they dare not ever show—"

I tuned out. Obviously poor Simon was brainwashed by his White Russian refugee parents. He was a right-winger, like Nabokov himself, who'd outraged his admirers by supporting the Vietnam War. And if gays had to suffer to promote the welfare of the masses, so what? One shouldn't just endlessly promote one's selfish interests. And anyway, we did believe that communists were wrong in thinking that homosexuality was a form of "bourgeois decadence," since it seemed to be spread throughout the social classes.

Only many years later did I understand that Simon was entirely right. That communism had been the worst scourge in history. That Mao and Stalin had slaughtered millions of their own people with a horrifying recklessness. That the abrogation of intellectuals' rights and kulaks' rights and gays' rights and the mass incarceration of inconvenient minorities wasn't due to the regrettable bigotry of an individual leader but rather was endemic to the whole system. These sickening excesses couldn't be chalked up as necessary sacrifices for the benefit of the whole but were deeply wrong and were preludes to even worse and more general illegalities affecting nearly everyone. No regime in history had been as destructive or as cruel or as irrational as the Soviet Union, unless it was Red China.

By the end of the 1970s I had figured that out, but that was very late in the day to come to such a realization. I had to read Nadezhda Mandelstam's *Hope Against Hope*, with its dry, undramatic recital of the agonies she and her husband suffered all because her husband wrote one short satirical poem about Stalin (though Mandelstam might just as easily have been subjected to even worse punishment for doing nothing "wrong" at all).

In his pioneering gay-inspired biography of Gogol, Simon had struck out against the Orthodox Church and its treatment of Gogol's homosexuality. Church fathers had taken advantage of Gogol's self-hatred and guilt by subjecting him to endless and cruel penances. What the priests didn't do, the doctors did—Gogol, already weakened toward the end, was repeatedly bled. Leeches were attached to his already infected nose. He was encouraged to turn the second part of *Dead Souls*, his funny social satire, into a serious religious drama. He worked on this impossible task for years and finally destroyed it just before he died.

For a distinguished Russian academic, Simon was daring in his political positions. He wrote a whirlwind gay history of Russian literature for a popular gay publication. With Michael Henry Heim he annotated Chekhov's letters and made of Chekhov an ecologist *avant la lettre*. In his biography of Gogol, Simon boldly demonstrated that the affection for another man revealed in

Gogol's letters surpassed the ardor of Romantic friendship. Simon marched. Simon signed manifestos. Simon taught gay courses.

He was lonely until one day he answered a personal ad in the *Berkeley Barb* in which a much younger man said he was looking for an "interesting older partner." Simon's was one of dozens of responses. Peter met with them all but was most taken by Simon. Peter was considerably younger and well-to-do and interested both in psychology and conceptual art. Simon's huge international culture and saturnine looks obviously fascinated him. Now they've been together some forty years.

From the very beginning he and Peter fussed over each other's health. They were hypochondriacs out of a nineteenth-century novel, endlessly worried about something too spicy or a draft or wet feet or tiredness, and they could be quite grumpy if they weren't sufficiently comfortable. They could also be irritated by other people's arrangements. I gave them a party in New York once and Simon literally threw up his hands when he realized that not only did he not know my guests, but that *they* didn't know each other (unforgivable). Of course my guests were just ill-assorted recent tricks for the most part—not really the stuff out of which successful parties are made.

When *Forgetting Elena* came out, it was reviewed in the *New York Times Book Review*, which still counted for something in those days. The critic apparently thought he'd given me a glowing review since forty years later he tried to call in the debt and asked me for a blurb or a recommendation or a review (I forget which). Actually the review was pretty confused and lukewarm, though some phrases here and there could have been used in an ad had there been one. The review treated the novel as a mystery and it was often shelved in bookstores and libraries under Mysteries.

The novel had taken so many years to be published that I was well into another one, called variously *Like People in History* and

*Woman Reading Pascal*, a much more realistic novel than *Forgetting Elena*. In the long years before *Elena* was accepted, I'd thought I'd gone too far toward the difficult and that I should write something about real people leading their lives. Since Richard Howard was by far the most original and colorful person I knew, I decided I should base a character on him and put him into a three-way friendship with "Maria" (based on Marilyn Schaefer) and a young heterosexual woman based on Sigrid, my friend from Time-Life. In fact I made Sigrid the main character from whose point of view everything would be written.

I must have had Henry James's *Portrait of a Lady* in mind, or perhaps George Eliot's *Daniel Deronda*, because I wanted to write about an heiress who falls into the claws of a fortune hunter. Today, in the era of prenuptial agreements and especially of divorce, an unwise marriage no longer has the same lasting, tragic consequences. Nevertheless, my basic plot idea was that a striking, rich young woman comes to New York from Baltimore (I'd spent a weekend there among the fox hunting set, friends from school). In New York she becomes best friends with a gay man and a lesbian and lives their exciting but (for her) unfulfilling New York gay life. At last, at the advanced age of thirty, she realizes that she wants a husband and children. Seemingly by chance she runs into someone who used to attend the debutante parties in Baltimore, one of those "extra men" so badly needed to keep cutting in during the dances. In American high society, I'd discovered, anxious rich parents do not sufficiently guard against two figures—the extra man and, especially, the riding instructor. If one of them is well mannered and good-looking, he can seduce the seventeen-year-old daughter of the family, and sometimes the mother, even though he hasn't a penny and his blood is red, not blue. For members of the "horsey set," the riding instructor is the real Trojan horse, capable of penetrating even the best-defended walls.

*Edmund White*

In my novel (just as in Eliot's and James's), my fortune hunter, Jimmy, is initially charming and accommodating. He once dated my Sigrid character years ago and now they take up where they left off. He weans her away from her friends—and destroys her life.

If truth be told, I'd been a little bit in love with Sigrid and we'd spent some time together, but ultimately I'd confessed to her that I was gay. I remember sitting with her on a Friday night at the Riviera Café in Sheridan Square. Armies of young gay men were marching past, loud and excited, and I wanted to join them—or make them go away. Sigrid said she would not have suspected I was gay and that it didn't make any difference anyway. The perfect answer. Of course I knew it did make a difference. I told myself that I couldn't afford children. And then I'd had not one but many cases of gonorrhea over the years. And then I felt claustrophobic if I spent too many evenings in a row with a woman.

I backed out of her life and she married Desmond, whom I didn't meet till some time later. Together they had a beautiful and talented daughter who resembles tall, blond Sigrid. In my novel the marriage is a disaster, and she discovers too late that he wants only her money. In real life Sigrid might have been a German Baltic baroness, but she had no money and her marriage seems much like another and survives to this day.

The interest of the book, if there was any, was in its presentation of heterosexuals and homosexuals joined through friendship—and the conviction that certain heterosexual women had in those days that gay people were freer than they were, that we were less possessive, more adventurous, and more devoted to our friends than they were, and that friendship provided the true through-line of our lives. As Marilyn told an ex who said he wanted just to be friends, "Practically anyone can be my lover, but it's very difficult to be my friend." I wanted to suggest that these "advanced" ideas might serve a gay man but not a straight woman. Not that traditional marriage was much better, I wanted to argue, just not disastrously worse. In the spirit of Elizabeth Bowen, I wanted to show a modern tragedy in which there were two choices and both were bad.

I was terribly insecure about my writing. More than ever. I was waiting for the first reviews of *Forgetting Elena*, and when they came in, they seemed genuinely uncomprehending. I was so afraid of being silenced again, of not being allowed to go on writing for publication. No one is sincerely interested in writing a journal that will never be published—or if he or she is, it's a sort of self-sufficiency or modesty I don't understand. If a writer has the desire to communicate by writing and be heard, then he necessarily cares about seeing his work into print. I suppose it's the difference between masturbation and making love—the real writer wants to touch another person. Reading the written word is participating in a dialogue in which one person is doing all the talking but in which the listening is also creative.

Yes, I wanted to reach readers but I also worried for professional reasons—I wanted to live by my pen. I wanted to be among those five hundred people in America who earn a living, even a meager one, by writing serious literature. If, as Schiller said, literature shows us what humanity would be like if it existed in a state of freedom (the author, not the characters), then I wanted to belong to that tiny minority that is genuinely free. Each time I give a reason, nevertheless, it ends up sounding too exalted; I wasn't interested so much in making money or enjoying freedom, I wanted to survive. For me, writing was essential to survival. Again, not because I had such beautiful or intense sentiments or because my ideas were so pressing and elevated (I didn't even have many ideas except during the five minutes every day when I took a shower), but because it was the label, *writer*, that mattered to me most in some primitive, essential way. To be sure, writers were far more important in the culture at large fifty years ago than they are now. Back then they were considered seers or the antennae of the race, in touch with the deep conflicts underlying our society. But even without that religion of art I still was frantic to be—and to remain—a writer. Yet I wanted to be one on my own terms. I wasn't willing to write TV scripts or bodice rippers or go on forever doing Time-Life potted versions of science or music or history (though I continued for several years to write just such books or parts of books to feed myself). No, I wanted to write a speculative work of fiction—yes, that was it: fiction was a form of speculation, a pure experiment in As If. Of course if you're interested in "immortality," then you'd better be a serious novelist. Look at the bestsellers of 1920 and you won't recognize a single title or the name of a single author.

In switching back to realism I'd somehow lost my ability to write. Or rather I'd lost my confidence. I'd turned away from the pure experience of writing *Forgetting Elena* (which, as Richard Howard said of Roland Barthes, was "intimate without being personal") to the no less highbrow but somehow compromised genre of the "problem" novel (*How Do We Live Now, We Who Are Androgynous?*). I was no longer inhabiting the center of my sensibility; I could no longer hear a hum when I was writing well. I'd gone back to writing scenes with dialogue and action, scenes in which the point was verisimilitude; I'd stopped being Beckett and become Updike (those would be the glorified comparisons).

David Kalstone, who'd just done an interview of James Merrill for the *Saturday Review*, came out to visit me in San Francisco, and the first thing I did was to read him a thirty-page chapter of *Like People in History*. He told me it was good—and I was so grateful to him, though he and I both knew it wasn't true. I was riddled with horrible, nearly paralyzing doubt. Sometimes I blamed my years of psychotherapy for this disease of self-questioning. In therapy, I'd learned to look at myself looking at myself and constantly interrogate my motives. So much subjectivity and second-guessing and constant scrutiny had made me inauthentic. Doubting my feelings had destroyed my inner orientation device—the only thing a writer has. Moreover, all those years of writing unproduced plays and unpublished novels had not been good for my confidence, either.

Later, in 1977, I wrote freelance for Time-Life Records a forty-page life of Anton Bruckner to go with some LPs. Bruckner was supposed to be one of the few musical geniuses in history so unsure of himself he could be talked into writing and rewriting his symphonies two and three times, constantly modifying them, sometimes for the worse. I knew I'd never be in his category, not even in terms of abjection, but I could see the resemblances. Like Bruckner I had started relatively late, received little encouragement, not emerged from the right artistic milieu. Other composers were also late bloomers, such as Janaček, but few were so indecisive, few could be talked into endless rewrites.

David's endorsement was kind and constructive and necessary. He gave me the permission I needed to finish the book and to go on as a writer, no matter how battered I might be. Even so, once my novel was finished, it made the rounds just as *Forgetting Elena* had done, but this new novel was never published. I had worked on it for five years. Anne Freedgood, the first person to whom we submitted it, did accept it, but made a mingy offer. Since I was convinced it was a "mainstream" novel that was worth real money, I petulantly withdrew it and told my agent to submit it to other publishers (once again discovering belatedly that she was sending out an earlier, unrevised version). When after two years no one had taken it, I went limping back to Anne, who decided she didn't want it after all. She argued that it was difficult, even impossible, to write a good novel about such a deeply passive character (what about Camus's *The Stranger*, I wondered, or all of those masterpieces by

Kafka with victims as protagonists?). Perhaps she was punishing me for having initially rejected her. Or perhaps like the other editors she was secretly alarmed by my middle-class gay characters. Low-life gays, as in the novels of John Rechy or Jean Genet or Hubert Selby, were easier to stomach since they seemed so exotic. What was hard to take was someone gay who might be in the next office or in the apartment across the hall. Although gay liberation had begun, it didn't penetrate the literary market for nearly ten years. Later I would meet editors who'd turned down *Like People in History* who were themselves gay and closeted but were afraid to speak up for my book. One of the most fearfully closeted gay editors, Peter Kameny, became so neurotic that he started hiding in the toilet at work. Even though he'd been among the most promising literature students his year at Harvard, the publishers finally fired him and he threw himself in front of a subway.

When eventually I realized that my novel wasn't going to sell, I wasted another year rewriting it, but even in its newest version everyone was indifferent or allergic to it. The horror of having waited so long to be published and then achieving my goal, only to have my next book turned down flat, filled me with dread. I felt that in choosing literature as a career I'd placed all my money on a single number and it had lost.

When I made this melodramatic declaration to a friend, he said, "What else were you planning to do with your life? Be an accountant? Civil engineer?"

David Kalstone was not only the warmest and most entertaining person I knew, he was also an expert in maneuvering in the world of academics and intellectuals. If I'd say something arrogant in an essay I was showing him that was destined for print, he'd write a tiny question mark in tentative pencil in the margin, and I'd instantly eliminate the offense. We went over every word the other one wrote.

I longed to have him as my best friend forever, but I recognized that his love for me was a constant source of anguish for him. I was ready to attribute my reluctance to sleep with him to a "neurosis" on my part, an inability to become intimate with the person I liked best, but I was fed up with conversations in which I was made to feel guilty for my tastes and aversions to begin with. David, I knew, nursed hopes that if he was patient enough, I'd overcome my "hang-ups" about "intimacy." I just wasn't attracted to him, putting us on a collision course.

Once we got terribly drunk and I asked David if as a Jew he considered himself superior to me as a gentile. He said yes. I was surprised since I must secretly have always considered WASPs to be superior to everyone else. I knew that Jews traditionally considered themselves the chosen people, but I hadn't suspected they actually believed in that high claim. David was an entirely secular Jew, but even he retained this in-the-bone sense of orthodox superiority. He could be humorously dismissive about the "dear Jews," and the sobriety of his clothes, the hushed elegance of his manners, his indifference to money (except as a means of financing his summer trips to Venice), all attested to his assiduity in avoiding the caricatural image of the Jew, but nevertheless he sometimes indicated that he considered his fellow Jews to be less alcoholic, better family men, more intellectually acute, warmer, kinder, and saner than all these slightly batty and cruel and dirty gentiles running about. Of course the whole Jew/gentile paradigm seemed almost far-fetched to us as friends since our intimacy defied all categories.

Our happiness together remains one of my most vivid and fructifying memories; when we are young and literary, we often experience things in the present with a nostalgia-in-advance, but we seldom guess what we will truly prize years from now. I always placed a high value on friendship, but even I had no way of guessing back then that it was more fun to get drunk with a friend than with a lover. Love is a source of anxiety until it is a source of boredom; only friendship feeds the spirit. Love raises great expectations in us that it never satisfies; the hopes based on friendship are milder and in the present, and they exist only because they have already been rewarded. Love is a script about just a few repeated themes we have a hard time following, though we make every effort to conform to its tone. Friendship is a *permis de séjour* that enables us to go anywhere and do anything exactly as our whims dictate.

The last few months that I was in the Bay Area in early 1972 I lived in Stephen Orgel's house. An ex-lover of David's from Harvard days, Stephen embraced me as a friend because David vouched for me. With what I later discovered would be his usual generosity Stephen allowed me to stay there and drive his car for the two months he was away. I'd come home late at night driving across the Bay Bridge and head up to the Berkeley Hills where I'd enter through the little garden gate beside the Princess plant and go into the low-eaved Arts and Crafts cottage with its ceramics from the period and its big, melodramatic Victorian prints of scenes from Shakespeare.

One night a young couple who worked with me—he was a Rhodes scholar and former football player, she was a blond gymnast and talented illustrator—followed me home. They were shocked by how drunkenly I'd weaved my way across the bridge and said they were worried about my chances for survival. They wanted to have sex with me, but I wasn't sure that I was ready for a three-way with a woman, not even such a beautiful, friendly, easygoing woman and a handsome athlete with the square-jawed face of the young Hemingway. Eventually, when we were all safely back in New York, we did try a three-way, and he and I later had a two-way, but I was always puzzled by their interest in me and by their sexual virtuosity. They were too beautiful for me. In those days we always assumed that a bisexual (especially, for some reason, a bisexual man) was really a homosexual in the closet. We would wait with amused smiles till he eventually declared his true colors, which we naturally assumed would be pink and mauve. But as I learned a decade later in Paris, the world is full of genuine bisexuals, though most of them keep a low profile, not because they're ashamed but because everyone distrusts and fears them. Tribes have only two ways of treating interstitial members; they either make them into gods or banish them. Yet as a trend if not a reality, androgyny and bisexuality were at the time being treated by the Sunday supplements as the taste of the moment. Articles and gossip columns were full of descriptions of just such young people, but I'd never been sure they really existed.

When the *Saturday Review* went under and I returned to New York after less than a year, I felt that I'd missed out on the best parts of California by not driving out of town on the weekends to camp under the redwoods, or beside the hot sulfur-water pools near the Russian River, or in the Zen monastery an hour away. I'd wasted my time smoking in bars and complaining because San Francisco didn't enjoy exactly the same advantages as New York. Older, more secure people can take pleasure almost anywhere they go, but young people like us—especially recent converts to New York— had to justify our strange, demanding, and by no means obviously rewarding religion by rejecting all other cults and sacred sites.

But God I was happy to be back in New York! I liked being able to find people on the street at two and three in the morning. I liked calling up all my friends and talking for hours on the phone. I liked the feeling that everything in New York was being *observed*. If I saw something strange on the street, it would end up in a cartoon in the *New Yorker* the following week. If the subway stalled, an article about it would be in the *New York Times* the next morning—and after all it was a national newspaper. If I got up in a restaurant and passed four tables on the way to the loo, there would be at least three conversations I'd be dying to join. The slightly glaucous narcissism of San Francisco had been replaced by the rabid egotism of New York.

Soon I'd stumbled into a part-time job back in New York as an editor and staff writer for the venerable hardcover quarterly *Horizon*. We had to think up articles of general cultural interest, but ones that wouldn't be dated by the time they finally came out after three months of lead time. It was a good job for me, given my wide-ranging reading, but I suddenly had much less authority than before and the editors were much more hesitant before committing themselves to a story idea. With *Horizon*, the illustrations were as important as the text and we usually started with them. An idea could be nixed out of hand if it didn't promise sufficient visual richness.

The most interesting story idea I thought up was to have Jan Morris write about Ibn Battuta, the late-medieval Arab traveler who traversed the whole Muslim world from Spain to China, from Turkey to Egypt and on into sub-Saharan Africa. Ibn Battuta made the trip twice—once when that world was still unified and then again decades later when it was beginning to fall apart. I knew that Jan Morris, in her earlier gender incarnation as a man, James Morris, a celebrated travel writer, had made the same trip herself.

Morris had just had her sex-change operation and published her autobiography, *Conundrum*. She came in to discuss the Ibn Battuta assignment, a hearty, middle-aged woman in a wool skirt and sensible shoes. Apparently she was back in Wales with her wife, and the two women were living together as sisters. Just the other day I read that now that civil partnership is permitted in Britain, she and her wife have married again. The English historian J. H. Plumb predicted that within a matter of minutes of arriving at the offices of *Horizon*, Morris would produce a cherished telegram from her son in India telling her that her plans for gender-reassignment surgery were all right by him. Right on schedule Jan pulled out the telegram. When she left my office, the woman at the next desk asked me, "Who was that?"

"Why do you ask?"

"Well, you can tell she's a woman who really knows who she is!"

I would see Jan occasionally over the years and she always seemed fearless, hyperproductive, and a bit solitary. Once in Australia a bunch of us writers at the Adelaide Festival were ferried off to the beach, but Jan stayed behind with the bus driver to chat. Later I asked her why she'd hung back with him and she said, "He's sort of my type." Once in New York I asked her if she jogged to keep her figure, and she modestly touched her full breasts and said, "It's rather hard for us older women to jog." Usually she spoke of her latest writing project; she had a well-organized, well-stocked mind, a capacious curiosity, excellent and penetrating powers of analysis, an eye for the vivid, life-giving detail, and an easy and generous flow of words.

When I first met her at *Horizon*, I told her that one day at the Gotham Book Mart I'd started reading a thick old book published in the 1930s about the first sex change in history, *Man into Woman*. It had so hypnotized me that I'd slumped to the floor and read straight through, never going back to my office at Time-Life as lunch hour became the cocktail hour. This was the book that also inspired David Ebershoff decades later when he wrote his brilliant novel *The Danish Girl*. The haunting 1930s book had black-and-white snapshots of the book's subject, the painter Lili Elbe (née Einar Wegener), before and after. In the after pictures she looked sickly and bony and nearly transparent in her cloche hat as she staggered around a garden held up by a matronly nurse. It also showed samples of her handwriting before and after, slanted letters versus round ones, and even of her painting (strong oils versus pretty pastels). She'd been so determined to become a real woman that she'd had a final operation in order to bear children—and this surgery killed her (I always wondered what the procedure could possibly have been). Her diary has heartbreaking entries of deep fear and superficial optimism. The doctor has vanished. She feels weaker and weaker, and her husband (an old family friend) attends her faithfully. Now an infection has set in . . .

Jan said to me, "If you think the book intrigued you, imagine the effect it had on me!"

But truthfully I couldn't imagine its having a greater influence on Jan than on me. It opened up a path that I never felt tempted to take but that burned its way right through my imagination. The "pre-op" Danish painter Wegener had never felt tempted by homosexuality, no more than Jan claimed to have been. Yet recently I heard someone, an ignorant young gay man, refer to her as "gay."

David and I were back to our old New York routine of diet dinners at Duff's and long evenings of reading. Our latest project was to read all of Dante, passage by passage, starting in Italian and then in English. We had all the books about Dante at our side and tried delving into every stylistic, exegetical, and historical complexity.

But the book never came to life for me. It felt terribly underwritten. Nor could I imagine Dante actually writing it—his account of its semidivine origins was all too convincing. It didn't seem like an act of brooding and hatching, of becoming. No, it was pure being, or rather it existed in an ungrateful, granitic state of having long already been. I might have said that it was too classical for my tastes, though it had thrilled me as a high school student to work my way through the first four books of *The Aeneid* in Latin. Virgil's account of Dido's death had made me weep in a way that Francesca's sorry fate in *The Divine Comedy* never would. I could enjoy the chaste beauty of Virgil's language, but Dante gave me no way in. When I voiced some of these doubts, David said, "Dante is not being judged."

I knew that. It was an error of judgment on my part, but I wasn't interested in being a critic, just a novelist. I didn't have to hand out grades to the classics; my only job was to filch what I needed from any available literary nest. In any event, *The Divine Comedy* seemed too confident, with no wound in its side, no crack in the bell, nothing vulnerable or hesitant, no stuttering. It interested me no more than a big full-dress late-medieval painting of the pietà, highly glazed and full of angels and donors, complete with all three Marys and a skinny, bleeding Christ. To be sure, in Dante Christ had several wounds in his side, but not one of them seemed to bleed my blood, no more than Dante's harsh judgment of his old teacher Brunetto Latini for having been homosexual seemed humane or feeling to me. I could see nothing in Dante but cold self-confidence and abstract rapture and an unimaginative application of the rules to desires, like stays pressing into bulging flesh.

My own confidence, of course, was worn down to the nub and I trusted none of my opinions. I felt foolish with my part-time job, my failed West Coast adventure, my roach-trap apartment, my minuscule salary, my frayed wardrobe. The government audited me, perhaps because I'd suddenly gone from earning a lot to earning so little and the IRS thought this hardly credible. I remember those two big auditors in their carefully pressed suits and big, polished lace-up shoes sitting on my dirty little mattress on the floor and near the overflowing garbage sack and smelling the roach spray as they opened their briefcases and worked through my records. Quickly convinced that I was concealing nothing, they turned green and hurried away. At that time a highly successful TV producer from England I knew intimidated me into inviting him upstairs to my place, where he forced himself upon me and virtually raped me.

Later he told a mutual friend he'd never seen such poverty. On reflection, I thought my poverty was a good partner to my obvious passivity.

And yet I had princely pleasures . . .

I met Elizabeth Bishop through David at a party for the magazine of poetry criticism *Parnassus*. Bishop looked almost exactly like my mother, with the same big eyes and heart-shaped face, but unlike my mother she was dry, precise, slightly fearful, and depressed, a ditherer. The only thing the two women shared was the face and a penchant for heavy drinking. All I remember of that first introduction to Bishop was that I referred to Nabokov's *Transparent Things* by mistake as *Silken Things* and Bishop snapped, "Why not *Silk Things*?" She volunteered that she also didn't like the word *wooden*. "*Wood*, it should be *wood*."

She was almost forbiddingly middle-class in the way she dressed and behaved, yet I knew from David that she was a famous drunk, that she'd drunk half her life away.

Not long afterward David and I were visiting Billy Abrahams, the beloved editor at Dutton, and his friend, Peter Stansky; together they had written *The Unknown Orwell*. They had a house in Duxbury, Massachusetts, and there we spent a night before going with them for lunch at a house in Wellfleet on the Cape that Elizabeth had rented with her girlfriend, Alice Methfessel. Elizabeth had a Brazilian friend with her, Linda, who started to throw the live lobsters into tepid water. Alice called out, "No! Surely *no* means 'no' even in your language!"

Elizabeth seemed fussed by the potential conflict between her Brazilian past and her New England present (Elizabeth and Alice both worked at Harvard). The table was covered with old copies of the *New York Review of Books*, the "cloth" that could be swept up later with the shells in it, but Peter Stansky was lost to us for the rest of the afternoon since he was hunched over, reading the tablecloth and making donnish exclamations that David whispered to me sounded like "Woof-woof."

As in so many situations in those days, I was the youngest and least well-known person at the table, not silent but certainly mostly a listener. I longed for literary celebrity even as I saw with my own eyes how little happiness it brought. For me, I suppose, fame was a club one yearned to join, obsessing over it night and day until the moment one was admitted, and after that never thought about again. But with one difference: literary fame, unlike club membership, was something you could lose as quickly as you gained. Now, in my nearly half century of being "on the scene," I've witnessed so many reputations come and go. Who in America remembers William Goyen (though his *House of Breath* is still popular in France)? Or *By Love Possessed*, the former "literary bestseller" by James Gould Cozzens? Don Marquis and his beloved *Archy and Mehitabel*? Of course, as Marcus Aurelius asks, who wants posthumous literary fame anyway? It will mean nothing to the dead author—and besides, as Aurelius points out snobbishly, the fools who will decide these things in the future will be no better than the fools deciding them now.

From the Cape, David and I went to Stonington, Connecticut, to spend the weekend with James Merrill. Merrill was in the midst of composing his answer to Dante, his epic poem *The Changing Light at Sandover*. I reviewed one book of it, *Mirabell*, for the *American Poetry Review*, and David read to me every scrap of the ongoing post-*Mirabell* project he could get his hands on.

Whereas Dante wrote mostly about historical figures, Merrill lent a mythical dimension to his own friends, many of them otherwise unknown. This strategy of elevating one's own experience had become more and more common since the collapse of a widely shared general culture (Proust is the star example of this new manner). Whereas Dante claimed he'd actually traveled into the afterlife and observed everything firsthand, Merrill communicated with his dead through the Ouija board, which all felt to me amateurish and "fun," the Delphic oracle reduced to a parlor game. Jimmy and his longtime lover, David Jackson, were doing endless sessions at a handmade board. I saw the letters and a few extras (*yes* and *no*, for instance) spelled out on a flat paper cutout. Some people (including Alison Lurie, in her memoir of her friendship with Merrill, called *Familiar Spirits*) later claimed that David had been losing his hold over Jimmy until he came up with his idea of the Ouija sessions— much as Mrs. Yeats, Georgie Hyde-Lees, recaptured the attention of William Butler Yeats through spiritualism. To be fair, Merrill himself versified these very doubts. A psychiatrist appears as a character in *Mirabell* to suggest that the whole thing may just be an example of folie à deux.

David Jackson had, apparently, once been a handsome military officer and a promising writer who'd published stories in the *Partisan Review*. But now he was a big mess. He smoked constantly, got drunk every night, teased everyone heavily but with the ostensible affectionate bonhomie of a diner waitress: "Hey, hon, looks like you've been putting on the pounds. Unhappy in love or just greedy? Or is it genetic? Well, you're still cute as a button. A very *big* button." His once wide-faced, strong-jawed American good looks, almost those of the young William Holden in *Picnic*, were now lost in the wasteland of drink and chain-smoking chatter. His mouth was often open as he tried, but failed, to follow the conversation. Yet this idiot was more savant than anyone suspected, since he could often suddenly join the general talk with a truly original and stinging zinger.

Jimmy just rolled his eyes with merry exasperation. He would lead us off to some other more amusing person or activity—a walk through the town, where many of the houses were pedantically and pretentiously labeled (*The house of a rich rope maker ca. 1800*).

The houses were small and pristine Greek Revival temples in wood painted white with small, perfect lawns. From Jimmy's top balcony we could look with binoculars down into the walled garden belonging to a famous literary agent, Candida Donadio, where Jimmy had once seen limping along the tall, tragic, solitary figure of her client Thomas Pynchon, the most elusive novelist in America—who eventually married Candida's assistant.

Jimmy's favorite books were E. F. Benson's Lucia series because Benson's English town (based on Rye, Sussex) he thought so resembled Stonington with its feuds, its petty rivalries, and its eccentric "characters." In Benson there was a lesbian named Quaint Irene. In Stonington, there was the photographer Rollie McKenna, a kindly soul who'd been around so long she had done portraits of Jimmy in the fifties and the eighties, of Richard Wilbur then and now, of Truman Capote then and now, of Dylan Thomas then. Eventually Rollie was virtually kidnapped and held hostage by a hostile, violent lesbian who beat her up physically and bilked her of her money, then left her to die penniless in a New England nursing home. From the start, Rollie's friends had suspected no good would come of the relationship and tried early on to intervene, though already she was creepily under the spell of her tormentor—a woman who'd fleeced two previous elderly ladies.

The town was crowded with Cheever characters, hard-drinking readers and writers with old patrician names and big houses along the coast and genteel jobs in the law or publishing. Jimmy, whose ugly Victorian was the highest in town, stood on his topmost terrace looking out and imagining all those lives below him. Stonington was his "two inches of ivory," as Jane Austen put it: on her birthday in 1816 Austen wrote her literary nephew, "What should I do with your strong, manly, spirited Sketches, full of Variety and Glow?— How could I join them on to the little bit (two inches wide) of Ivory on which I work with so fine a Brush, as produces little effect after much labor?" Merrill started with his own two humble inches, but abandoning immediately the brush and using the knife of his keen wit soon turned them into a vast scrimshaw carving of the past and the present. He may have been a social satirist, but in Jimmy's hands satire was transformed into epic—and malice was changed to bliss.

One of the guests that weekend was Alfred Corn, an erudite and handsome poet I'd known since the sixties—*Forgetting Elena* was dedicated to him and his wife at the time, Ann Jones, who, much later, after their divorce, became a brilliant Renaissance scholar. Al had brought along a copy of John Ashbery's newest poem, "Self-Portrait in a Convex Mirror," a long poem that was the best thing of John's any of us had ever read.

Alfred was three years younger than I, and he and I shared a fascination with Jimmy Merrill and David Kalstone as well as Richard Howard. We could both be ill at ease at a social event hosted by any of these guys. Al and I were probably the youngest people at the joint fortieth birthday party in 1969 for Richard and John Hollander, another poet who seemed to have read everything. John and his then wife, Anne, lived in an immense West Side apartment, and despite its many rooms it was crowded with guests. Not knowing anyone, Alfred and I stepped back and were content to watch things as they unfolded. We witnessed the, to many, historic moment when John Ashbery was introduced to the critic Harold Bloom. John was John and was so drunk that when he stumbled out at the end of the evening, Bloom said in his best orphic manner, "I revere the poet but I deplore the man."

Merrill was the patron not only of writers but also of performers who matched his taste for refined and sometimes absurd entertainment. I can remember one afternoon attending with David a performance by the Little Players, a finger-puppet troupe Jimmy subsidized. Five puppets were putting on plays or operas in which they impersonated classic characters from Chekhov,

Maeterlinck, Wilde, and Shakespeare. Though they had no legs, they once danced the entire *Giselle*. Two shy older men, William Murdock and Francis Peschka, hand-fashioned the puppets and did the sets and lighting entirely themselves, often writing their own adaptations. The afternoon we went, we sat in a well-appointed but small living room on the Upper West Side for Racine's *Phèdre*.

Jimmy had met an Egyptian from Alexandria named Bernard de Zogheb, who wrote texts in a hilarious macaroni language consisting of morsels of French and Italian. He'd already done *Le Sorelle Brontë* with the Little Players. Now Zogheb, who'd been a tourist guide in Egypt and mixed up all his languages, asked Merrill to tell him the story of *Phèdre*. Jimmy said, "I can find you a copy in a day," but Zogheb countered, "Oh, no, I don't want to read it. Just tell me the gist of it."

Once Jimmy had summarized the plot for him, Zogheb wrote out his ballad opera—that is, new words to familiar pop tunes. Thus to the tune of "Honey," Phaedra (played by the Lady Bracknell–like puppet personage Isabelle) sings:

*Ah, Zeus, come son pesanti*
*Tutti le quel ornamenti*

Which is a very funny translation of "How these vain ornaments, these veils burden me," I'll admit.

I guess the whole matinee, as was widely intoned, could be called "a delight." But a smoldering little Marxist inside me resented all of these well-heeled cultural figures in the audience cooing over the Players' wit and charm. Phaedra's maid, Oenone, was played by Isabelle's puppet maid Elsie Lump. I thought humor about maids was on a par with tasteless *New Yorker* cartoons about bums.

After the "opera," a select inner group filed over to the nearby Central Park West apartment of the duo pianists Arthur Gold and Bobby Fizdale, where caterers (quietly paid by Merrill) served twenty guests a light supper. David Kalstone was a little in love with

Bobby Fizdale. Bobby and Arthur had been lovers years before, but now they were more close companions and artistic partners. In the old days the two had spent a lot of time in Europe with titled people and composers, performing concertos for two pianos by Poulenc, Virgil Thomson, John Cage, and Paul Bowles. One of Jimmy's favorite pieces of music was Fauré's *Dolly Suite* played by "the boys," Gold and Fizdale, a lemony, edgy, sometimes sad, sometimes frothy duet written for Debussy's stepdaughter.

I remember those mornings in Stonington when the high-ceilinged rooms were full of sunlight, we were drinking our morning coffee, Jimmy had just come down from his workroom with a draft of a poem to his newborn goddaughter Urania living just downstairs, and the naïve sophistication of *Dolly Suite* was playing tag with our caffeine highs. David and I had both loved "Urania" but asked Jimmy (heart in mouth, for who were we to correct the master?), "Isn't it just a bit . . . cold?" Jimmy slapped his forehead and said, "Oh, God, I left out the human feeling!" He then dashed back upstairs and descended half an hour later with a version that made us weep. *Dolly Suite* was the theme music to those glorious, preposterous days.

By the time I knew the "boys," Arthur's hands were acting up and Gold and Fizdale were turning to writing cookbooks and biography, producing a much-acclaimed life of Misia Sert—one of the principal patrons of the Ballets Russes and a Polish beauty painted by Renoir. Sert was also a friend of Cocteau and Picasso, and Mallarmé had written verses on her fan. Wits and women who organize salons are the hardest subjects for biographies since they say clever, quickly forgotten things and facilitate everything and create nothing. They're crucial cultural figures whose fame and utility vanish when they die.

Misia was a perfect topic for the boys, however, since they were as worldly as she in their way. They were great hosts who cooked so well they had their own TV show. They had known musicians on every continent and were close friends of both Balanchine and Jerome Robbins, not to mention the dancer Tanaquil Le Clercq, who had been Balanchine's wife and star until she contracted polio and eventually he dropped her. The boys were so social that their list of tony acknowledgments was like a page from the *Almanach de Gotha*; so reluctant were they to leave out even the dead, if they were sufficiently titled, that they flagged the names of deceased aristocrats with a cross, and more crosses were lined up in their *remerciements* than at the Omaha Beach cemetery.

They knew everyone. Bobby said to us, "It seems we're staying with the Contessa Grimaldi in June, and then it seems we're invited to the house of the Della Corte di Montis."

Jimmy whispered to us, "Those seems are well sewed."

I was invited with David to their large apartment several times. They'd give us a wonderful dinner, then we'd play charades or Encyclopedia, a grander form of Dictionary in which the guests were asked to write fake entries for a name or event. We were then instructed to guess which version was the real one copied out from the *Encyclopaedia Britannica*. If anyone already knew the true identity of the person or place, he had to own up to it right away. We were all in stitches when one of the guests, Maita di Niscemi, a Sicilian princess who worked on Robert Wilson's scripts, kept admitting that almost everyone we mentioned was a cousin or aunt of hers.

At these dinners Tanny Le Clercq in her wheelchair (she was teaching ballet to a company in Harlem), Jerry Robbins, David Kalstone, Maita, Johnny de Cuevas (whose father had been a marquis and had had a ballet troupe and whose mother was a Rockefeller), were all in attendance. It was heady stuff—and they were all so clever at recognizing passages from Shakespeare or the Bible that, as usual, I felt intimidated and kept wishing I'd majored in English rather than Chinese or kept going to Bible-study class.

One afternoon Johnny de Cuevas brought along a kilo of caviar from the very same Caviarteria, he said, where his father had bought his supplies.

David had a lingering resentment against Bobby Fizdale for breaking off their affair some time ago. At a Valentine's Day party Fizdale held up to his sleeve a heart cookie that Maita had baked and asked, "What does this symbolize?" Crossly, David replied, "He who gets slapped." When David had asked Fizdale why he didn't want to continue the affair, Bobby had said that he had only one more goal in life and it wasn't romantic; his only remaining ambition was to meet Mrs. Lytle Hull—a queen of society, as I learned, a rich patron of the opera and the first Mrs. Vincent Astor.

David was going away for the summer. He would be sailing on the *Queen Mary* with James Merrill. David would spend June, July, and August with Stephen Orgel in Venice. Before leaving he made *penne arrabbiata* for just the two of us, then we settled in for a long reading of Elizabeth Bishop poems, after which David read me what he'd been writing about Ashbery. We drank a fierce amount of white wine. At the door, as I was leaving, David grabbed me, as I knew he would, and began to give me a long, wet kiss with tongue, as I knew he would. He had a sweet smile while he kissed me, which felt oddly too heterosexual to me—domestic, normal. Everything about the moment I hated. I was as repelled as Diana by Acteon, and in a spontaneous rage I stamped my foot, let out an angry groan, and left. David was deeply offended. He decided not to see me again, which I found out for sure only later but which I sensed right away.

On the ship, however, Jimmy Merrill convinced him that there was too little love in the world to go around, so little that one should not spurn it in whatever form it came. David decided to forgive me and to go on with our friendship—sexless and ultimately satisfying to both of us. Later he referred (not often, only once or twice) to that decisive night as the time I "stamped my foot." To be sure, I had twice tried to sleep with him but was impotent both times. I decided that was okay, I could just lie there and let him do with me what he would, and hoped that my evident lack of excitement would be more eloquent than words. But somehow that bodily "statement" hadn't proved my point. He had kept thinking that if he applied himself a bit more strenuously, I would respond, like a stain to scrubbing.

Now David wrote me an eloquent letter from Venice—and entirely characteristic of his generosity, he was able to change tactics with me and recast his love for me into friendship. We went on to have twelve years of an unforgettable and inimitable friendship, which ended only with his early death.

As if the gods were punishing me for not loving David, they made me fall in love with the boy across the street, Keith McDermott, an actor who was in his mid-twenties but who looked as if he were seventeen—and someone who wanted my friendship but not my love. I could see Keith struggling with the same revulsion for me that I'd felt for David—and the same strong sense of attachment and friendship. But Keith had a more inventive strategy than I did with David, creating a "chastity club" and naming it after a saint (he was a lapsed Catholic). He invited me to be one of the two charter members. The idea was that we could sleep together and embrace but not have sex. Keith said that he was sick of sex and needed a break from it. Over the many years that I knew him he would often go off on retreats, stop eating meat or give up drink, or enter into a strenuous period he dubbed "health and beauty month." He was small, blond, beautifully built, an excellent gymnast. He was physically fastidious and conscious; he seemed to have no habits, certainly no bad ones. Every movement he made was willed.

I had met him through Larry Kert, the Broadway star, who'd

played Tony in *West Side Story* and was the lead in *Company*. Larry would call me up on a rainy day whenever he was horny, and I'd hurry across the street. Keith was also a part-time pillow boy and houseboy.

Larry had a curious way of treating us both like cheap sex toys, completely interchangeable and disposable, but when he engaged with us as people (as artists or just conscious suffering beings), he treated us with an unexpected seriousness and respect.

Soon Keith and I were living together on West Eighty-sixth Street and Columbus Avenue in a large sixth-floor apartment that cost four hundred dollars a month. I had a small bedroom and a study full of light. Keith had a large bedroom. My teenage nephew, Keith Fleming, also came to live with us and had the former maid's room. His mother (my sister) was hospitalized and was incapable of taking care of him.

There was a kitchen, a storage room, a butler's pantry, a dining room. I suppose it was an example of what had been called in the late nineteenth century "a classic six," the standard middle-class apartment of the period, but what by now seemed an unimaginable luxury. Keith McDermott had understood we'd just be roommates and had been explicit about that. But I couldn't resist tormenting him with my large cow eyes full of tears and yearning.

Those years in the classic six on Eighty-sixth and Columbus were emotionally painful but artistically productive for me. I was so miserably in love with Keith that I started seeing a therapist again—but this one was a gay shrink at least, Dr. Charles Silverstein. Keith was the cause of both the suffering (unrequited love) and the creativity (he was always rehearsing or drawing or writing). He treated every action as an aesthetic occasion. We bought pink and ocher porch furniture but even it was too "heavy" for his tastes and soon he'd dragged it out into the hallway. Nothing short of total Japanese austerity suited him. But I wanted to have people to dinner, a bourgeois failing that awakened his scorn. At three in the morning Keith would be "writing" on large sheets of paper in illegible script. He and another actor would be memorizing scenes from Noël Coward—but backward, reciting the reversed scenes with all the same artificial panache of Coward and Gertrude Lawrence on the few old recordings we owned.

Although Keith was at that time a Broadway actor, he idolized Robert Wilson, the avant-garde theater director. Keith even ended up sleeping with Wilson at our place. Soon I was willingly drawn into the revels. I was so lovesick over Keith that a couple of times I organized orgies, just so that in the melee of bodies I could touch Keith without his knowing it. When Keith moved to the West Coast, Bob Wilson and I got together a few times alone. He was a tall, handsome Texan who dressed in formal, dark clothes. He was my age, just a little younger, but his demeanor, that of an Eastern European diplomat, was ageless. Paul Schmidt, a poet and Russian scholar, had lived with Wilson for one year right after Wilson got out of the Waco high school and Schmidt finished serving in the army. Schmidt claimed that Wilson spent the whole time arranging their few sticks of furniture down to the last millimeter—and indeed Wilson's striking stage tableaux depend on precise and innovative lighting and sets and even props.

Keith and I worshipped everything being done by Bob Wilson, including his 1976 staging of *Einstein on the Beach* with music by Philip Glass. It was performed at the Metropolitan Opera House and to us felt like the premiere of an opera by Wagner—something awesomely new and revolutionary, a new chapter in the story of the human spirit. It wasn't the music so much that impressed us but the ingenuity and grandeur of the stage pictures. I wrote an article about the event for *Christopher Street* in which I praised the opera at the top of my lungs. I've never felt foolish afterward about my enthusiasm; I'm just happy that I had the wit to recognize at the time the advent of one of the great artistic moments of my generation, though I was far from alone in my praise. The opera was five hours long and people were free to come and go as they liked; I recall there was a sound booth from which one could watch and hear the performance while chatting to friends. Many people (stoned, to be sure) stood in the aisles weeping. Yet the whole event was cool—a train, a trial, a rocket launch. In many of the sections the chorus merely sang numbers over and over ("one, two, thirteen . . .")—not a bad liturgy for Einstein. The rumor was that the cost of mounting the production burdened Wilson with an enormous debt for the next decade.

LSD was an occasional part of our lives in the 1970s. I would never have dreamed of dropping acid every weekend or even every month or even every half year. For me it was too big an event, a quasi-religious ceremony, and far too dangerous. Acid was much stronger in those years, lasting for twenty-four hours and sometimes driving people we knew around the bend. I remember one weekend at a house out on Fire Island when our host discovered that he'd invited too many guests and didn't have enough beds for everyone. His solution was to mix LSD into the drinks, unbeknownst to the guests. Then he pulled a few mattresses and pillows into one room, which he declared the kiddies' room, and herded us all in there gabbling and sobbing and laughing for the next twenty-four hours. We went on a stroll around the community, which at least had no cars so we couldn't get tangled up in traffic and damaged, though I suppose we could have gone swimming at midnight and drowned. We visited one house where the house pet was an Irish wolfhound the size of a pony. Though the dog was so sweet he was called Baby, his demonic owner decided to terrorize us by showing us his enormous claws, as big as a pterodactyl's, and saying, "He could tear you apart with these—just rip out your throat." We were so infantilized by hallucinogens, we sobbed at the thought and our teeth chattered with fear.

Everyone, I suppose, has different notions about how much drug use constitutes abuse. In the early 1990s a French psychiatrist interviewed me and wrote an article about me as a typical drug addict of the 1970s. I thought she was overreacting, though I humored her since she was so keen on her article. In the 1970s I almost never bought marijuana but I'd smoke a joint if someone offered it, usually about once a week (not often by human standards though excessive for a presidential candidate, it seems). Over the decade I probably went on twenty acid trips maximum, none of them good but all of them memorable and life-changing. I didn't know people rich enough to afford cocaine, though occasionally a well-heeled trick would get me high. Most of my drug use was connected to sex. Marijuana and quaaludes (a muscle relaxer) and a glass of wine or two would make me available to almost anyone's desires. I understood why prostitutes were often high.

Quaaludes also made me sloppy. One night at Ruskay's restaurant on Columbus Avenue I must have tucked the tablecloth instead of a napkin into my belt. When I got up to leave, I trailed the plates, glasses, and silverware behind me as I staggered along, saluting friends obliviously, heading for the exit, a big smile on my face.

My main problem, however, was drink. I never drank during the day, but in the evening I started sipping wine with dinner and kept on until I passed out. I could easily get through two bottles a night. In 1983 when I couldn't get up the ladder to my loft bed, I decided that I'd become so absurd I should stop drinking forever—which I did. A year before I'd stopped smoking. Soon I'd gone from a skinny, boyish smoker, always talking and grinning drunkenly in the evening, to a fat, old-mannish sobersides who went to bed early. A profile in the newspaper referred to my "matronly" chin.

\*     \*     \*

Keith, like many Americans, had not grown up with classical music, though he was eager to be introduced to it. We were so poor we didn't have many 33⅓ records but would listen over and over to the few we had, especially a magical recording of Schumann's *Kreisleriana* played by Alicia de Larrocha, of all people (since she was Spanish, we thought she was supposed to play Spanish music exclusively, just as gay writers were by then only being allowed to write gay fiction).

To support my nephew, I had to take a job with a chemical company that had, last time I looked, generated sales of more than six billion dollars in one year. This was by far the worst job I ever had as a grown-up.

I was in the public relations department and my first task was to try to justify to stockholders and government regulators why the company should be making flammable children's pajamas. Then I was supposed to justify its extensive holdings in South Africa under apartheid. I was sick to my stomach every day. We were supposed to be in the office from eight A.M. to eight P.M., at least, six days out of seven. I was in charge of shepherding through production the annual report to stockholders, a glossy four-color magazine that was designed to explain why the company was losing money. All of the vice presidents, and there were a great number of them, were tightly guarded by high-paid executive secretaries warding off every disturbance and insuring their constant repose within their calm offices on the highest floor. They struck me as fetuses being maintained in a warm chemical bath under artificial light. I would regularly send around to each of them a request for information that I could include in the annual report. But, invisible in their luxurious offices, each of the twenty vice presidents would then forward my request to the next vice president, making sure that none ever answered. Everyone in the building was afraid to make a decision, and the entire organization was paralyzed with fear.

Even the annual report couldn't be turned out by the company, but must be handed over to an expensive freelance outfit that specialized in business publications. I wanted a brilliant fashion photographer I knew to take the executives' group picture, jazz it up, but my boss—a duplicitous, angry woman (and the only female vice president)—met my friend Edgar and explained, in a voice shaking with rage, that no gay person was ever to be allowed on the executive floor, and what had I been thinking?

My only consolation during this difficult period was the two Keiths, my nephew and the actor I was in love with. While living with me, my nephew reawakened to all the beauties of literature and began to write with great fluency and charm. At my suggestion he read Lord Chesterfield's *Letters* and the Abbé Prévost's *Manon Lescaut* and Stendhal's *Charterhouse of Parma*. He worked hard at after-school jobs and got terrific grades at the private school around the corner where I sent him. But my greatest pleasure came from our long conversations about life and literature—which were of course held under the benign and refined supervision of Proust. My nephew loved music and became an accomplished composer and singer, but his greatest ardor was for literature, in which even as a teenager he was able to find the words he needed for his own life. Although he was just sixteen and his girlfriend fourteen, both of them were reading *Lolita* and *Manon*—which were versions of their own loves and passions and misadventures. Although since then I've taught creative writing and literature to hundreds of students over three decades, I never had such eager students as those first two. They were able to move quickly beyond the language of the eighteenth century and the nineteenth century or even the elegant ironies of Nabokov to find the unclouded mirror they were searching for. My nephew went on to write a haunting memoir about that time, *The Boy with the Thorn in His Side*, and *Original Youth*, a biographical study of my first sixteen years, which was a factually correct version of the period covered by my semiautobiographical novel *A Boy's Own Story*.

When I started work on a new novel, I'd put in little bits here and there just for him—allusions only Keith would get, funny turns of phrase and sexy descriptions of dark-skinned girls intended for his amusement.

Keith McDermott was less a reader then than my nephew, less hungry, but he nevertheless rode his own interests hard—his taste for the very first recordings of Steve Reich or for the plays of Robert Wilson or the dance inventions of Lucinda Child. More than my nephew and more than me, he wanted to be original and experimental—and this urgency and formalist absolutism he brought into our big, underfurnished apartment.

Before I started working at the chemical company I was trying to eke out a living writing managed textbooks. They were histories of the United States or introductory psychology texts designed for college freshmen or sophomores. Well-established academics outlined the content and photocopied numerous articles of the latest research and would present the whole bundle to me along with a cut-and-paste collation of the best passages in already existing competing textbooks. My job was to synthesize all this material into vivid, crystalline prose—for which I'd receive a flat fee of three hundred dollars a chapter. I had a secretary who'd show up every day to whom I'd dictate my synthesis—then, promptly at one, we'd have sex.

Although I remember nothing of the thousand-page psychology textbook, I wrote not one but two thousand-page histories of the United States. Both of them were lousy and never "took off" in the way that the editors had hoped—never becoming widely adopted, though the second one was a harbinger of "political correctness" and had far more information on African-Americans, Native Americans, Asian-Americans, and Spanish-Americans than was typical for the time. Nevertheless, I learned a lot from them. When I wrote a review of one of Gore Vidal's books of essays, for instance, I was able to criticize his assumption that all the founding fathers were greedy and acting out of self-interest. I had just read the most recent statistical analyses of what happened to the personal wealth of the founders— and in almost every case the Revolution diminished rather than augmented their fortunes. The founders had clearly been for the most part idealists. Years later when I came to write two historical novels, *Fanny: A Fiction* and *Hotel de Dream*, all that American history helped me orient myself into the intricacies of born-again fervor and utopianism and abolitionism in the 1820s (*Fanny*) or of urbanization and sensational journalism and "vice" in the 1890s (*Hotel*).

While writing U.S. history, I, of course, still wanted to write fiction. I was talking to John Ashbery, who had been to see a shrink who specialized in writer's block. The conversation he reported:

Shrink: So tell me what your daily schedule is.
Ashbéry: Well, I wake up and get up and—
Shrink: You do what?
Ashbery: I get up—
Shrink: You must never, never get up. Okay, pee and make a
    cup of coffee, but then get back in bed if only for half an hour
    every day and write longhand in a notebook.
Ashbery: Why?
Shrink: That way your inhibitions will still be low and you'll be
    closer to your dreams. That's the surefire way out of writer's
    block.

I followed the shrink's advice. I didn't have writer's block, though all my failures with plays and fiction had left me feeling wounded. I would feel sick with fear every time I'd begin to write something made-up. I couldn't afford to have writer's block in any

Edmund White

literal sense; I had to keep writing to survive (and support all these new people, now that I was a "family man"). I could, however, have kept on doing nothing but churning out articles and reviews and ghostwriting, as so many other people in New York did. A novel was a long-term project that no one would finance, at least not in my case. It took years out of one's life, with no promise that it would ever be published. If it was published, there was no assurance it would earn any money or even be reviewed.

But my sense of personal identity required that I write fiction. If I thought that my only take on life would be the clever remarks or vague thoughts I might be able to cook up on the spot, then I wouldn't be able to recognize myself.

I knew I had to keep on writing or else I'd let the ambient cultural noise drown out my thoughts, which weren't paraphrasable wisecracks or wisdom but rather a way of looking at the world or the self. French people dismiss the cultural chatter and self-centered attitudinizing of Paris as *parisianisme*. A similar noise is generated by hip New Yorkers, though we don't have a word for it and perhaps we haven't isolated it yet as a reprehensible phenomenon. This "newyorkism" is so opinionated, so debilitating, so contagious with its knowingness, its instant formulas that replace any slow discoveries, that only people who are serious and ponderous can resist its blandishments, its quick substitutes for authenticity. No wonder the psychiatrist had said one should write first thing in the morning—before the tide of newyorkism swept over one, washing away actual honest thought and replacing it with trendy pronouncements.

But I don't want to suggest that for me the value of real writing was as a shield against newyorkism, that it substituted private feelings for public catchphrases. What it really did was to set up an idealized construct of life as a rival to actual, formless life in all its messiness. Because fiction depended on telling details and an exact and lifelike sequencing of emotions, and on representative if not slavishly mimetic dialogue, and on convincing actions, it required heightened and calculating powers of observation. Living-as-a-writer was different from living *tout court* to the degree that for a writer even the dreariest, most featureless evening among dullards became a subject for satire, a source of "notes" on the new bourgeoisie, a challenge to one's powers to discriminate among almost interchangeable shades of gray. Living-as-a-writer was not so different from living-as-an-analysand in that both novelist and psychoanalytic patient must remember their experiences, their aperçus, their ignoble hours and their petty minutes as well as their generous seconds in order to—well, to write it all down, or to report it to the shrink. Of course shrinks don't encourage patients to prepare, and the dream report is just another form of resistance, one of the most boring as well. And I can't say that I was ever a note-taker. My sister thinks I have a lousy or at least highly selective memory. Marilyn used to tease me for being so unobservant, saying that she could dye her hair blue and I wouldn't notice. So perhaps finally living-as-a-writer is more a project than a set of strategies. Perhaps it's only a good excuse for not buckling down at the chemical company.

# Chapter 10

I was approached in 1975 by an English book packager called Mitchell Beazley, who asked me to "audition" for *The Joy of Gay Sex*. Someone had suggested me but I didn't find out who till later. They were planning to follow up their international success, Alex Comfort's *The Joy of Sex*, with two new books, *The Joy of Gay Sex* and *The Joy of Lesbian Sex*. The look of each book, the format, the cover, everything would resemble the concept of Comfort's book, which had been a huge bestseller in many languages. These new books would be widely and openly distributed, and this way of packaging them was already an act of defiance, I thought. With each of these two new ventures, however, the book packager would team a writer with a shrink. Mr. Mitchell and his American editor, Frank Taylor, got in touch with me.

Frank Taylor had been married and had had four sons. He had been the editor in chief of McGraw-Hill, had accompanied Nixon to China, and had produced the Arthur Miller–scripted movie *The Misfits*—and only recently had he come out. He was in his sixties when he went into his first gay bar, Uncle Paul's on Christopher Street. There he'd seen a young man he thought was attractive, but the whole idea of approaching the fellow terrified him. At last, on his way out, he handed his card to the guy, who said, "But I've been in love with you since I was nine."

When he was a child, this young man's parents had written mysteries under a pseudonym. They were Frank's authors, and once during a visit with them at their home he'd met their little boy, who was visibly upset, frightened because he was about to be operated on for a bad heart. "You put me on your knee," the young man told Frank in Uncle Paul's, "and very calmly explained everything to me about my heart in scientific detail. And that's when I fell in love with you." The Frank I met in New York in the 1970s was already the happily-in-love Frank I'd later catch sight of in Key West in the 1980s accompanied by this same young man.

Now Frank asked me to write sample entries for *The Joy of Gay Sex*: on something hard (sadomasochism), something soft (kissing), something technical (cruising), and something psychological (coming out).

For me that kind of writing assignment felt like Method acting. I first had to establish who I was. In this case I thought someone kind but with an edge, someone worldly but patient, someone breezy most of the time but capable of being solemn. A slightly less clever but still amusing version of Cocteau, I thought. Someone who can whip off an epigram but is never a bitch, who thinks in paradoxes but doesn't insist you admire his wit. Just as pianists talked about something mysterious to nonmusicians called attack, I had to scrunch around on my stool while stoking (today we'd say "programming") my head with just the right elements of worldliness and compassion and reassuring didacticism. Then the writing went quite easily—as well it might, since I couldn't take it too seriously at the risk of seeming preposterous in my own eyes. It was that rarest and most agreeable thing of all for a writer: an assignment.

But I did take the project seriously because I wanted to escape the living death of the chemical company. As a writer I enjoyed competing with other contenders, especially since I didn't know the names of any of my rivals for *The Joy of Gay Sex*. Part of me—most of me!—was frightened, however, of doing something so tacky, and to this day I wince when I'm introduced as a reader at an Ivy League university, say, and the presenter makes a meal out of this particular title. ("Tonight we have with us the only"—chuckle, chuckle—"actual sex symbol I've ever met," har-har. "He is the coauthor of *The Joy of*"—heh-heh—"*Gay Sex*".) Back then, with just *Forgetting Elena* to my credit, along with a growing list of Time-Life Books I'd written or partially written, such as an anthropological look at *Homo erectus* called *The First Men* (har-har), or one about the *Hindenburg* (*When Zeppelins Flew!*), not to mention my forty-page LP-accompanying bios of Mendelssohn, Bruckner, Handel, and other composers, I was afraid my fragile literary "career" would be derailed by a sex manual. When I saw the Random House editor Anne Freedgood at the ballet and told her about my new project, she laughed insultingly and patted me on the sleeve and said, "Good. That's perfect for you."

I was the writer selected for the project and I was able to quit my job. I didn't have the nerve to tell my dragon-lady boss about the exact nature of my new assignment. I just said I had a big book contract and put in my notice. Bertha Harris, the literary half of *The Joy of Lesbian Sex* team, and I used to joke that if we were ever interviewed on television and asked why we wrote sex manuals, we'd say, "For the sake of our children," since she had a teenage daughter to support and I had my nephew.

At first my boss was panicked because she thought she'd be overwhelmed by work, but she quickly became sly and suspicious and had me barred from my office before the two weeks' notice period was up. She had not liked me ever since the CEO of the company had praised a brief, clear paraphrase I'd done of a sociological book he was supposed to read, *The Coming of Post-Industrial Society*. She'd become one of the only female officers of the company by being cunning, not through intelligence. So many of the women who succeeded before the feminist era were truly loathsome. They knew they were tokens and were never given any real power, and they maintained their positions through the vilest sort of feminine wiles.

Patrick Merla, my assistant at *Saturday Review* had suggested me as a coauthor of *The Joy of Gay Sex*. To my surprise I discovered that my coauthor was my own therapist, Dr. Charles Silverstein. He said that I could be his collaborator or his patient but not both, so I chose collaborator. We had just three or four months to turn out the book. I remember working so hard that I never had time actually to have sex. I would be describing Anal or Oral Sex and would get so excited but would have no time for anything but Masturbation.

We were a good team. Charles, who'd come out late and moved directly into an affair, then another, knew little about the apparatus of gay life, which I was an expert on, though one of his sidelines was sex therapy (cures for impotence and retarded or premature ejaculation), and he brought that to the table as well as a warm, reassuring personality. I was still cynical and cold from having endured my early years of gay life before the era of self-acceptance. If it had been up to me, the book would have been called *The Bleakness of Gay Sex*. Charles introduced the right note of physical closeness and emotional intimacy.

For the longest time I thought being gay was a sort of scandal. It seemed deeply unnatural, not only because it did not make babies but also because it seemed to violate anatomical design. Worse, no man had been brought up to take charge at the office but surrender in bed. In the days when I'd gone out with women, everything had seemed easier, more familiar, more reassuring—but, perhaps, too often sickeningly so. In college I'd dated a woman who adored me so much that I found myself preening, glowing with self-satisfaction. I thought that gay life, by contrast, toughened me up for this Spartan, competitive, dangerous activity of being a New York writer.

During the 1970s I began to question many of the basic assumptions of our culture. We now saw that for the thousand-year period before Christ the pagan world had accepted boy love as a viable alternative. In the classical world numerous debates, which in their written form ran to hundreds of pages, had argued the relative merits of heterosexuality and pederasty, with the pederasts usually winning. K. J. Dover, a professor of Greek at St. Andrews who happened to be heterosexual, published in 1978 a careful study of all the actual sex practices and romantic conventions between two males in ancient Greece. Such works, and later Foucault's *History of Sexuality*, provided both a long pedigree for male-male sex and dramatic evidence of how much homosexuality differed from epoch to epoch. If there was nothing exclusively natural about heterosexuality, there were also different "homosexualities," not one homosexuality. This discussion lay at the heart of one of the major culture wars of the 1970s, between essentialists (who thought homosexuality was the same no matter when or where it appeared) and the social constructionists (who thought Alcibiades' homosexuality bore no resemblance to Michelangelo's and that his bore no resemblance to mine). Of course you could be a bit of both and claim, as I would, that the rules of homosexuality might be determined by your society (active or passive roles governed by age, bisexuality permitted or not, anal or "intercrural" penetration preferred, same-sex marriage legalized or not), but that the overpowering attraction to a member of the same sex despite rigorous taboos in certain cultures might actually be innate and biologically determined.

These debates that "naturalized" homosexuality (or that at least showed it was omnipresent, eternal) were backed up by new biological studies of homosexuality throughout the animal kingdom and new ethnological studies of homosexuality in other cultures. At this time I was beginning to read Foucault. His central idea had a liberating effect on me: that we are all—philosophers, children, and chemical engineers alike—constricted as to what we can think by the prevailing discourses of our period. As he put it, "We cannot think no matter what no matter when" (*On ne peut pas penser n'importe quoi n'importe quand*). Like me (and it sounds absurdly pretentious to put it that way), Foucault was a positivist who rejected metaphysics and all grand spiritual generalities à la Heidegger or class conspiracies à la Marx. Foucault disliked all general principles and held out for particularities, though he did recognize that at each historical moment people could think only certain thoughts and not others—and that these restrictions applied to the entire population. According to Foucault, no one was immune to the subduing power of discourse.

I felt that in the case of homosexuality no one before 1969 had been able to think of homosexuals as something like a minority group. Before that date there were many competing theories, all dismissive, and in the beginning of *Cities of the Plain* (*Sodome et Gomorrhe*), Proust presents at least five etiologies, many of them contradictory. He is obviously caught up in a delirium of theorizing. All other books touching on homosexuality then and later (from André Gide's *Corydon* to James Baldwin's *Giovanni's Room*) cannot resist subscribing to a theory; indeed, they seem obliged to theorize. One sign of post-Stonewall liberation is that all this scaffolding of theory has fallen away; now no one friendly to homosexuality feels he or she must explain it, any more than a thinker or writer is forced to explain heterosexuality. Novels and plays treating homosexuality as a theme no longer indulge in presenting the characters' etiology. Now characters are simply shown inhabiting their difference.

None of these ideas was racing through my head when I coauthored *The Joy of Gay Sex*, but Charles and I had certainly been influenced by all the intellectual activity bubbling through the Gay Academic Union. What we discovered in working on our book (aimed at an inexperienced young or old man living in the provinces, far from centers of gay sophistication) was that whereas sexual technique and the divide between male and female cultures were the primary problems for heterosexuals, in gay life your partner's body was no more a mystery than his priorities and patterns of communication. No, the problem was gay life itself— coming out, dealing with religious prejudice, coping with the straight world of employment or with the problems of friendship, housing, and family, and handling such thorny practical and legal problems as how to leave your property to a gay lover. Then there were the lifestyle questions (cruising, "marriage," fidelity or open relationships, role-playing).

My own problems in dealing with being gay were crippling—I'd devoted decades in therapy to coping with them and as a teenager had often been suicidal. But in our sex manual I decided to take a jaunty, relaxed tone, to "act ahead of my emotions," as a friend undergoing therapy put it. That I'd turned away from straight therapists trying to cure me to Charles Silverstein, an openly gay man, revealed that even I had been shaped by the new intellectual and cultural currents before I began working on *The Joy of Gay Sex*.

One of the ironies of writing about such a highly charged subject was that when the book came out, we were criticized within the gay community for being too conservative, for warning people, for instance, against such potentially damaging and outré practices as fist-fucking, whereas just four years later, when AIDS appeared in 1981, we were accused by that community of having been unalarmed by promiscuity. The idea that we'd erred somehow in not foreseeing an unprecedented disease no scientist in the world had predicted strikes me as bizarre and unfair. The publisher certainly made a mistake, however, in not withdrawing the book immediately and replacing it with an AIDS-conscious edition. It took several years before the book was revised.

I was never quite sure how I felt about having coauthored *The Joy of Gay Sex*. I discovered that having a "bankable" book made me more attractive to publishers, but its sexual nature turned my name into a bit of a joke. That such a book now existed—and as a companion to the bestselling *The Joy of Sex*—caused it to count as a liberating publication, and in certain circles I seemed to be striking a blow for gay freedom. Amazingly, no one tried to ban it except in a province of Canada where a lady had thought she was buying *The Joy of Cooking* and was so horrified by what she found under "chicken" that she convinced the local bookshops to withdraw it from their shelves, a form of de facto censorship that the Candian version of the ACLU instantly and effectively opposed.

# Chapter 11

David Kalstone invited me to join him one summer in Venice—then another, then another, on and on for several years. Stan and I had visited Venice that first time, but I hadn't gone back in ten years. David introduced me to his Italian summer world, which was *dolce* and *soave* and *raffinato*. Funded with a few thousand dollars here and there by the Merrill Foundation, I was able to afford my flight and pocket money, but David paid the rent and financed the major treats, such as dinner once a season at Harry's Bar and a day beside the Cipriani pool once every week or two. At the pool everyone was so old that Gore Vidal had reputedly referred to it as Lourdes. It was there that Marguerite Littman (an American socialite and AIDS fund-raiser in London whom I interviewed years later) said to Tennessee Williams as they looked at a cadaverous girl shambling past in her bikini, "Look, anorexia nervosa!" to which Williams replied, "Oh, Marguerite, you know everyone."

At Harry's Bar the waiters were like characters in Goldoni's *The Servant of Two Masters*, whirling chairs through the air and posing them beside an already crowded table or catching plates of pasta hurled out of the kitchen and rushing them upstairs (social hell) or to the backroom on the main floor (purgatory) or to the front room (heaven). There in heaven we'd see, sitting by the front door every time, a couple of elderly gay men from Kansas who came bedizened with their heavy gold necklaces (David called them "the chain gang"). They never spoke to anyone or to each other, but just sat there at the price of hundreds of dollars an hour absorbing old-fashioned gin martinis and looking on at each arrival and departure with all the attention they'd lavish on pigeons in San Marco. There we once saw Lady Diana Cooper, ancient but with startling sapphire eyes (David would have marked the word *sapphire* in my manuscript and then written in the margin, "The sin of aristocratic admiration," which he considered a failure of taste as much as a breach in style). She and her husband, Duff Cooper, the British ambassador, had been the social leaders of postwar Paris. During the winter she lived alone in London in "Little Venice," mostly bedridden, and there she would receive the Queen Mother for tea.

Those first two summers David lived on a *rio* between the Salute and the Guggenheim Museum across from the Da Cici *pensione*. Twice we saw Ezra Pound just before he died in 1972 with the violinist Olga Rudge walking slowly along. Pound no longer chose to speak, though he could. He was small and frail and carefully dressed and had a white beard and a cane. This is the man, I thought, who'd described his virulent anti-Semitism during the war years to Allen Ginsberg in the 1960s as "that suburban vice." This was the man who'd invented Chinese poetry for our time and culture. Who'd been locked in a cage by the American army and been befriended by a black soldier and written about it in *The Pisan Cantos*. Who'd translated Egyptian poetry and troubadour poetry and parts of the Confucian Analects, launched vorticism in the plastic arts and imagism in poetry, drastically cut and rearranged *The Waste Land* for T. S. Eliot, written an opera (both words and music), written the *ABC of Reading*, and had made such an impression on me since my adolescence, and whose poetry struck me as faultless if daunting. Accompanying Richard Howard to

Princeton once for a class he was teaching, I'd heard him say to his students that the two poets in English with the best "ear" were Herbert and Pound.

David, from the early 1970s up until 1985 (the year before his death), mounted a campaign to conquer Venetian society. As a goal for any other person, he would have laughed at that idea—since he was the first to recognize how vapid Venice could be. He often said, "Venice is as intellectually distinguished as Akron, Ohio." But if it was small and closed, that made it all the more interesting to the novelist in David. For he had always wanted to write a novel and now began one that opened with a Harvard-educated professor at last getting a job back at his alma mater. He bends down and kisses the ground in Cambridge—or did he put lipstick on so that he could leave the imprint of a kiss on a window? I forget which, but the kiss seems a safe bet.

Though David lived in New York and worshipped the New York City Ballet, I think the city otherwise failed to stimulate his imagination. Manhattan was too big, too kicked-out—historical, yes, but all the evidence of its past worn down and built over and nearly erased. In Venice, by contrast, people bore historic names and lived in historic family palaces that in their way were in perfect repair. Behind the water gates of a palace could be seen the old wooden hood (the *felze*) of a gondola, an intricately carved fitting that protected the family from prying eyes or, in the winter, from icy winds. In the grand *salotto* were the ceilings by Tiepolo, and there, sitting around in gilded chairs in the dim light, were descendants of the very people pictured in the nineteenth-century watercolors in the hallway—ancestors at receptions in these rooms that were the same then as now. Here the pink marble floors were cracked and tilting, the plaster putti slightly grayed and missing a wing or a finger, but the same luminous and elevated luxury everywhere.

Most of David's conquests were effected at the Cipriani pool. One would get into a boat just next to Harry's Bar and a few moments later have been sped past San Giorgio and deposited at the hotel, then helped out by the uniformed arm of a young, golden-haired demigod. Led by one of the *bagnini* to a chaise longue by the pool, one would then enter the changing rooms and put on a swimsuit. This was the realm of wens and warts, of bellies and sagging tits—all outfitted in bathing costumes by Hermès or Valentino, and all cosseted on wonderfully upholstered deck lounge chairs with crisp white piping, and supplied with abundant white towels the size of bedsheets. At the shallow end was Patricia Curtis, standing in the water but resting her hands, heavy with family diamonds, on the poolside. Her family had been living in the Palazzo Barbaro for a hundred years, ever since an ancestor had quarreled with someone back home in Boston and in a rage moved his wife and children to Venice. Here they had played host to Henry James and John Singer Sargent and scores of other American visitors and expatriates. Now Patricia was watching her eccentric, fairly mad brother oversee the family's loss of the palace; her son scarcely spoke English and handled the transfer of luggage from the Orient Express to the various five-star hotels in Venice.

Over there was John Hohnsbeen, a handsome guy from Oklahoma with cornflower-blue eyes and lips so full they looked as if they'd burst. He'd been a Martha Graham dancer and his body was still well-knit and powerful. He lived with Peggy Guggenheim and ran the museum here for her. John was an unabashed social climber and had had great success—at his fiftieth birthday party, which I attended, there were four "royals," including the pretender to the Hapsburg throne.

John looked no more than thirty and said the secret of his youthful appearance was tuberculosis. At twenty he'd been tubercular and sent off to Switzerland for the "sleep cure," in which the patient was put into an induced coma for long periods for a year. Apparently it not only cured TB, it ensured eternal youth. When, awakened like Sleeping Beauty, he'd returned to New York, his lover, the architect Philip Johnson, designed for him an all-white apartment. John had astonished his old fraternity brothers by striding about in a white silk peignoir with the only touch of color in the whole place being a drop of blood on his handkerchief. John was a born "capon," a walker for rich and elderly straight women. I remember he used to visit a woman named Mrs. Walker in England who was a great-granddaughter of Johnnie Walker—that same Walker of whiskey fame with the top hat and cane, a Regency rake. John had never worked at any real job. He and Johnson had been lovers for a decade, and after Johnson moved on, he felt so guilty he paid John alimony for years. John had dabbled at being an art dealer at the Curt Valentin Gallery and elsewhere, but he didn't have much to show for it beyond a good abstract wall sculpture by Hans Arp. I went to bed with John once but I'm afraid I wasn't aggressive enough to interest him.

When Peggy died in 1979, she left him nothing but a Picasso drawing. Guggenheim curators from New York moved in and found snails crawling up the backs of paintings. John was suddenly out of a job, money, prospects. His wealthy ladies all seemed to have evaporated. He limped back to the States and lived quietly until an unglamorous uncle whom he'd scarcely known suddenly died and left John a small fortune. His Oklahoma family, which he'd always shirked in favor of his ladies, had come through. Finally John was able to summer in Venice again and winter in Key West (later Fort Lauderdale, when it became the gay capital for "silver daddies"). He rented a wonderful ground-floor apartment across from the Palazzo Albrizzi, though soon enough Venice became more and more difficult for him. By his seventies his emphysema had become so bad he could walk no more than ten paces without stopping and gasping—and Venice, a city without cars, requires lots of walking since gondolas cost hundreds of dollars a day to hire. In the end, in a suicidal but I thought rather heroic gesture, he decided to pay a call on a friend in Santa Fe where, everyone warned him, the altitude was so high that he'd never be able to breathe. John, however, wasn't about to have his social schedule interrupted by mere health. He went, was quickly hospitalized, and did indeed die in Santa Fe.

Besides John, another of David's and my favorites in Venice was Maria Teresa Rubin, who headed the Save Venice Committee and who'd not long before divorced the composer Ernesto Albrizzi. His older brother Alessandro, the head of the family, who was also a New York decorator, gave us a tour of the Albrizzi palace, starting with the massive beacon in the front hall (some thirty feet high) that had once crowned the ship sailed by the last admiral of Venice, an Albrizzi ancestor. The palace had always belonged to the Albrizzis, and in the various salons were paintings of Albrizzi doges and other Albrizzi grandees. In the dining room were life-size stucco angels swooping down out of the ceiling like dive-bombers. Maria Teresa lived on the top floor and had a separate entrance and elevator. I suppose her ex-husband let her live there because she was raising their children.

Maria Teresa had a lovely, smoky gaze in which, from time to time, the smoke would clear to reveal the fire. She was slender with blond hair and high cheekbones. Someone must have once complimented her on her smoldering glance since she knew just how to work it, when to let it flare forth. She saw more "wickedness" in what the people around her said than they actually intended. Maybe that was her way of keeping herself interested in a fairly routine social life. She had a handsome young lover, Vladimir de Marsano, whose father was an Italian aristocrat living and working as a banker in Switzerland, and whose mother was a Serb. He'd grown up speaking Dutch to the nanny until one day his parents laid down the law and said, "We think it's time you had a grown-up language of your own, and we suggest French," and Vladimir was equally proficient in English and Italian. Vladimir was in his early twenties then and Maria Teresa in her forties, and they made a dashing, attractive couple. I suppose it helped that Vladimir, as a count in his impeccably tailored clothes, unlike a lot of young men his age didn't resemble a willfully sloppy American college boy. He was affectionate, mysterious—we were all dying to know if he might not be a little gay around the edges, but he'd always meet our questions with a delighted laugh and an enigmatic smile. He had plenty of spirit that he usually held in check, and we knew not to press him too far. He, too, thought everyone was joking around him, which I think was less a form of paranoia than a disposition toward *leggerezza*. What I mean to suggest is that he was wonderfully *serviable*, polite and patient to a fault, always on the lookout for something fun and new and light, not too cultured himself but cultured just enough to maintain his membership in his upper-class world, affectionate and teasing with everyone, including much older and far less polished friends, capable of sweet friendliness—without ever showing his cards.

Another poolside habitué was Harry Mathews, the experimental novelist and the only American member of Oulipo, the French writers' club that proposed mathematical models for works of fiction and poetry. He'd had an aristocratic mistress with the lovely first name of Loredana and was often in Venice. He and David were best friends (but who did not count David as his or her best friend?), and they had lots of worldly interests that I could not share—a new Venetian restaurant out by the Arsenale, new Missoni sweater designs, the new director of the Paris Opera, and Maria Teresa's newest affair with someone they nicknamed Bambu, who would eventually become the most powerful arts bureaucrat in Italy. His real name was Vittorio Sgarbi and he was also, at some point, the Italian equivalent to the British layman's art-history guru Sister Wendy, since he often discoursed on painting on television.

David had asked me to review one of Harry's most difficult books, *The Sinking of the Odradek Stadium*, for the *New York Times Book Review*, which I'd done before ever meeting Harry (the *Times* editors didn't want reviewers to know the authors they were critiquing).

I loved this hilarious, improbable novel and wrote a long essay about a later one, *Cigarettes*, also funny and utterly original. Harry was and certainly remains a great writer—one of the best I've ever known, though he's never enjoyed the celebrity he deserves. He always had money, though he downplayed that, and later he inherited a large family fortune. Eventually he owned apartments in Paris (next to the prime minister's *hôtel particulier*) and in New York (at first on Beekman Place) and houses on Long Island and in Vercors (near Annecy in the southeast of France) and two adjoining houses in Key West. Merrill seemed more relaxed about his money than Harry was with his. It did strike me that almost all the poets I knew were rich or had rich wives.

David had such terrible vision that he was capable of saluting a passing pigeon on the Giudecca, convinced it was a lady he'd once met. Nevertheless he loved to watch and assess all the little dramas playing out poolside at the Cipriani. On some days before he headed off for the afternoon we'd eat a diet lunch of prosciutto, salad, and a few slices of mozzarella. No bread, no wine, no dessert. Soon we'd be sick with laughter as we played bitchy *alta borghese* house-proud women, calling out, *"Cara!"* and typifying everything as *carina* ("cute") and *casalingha* ("spotlessly domestic"), and archly complimenting each other on little flaws one would more likely feel embarrassed by: *"O, cara, quanto i tuoi capelli sono bellissimi con questo nuovo colore."* Everything, even the dim matronly prospect of one day succumbing to the vanity of a dye job, sounded brighter and funnier and more tolerable to us couched in a prosperous housewife's lightly carping, subtly "intimate" Italian.

What were we doing? I could imagine Simon Karlinsky turning away from our campiness with a fart-sniffing scowl of disapproval. Perhaps by impersonating two middle-class, middle-aged Italian women we were celebrating our tentative hold on the language, rehearsing roles that steered us away from the dangerous shoals of spurned love and put-upon chastity, and finally just indulging in the sublimely silly play unique to friendship.

For us Venice was such a complete contrast to New York. In New York, David could scarcely go out at night, too blind to negotiate the ill-lit, dangerous streets. Venice was safe, and a pedestrian city where every bridge step was lined with white stones. No Venetian was going to mug a tourist—how would he run away in a town without cars or motor scooters, where every boat was licensed and known and counted? With so many eyes behind every shutter, he'd be sure to be identified and denounced right away. If he was Venetian, his neighbors would know him. If he was a "foreigner," that would register as well with the locals.

New York took its duties seriously and shrugged off its pleasures, whereas Venice was devoted to the delights of eating a sherbet, of visiting the tailor, of looking at the latest *nouveautés* (not all of them hideous) from the glassworks on Murano, of buying fish and vegetables under the Rialto Bridge, of dropping into the pasta shop and purchasing coal-black linguine flavored with squid ink, of watching the flush-faced, black-bearded butcher cut tidy little veal chops in his minuscule shop, of stopping at the *drogheria* and knowing the words for mustard (*senape*) and anchovies (*acciughe*). Even for its part-time residents, Venice represented the pleasure of knowing how to slip through the throngs of tourists (the sheep or *pecore*, as David called them) following their guide holding aloft a red umbrella and turn into a quiet *calle* before stepping onto the *traghetto*, the gondola that ferried people across the Grand Canal. David, usually so fearful and unphysical, knew just how to step onto the boat without slipping, stand all the way across without staggering, leave a few coins for Charon on the gunwale without under- or overtipping.

I can picture David with his face tanned and his hair silvered by the sun, wearing his azure-blue silk shirt and hand-sewn beige silk-and-wool trousers and black gondolier slippers and gold seal ring emblazoned with the Venetian lion. Neither of us was good at sustained conversation in Italian, though both of us could chat with waiters and shopkeepers. I'd stay behind at his apartment in the afternoons writing while he was off at the pool; around six he'd come back with the latest and a fresh bottle of Campari and a lemon. David had always taken a demanding book with him—a new study of Spenser, say, or Ashbery's *Three Poems*—though he seldom read more than a page or two. He was too busy being debriefed by George Smith, an American industrialist who ran a Goodyear factory in Bergamo and lived in a villa surrounded by German shepherd attack dogs and barbed-wire fences as protection against kidnapping for ransom, which was common in Italy in those days. George, with his cigarette holder, hairy barrel chest, and the handsome face of a society band conductor, was gay but celibate. He had converted to Catholicism and hoped to be made a papal baron; celibacy was not too high a price to pay for such an honor—or for his eternal salvation. His snobbism and his social-climbing form of Catholicism reminded me of Somerset Maugham's Elliott Templeton in *The Razor's Edge*, though George was humbler, less of a termagant than Elliott. His emotions he poured into his relationship with his adopted son, an upright young man of Bergamo whom George was about to marry off to a local heiress. I hitched a ride with George once as he was sped from Mestre to Bergamo in a Mercedes limousine driven by his uniformed chauffeur. I stayed over one day at the barricaded house, illuminated all night by spotlights and patrolled by the attack dogs. I remembered Hervé Guibert's description of the fading Italian movie star living in a villa protected by German shepherds that obeyed commands only in German (*"Auf! Sitz!"*), and who kept all her old movies in a refrigerator, extracting one every evening on a rotating basis and watching it as the dogs prowled outside. I visited George's plant, where I had a delicious three-course lunch in the company cafeteria. In Bergamo, at least, the employees spoke softly, wore clean uniforms, and seemed more like skilled watchmakers than assembly-line workers.

Though George was devout, he didn't radiate disapproval. Quite the contrary; he lived for every morsel of gossip, which "amused" him. He was as sophisticated as a playboy and as pious as a peasant. He'd sit beside the Cipriani pool in his swimsuit, exposing his hairy chest to the sun, puffing on his cigarette holder, drinking the first of many cocktails, listening to an account of the complicated maneuverings of the Franchin family or the Franchettis, I'm not sure which—in Venice in those days you had to choose one family or the other. The American painter Cy Twombly had married into the Franchettis, who'd once owned the Ca' d'Oro (now a Venetian museum on the Grand Canal) and who counted among their forebears a composer who'd based an opera on the life of Christopher Columbus. They were Jews ennobled for a gracious loan to one king or another. All of the gay men in town worshipped Christina Franchetti, who was Cuban and stayed up all night reading Stendhal or George F. Kennan or Gyp (the pen name of a turn-of-the-century French society novelist). She'd sleep all day, then at sunset head off to Harry's Bar for breakfast, then hop a boat to the Cipriani, hoping to encounter a few stragglers still lingering by the pool (like Proust haunting the cafés at midnight after the asthma-causing dust had settled). She had her laundry sent off to London. She sometimes made spaghetti for friends at two in the morning. Her husband, Nanuk, a deaf and unpleasant Franchetti, seldom bothered her, but he had gambled her money away. She had a hard time paying for the necessities of life (rent, food), but she charged the luxuries (Harry's, the Cipriani, books, couture clothes) to accounts she never settled. She spoke in a thrilling baritone voice and had the slow, exaggerated intonations of an opera diva, and her gay male court was always faithful, regarding her mildly diverting remarks as sidesplitting.

No one I knew in New York was celibate or devout, nor were any older gay men there receiving alimony. Nor did I know of any bisexual aristocrats. Of course pockets of idle friends gossiped about each other in New York, but with no central, highly visible group of that sort to concentrate on. In New York, society had broken down and splintered. Decade after decade of new rich arrivals and members of café society and well-heeled fund-raisers for charities as well as celebrities from the theater and television had brushed aside the old hierarchy explored by Edith Wharton (which even she had pictured as already dissolving). Too many different social scenes competed in New York for any one of them to seem glamorous. New York "society" events had a cheerlessness because of an insufficient sense of privilege or pleasure or exclusivity and an excess of duty connected to them (all those cancer benefits). Everyone in New York felt he or she should work, even those with enough money not to; idleness wasn't socially acceptable, and women with tens of millions of dollars ran bookstores or opened thrift shops or attended charity board meetings or started restaurants, for which they'd taken dozens of cordon bleu cooking courses. No one in Europe would become a chef unless his father had been in the trade; certainly no one would do something so repetitious and fatiguing and hot and smelly and financially perilous for "fun." All these "jobs" meant everyone over fifty went to bed early, at ten—which contradicted the late-night *dolce far niente* habits of real society. Nor did the very rich mingle with the merely rich in New York. Everyone socialized with people of exactly the same level of wealth, and no one rich on any level received artists and writers. Early to bed and no bohemians had made Jack and Jackie a dull boy and girl. New York publishing, for instance, was full of heiresses. They, too, had to have jobs, and luckily their family money allowed them to take interesting if poorly paid positions. When I'd worked at Time-Life, my researcher would descend at ten in the evening after laboring long hours under a deadline and at the curb find her family driver waiting in the old Lincoln Town Car. The miserable salaries paid in publishing could have been sufficient only to people with great fortunes and private incomes. Publishers had figured out that heiresses had good, expensive educations, low expectations, and so much guilt about their wealth that they were sure to work harder than everyone else.

New York nightlife catered to the affluent young, the only people who stayed up late, whereas Venice had almost no late gathering places beyond a bar next to the Gritti Palace, Haig's, where (as David liked to pretend) the "disreputable" people hung out. We'd stop in late at night (in Venice meaning midnight), and David would insist that everyone present was a heroin addict or jewelry thief or committing incest with his druggy, stringy-haired sister in the family palazzo: "There, that's her in the dirty Ungaro!"

In New York everyone we knew was a liberal, whereas in Venice we met several genuine and unreconstructed fascists. One particularly drunken evening we were lured back to a grand apartment next to Count Volpe's house, and there a young father, who was the son of a famous designer, showed old black-and-white movies of Hitler standing and saluting in an open car. The father shouted at his five-year-old, "Clap, darling, clap—our Führer!

Wave to the Führer!" At first we thought it must be a joke in bad taste, so bizarre and unexpected a display was it. After a time, realizing it wasn't a joke, we then had to make our hasty retreat.

In New York in those days you could assume everyone you would ever meet, on whatever level of society, was left-leaning and certainly tolerant. We knew no Archie Bunkers. One of the curious aspects of New York was that at that time its most illustrious citizens were all imports from the hinterlands or from Europe or Asia, whereas the natives were the rednecks.

One year when I arrived in Venice, David had already made a conquest of Peggy Guggenheim. John Hohnsbeen had introduced them to each other and they'd instantly become friends. Peggy had for years and years been intensely romantic and sexual, but now she'd put all that behind her. "It's not dignified," she told us. Peggy believed she owed her admirers—her observers—a modicum of dignity and as a result was permanently idle. David called her "the laziest girl in town," but she wasn't lazy but bored. She had a few occupations but no passions except her dogs, her Lhasa apsos, whom she called her "babies." And she had one obsession—arranging for her babies, and herself, to be buried in the garden of her palazzo. It was against commune rules to be buried anywhere but in a cemetery, but Peggy was willing to give her entire art collection and her palace to the city of Venice in exchange for having the rules bent in her favor. She eventually succeeded. In her garden she had a Byzantine stone chair, and now she and many of her dogs are buried in the ground that surrounds it.

Although nothing interested her, she had a sense of her status, which in her eyes was something like the public position of a monarch. When a visiting big shot came to town, Peggy would give him or her a cocktail party and wear her Fortuny gown, which made her look all the dumpier (since it clung to every bump and declivity of her body), but the gown, too, had a historic significance.

The dress was beige silk and made of hundreds of tiny pleats. Peggy told us that she would roll it up and tie it in a knot and mail it to London for cleaning. When she turned eighty, she posed for photographers and granted dippy interviews to the press. Smart or dumb, she was still Peggy Guggenheim.

In her heyday she'd lived with everyone from Samuel Beckett (who according to legend was always so drunk or depressed he refused to get out of bed, prompting Peggy to nickname him Oblomov, after the lazy Russian literary character) to Max Ernst (whom she'd spirited away on a plane to the States, where he quickly dumped her for the younger and more beautiful Dorothea Tanning). She'd been advised in buying art by Read, who'd drawn up a checklist of paintings to be acquired—and this she'd systematically followed. She gave Berenice Abbott her first camera. She'd opened a gallery in New York during the war years (Art of This Century) in which she'd given a first show to Jackson Pollock, whom she also slept with. Right after the war she'd brought Pollock to Venice for the Biennale. At gallery openings she'd wear one abstract earring and one surrealist earring to show—in her loopy way—how impartial she was. Now in Venice she hung all her earrings on the metal bedstead that had been designed for her by Alexander Calder. Like Gertrude Stein she'd gone on buying art after those first glory years, and for both Guggenheim and Stein, the later "geniuses" were all duds.

Peggy had the last private gondola in Venice. She was cheap, however, which meant she didn't want to hire a normal gondolier who belonged to the union and earned high wages. Instead, every spring she'd look around for a retired gondolier who could be engaged for less and who would fit into her livery, which she didn't want to modify. I remember that one summer David helped her line up a gondolier who'd conducted funeral boats to San Michele. If, after boarding, Peggy didn't give him a specific goal, he'd automatically start heading for the funeral island and singing traditional dirges. Perhaps she was cheap because her father (who'd installed the elevators in the Eiffel Tower and who'd died in the sinking of the *Titanic*) had sold his share of the partnership to his brothers before the discovery of the family copper mines in South America. Peggy had inherited just half a million dollars, which she'd parlayed into a huge estate through her wise art investments. But she'd never been cash rich, not like her cousins.

In the gondola, she'd have something she wanted to show us—the Cima da Conegliano painting of St. John the Baptist at the Madonna dell'Orto, or the Carpaccio pictures of St. Jerome and his lion frightening the friars at the Scuola di San Giorgio degli Schiavoni. The gondolier would pull up next to the church and help us out. Red-faced Dutch tourists or camera-armed Americans would watch this strange event with bewildered curiosity. Or Peggy would sit back with her eyes half-closed and listen to David reading to her from Henry James's *The Wings of the Dove*, which she thought of as "her" novel—since it was about a rich American girl in Venice who's very nearly exploited by attractive and devious compatriots with too many scruples to be true villains. She'd ask us to read it to her summer after summer, and it was always new to her. She never remembered it from one year to the next. She liked its Venetian setting and imperiled American heiress-heroine, the constant muted skirmishing over sex and money and love.

Once, when we were being punted along, a young man ran along the *fondamenta* for five minutes shouting, *"Principessa! Principessa!"* She dimly nodded toward him. "I think he's a man who used to work for me in the kitchen." When I asked her why he called her a princess, she said, "They like titles and are disappointed if one doesn't have one."

Peggy was always patting the back of her right hand with her left. When I asked her why, she said that she had rheumatism and doing this was the only thing that made it feel better.

Sometimes we'd eat a meager, uninspired meal in her dining room, surrounded by major paintings. It might be a lackluster chicken broth and then pasta in a tomato sauce followed by fruit. John Hohnsbeen had told us that Peggy would count the apples in the pantry every day to make sure the servants weren't eating more than one each. Conversation was tough sledding, though David was up to any demand and was always lavishing on Peggy his best gossip. She would look wide-eyed at him and say in foghorn tones, "How very amusing." Or she'd say, "That's outrageous, I love it." Of course, Peggy never actually sounded either amused or outraged about anything whatsoever. She'd merely been saying these same words for half a century.

I once asked her where she'd picked up her strange accent with its hooty vowels, and its bored falling intonations so in contrast to her antiquated adolescent vocabulary of excitement: "How positively thrilling," she trilled as a dismissive aside. In reply to my impertinent question she explained, "I went to a girls' school, the Jacoby School, on West Seventy-second Street, which was for rich Jewish girls. We weren't admitted to any gentile private schools and there weren't very many of us. But we were very close and we invented this way of talking and so we all spoke this way."

Often we'd take her out to dinner at some local restaurant where she could walk with the babies. She had weak ankles but still had good legs, which she showed off with short skirts and sandals.

She never talked about her feelings or her thoughts, though surely she'd had some, enough to write a funny, insolent autobiography, *Out of This Century*, in which she said that the day the Nazis marched into Paris she marched into Fernand Léger's studio and bought a 1919 painting for just three thousand dollars. She had a funny, mashed-in nose, and as a young woman had gone for a nose job to get rid of her large "hook." The doctor, however, had botched it, and Peggy had decided not to try it again. She accepted her potato nose with typical fatalism.

We felt that we were living with an extinct volcano, someone who'd been so often aroused and then damped down that she'd been left confused and indifferent. Peggy knew everything about Venice and enjoyed showing us strange facades, memorable little churches. She'd moved there right after the war, when she'd bought her palace for a song. It had just one floor above ground (it had never been finished) and had belonged to the Marchesa Luisa Casati, an art nouveau vamp who'd prowled the terraces with her leashed cheetahs and live snakes. Peggy had filled it with art, then decided to turn it into a museum, where she sometimes sat at the entrance and sold catalogs and tickets. She told us that once a woman asked her if Peggy Guggenheim was still alive and Peggy had said no. As she told us this story, she patted her hand, which unintentionally gave the effect of her reprimanding herself. Out front of the palazzo on the water side she'd installed an equestrian statue of a nude man by Marino Marini. The artist had given the horseman an erect penis that Peggy could unscrew when the cardinal came calling in his boat. Now the penis is soldered in place, I've been told. I've never been back since her death.

She gradually became more irritated with John Hohnsbeen for not spending his evenings with her. John had so many friends everywhere and wanted to go out and not be trailed by Peggy and the babies. She pretended that he was leaving the museum unprotected at night against robbers, but it seemed to us that she was mainly lonely—and that almost by reflex she nursed romantic hopes, or at the very least hoped John would go through the motions of courting her.

Although John lived decades in Paris and Rome, then Venice, he never learned either French or Italian and spoke English to everyone. Peggy could speak several languages, all with a strong accent and in short bursts with the inattention that typified her utterances even in English. She seemed elsewhere most of the time. When people talked to her, she often misunderstood them, or she'd cover her confusion with a habitual widening of her eyes: "Oh, really? How very amusing!" As I was to see with other famous people I came to know later, it didn't much matter how a "legend" like her behaved. If a friend was bored or alienated and dropped out, the next day there were always new people, attracted by a celebrated name and what amounted to open house.

## Chapter 12

David and I became closer and closer, perhaps because we shared these Venetian adventures that would have struck our New York friends as slightly glamorous but decidedly irrelevant and snobbish. New Yorkers constituted a kingdom that recognized no equals, no other powers, and took no prisoners. David's and my friendship was a strange tree to grow in New York, where so many relationships of all types were corrupted by self-interest. The idea of having important friends who could impress others and predispose them in your favor was a typically New York notion. I remember that when I moved to Paris in 1983, my French editor (Ivan Nabokov, the nephew of the writer) wanted to give me a launch party. I thought I should invite the press and the few famous friends I had in Paris. Embarrassed, Ivan explained that in Paris you could have a party for the press and then on another night one for your friends, but you wouldn't want to mix them. I was stunned by this idea, and when I'd absorbed it, I felt vulgar for not having known it all along. Now, perhaps, Parisians have become almost as cynical as New Yorkers, but then they still had a cult of friendship that made it sacred and nearly invisible to the public. There's no word in French for "name-dropping," and *arrivisme* isn't really the same as "social climbing."

My friendship with David was disinterested—neither of us had anything to gain from knowing each other—or nearly so. He might have paid for some things, but neither of us was ever using the other. David advised me about worldly things and introduced me to people who are still close friends, and once in a while I helped him with the wording of an essay. All the odder that just such a friendship should flourish in a city where people quite openly talked about "networking" and "contacts," as if anyone moderately clever would devote his time at a party to such admirable activities and not waste it on unprofitable friendships. It was said that you could tell who were someone's best friends because they were the ones he never saw—only a true friend would accept being endlessly put off. Of course most friendships here in New York are conducted on the telephone (and now, I've noticed in supermarkets and movie theaters, on cell phones), and David and I "checked in" with each other three times a day: "My dear, you won't believe what happened to me on the way home from Mary Ellen's *very dull* party!" To be fair, no wonder people social-climb in New York, since it has more genuine social mobility than London or Paris, where clothes, accents, and manners reveal all too much about origins and where there are no more than three degrees of separation between any two people. Everyone already knows every single bad thing about you. In all three cities, people practice what Paul Valéry called the "delirious professions," those careers that depend on self-assurance and the opinion of others rather than on certifiable skills. The delirious professions, I'd hazard, comprise literature, criticism, design, the visual arts, acting, advertising, all of the media—but not dance, for instance, where you can either do your thirty-two tours jetés without "traveling" downstage, or you can't. If you can do them, you can dance in any company in the world without further ado. But all the delirious professions, having no agreed-upon standards, require introductions and alliances, protectors and patrons, famous teachers or acclaim by someone reputed. In short, they depend upon that most mercurial of all possessions: reputation. Socially static cities such as Paris have less obvious social frenzy, and the rise of a Rubempré or Rastignac is all the more remarkable because it's so rare. But in a mobile city such as New York, people's ambitions are much more pressing and obvious. In New York *pushy* can be a compliment, *aggressive* is unqualified high praise. I remember how some Swedish friends of mine laughed when an American engineering firm ran an employment ad saying they were looking for "aggressive" applicants. Or was that "candidates"?

I learned all sorts of things from David. How to entertain simply with just a few dishes and everything prepared in advance. How to befriend people who are older, richer, and more famous by being useful to them—helping them send packages, find a caterer, work out a seating plan, bringing back from Europe those heavenly sleeping suppositories (Suponoryl) that weren't available here—an office that I'd repeatedly perform for Jimmy Merrill. How to keep a short book review simple and unassuming by cutting all of those pointless, show-offy references to Gramsci and Rousseau. In fact, David had a horror of general ideas and liked to quote William Carlos Williams's remark "No ideas but in things." David was erudite but never made a show of it, as if he assumed that people could sense a reference even if he didn't make it explicitly. For that reason, perhaps, his essays and reviews were less noticed than they might otherwise have been. He was too subtle, too graceful. He didn't make pronouncements the way Harold Bloom did, nor did he lay bare all the formal trappings of a poem as Helen Vendler did. He knew Bloom and Vendler and envied them both, though Bloom cheered him once by saying, "Of course I'm not a real critic the way you are, David; I'm unable to do a close reading of a poem with your style." David was so subtle that his friends laughingly compared him to Proust's aunts, those ladies in *Swann's Way* who think they're thanking Swann for the wine by making an extremely indirect reference to it.

I learned to admire but not to imitate David's way of writing biography (in *Becoming a Poet* he examined Elizabeth Bishop and her "opposite," Robert Lowell, and her "covering cherub," Marianne Moore). David had found a compelling middle path between gossipy narrative and academic close reading. He had a gentle, almost indirect way of starting with a few facts in his subject's life (Bishop's witnessing as a child her mother's mental breakdown) or a scrap of correspondence, then relating it to her poems and stories—not as a "theme" (thematic criticism was the more primitive pursuit Howard Moss performed in his *Magic Lantern of Marcel Proust*) but as a "strategy" or a trauma to resist or transpose. I think he understood that real writers don't just idly render one subject or another but conceal or dramatize or convert into other terms the hidden dynamics of their own lives. In her greatest poems, such as "The Bight," "The Moose," "At the Fishhouses" or "In the Waiting Room," Bishop rehearsed and disguised her childhood fears. David wasn't psychoanalyzing her; he was never reductive, he never mentioned sex, he never talked about repression or "screen memories" or displacement, but he did see a writing career as a series of skirmishes with one's own younger self and also with one's contemporaries. In her case, Bishop had Lowell's example as a public, political poet to resist and reject. Although she'd once contemplated marrying him, she defined herself as indeed his opposite, just as she saw Marianne Moore as her mentor and would write to please her (and finally to surpass her). The day she ignored one of Moore's strictures was the day she declared her independence.

Writing was torture for David. Maybe he'd been handicapped by being made a full professor and tenured at a young age. His boss at Rutgers, Richard Poirier, was a devoted friend from Harvard days and looked after him. I once attended one of David's classes, a session on *The Tempest*, and I was impressed with his way of provoking discussion while always keeping it on target and eventually leading it back to conclusions that only David's subtle mind could have worked out. He'd written a book on Sir Philip Sidney and one on contemporary poets (Robert Lowell, John Ashbery, Elizabeth Bishop, Adrienne Rich, and James Merrill) called *Five Temperaments* (an allusion to Balanchine's and Hindemith's *Four Temperaments*). He'd fiddle with the phrasing of a paragraph for days on end—and accordingly, his final drafts were always both efficient and felicitous. Nevertheless, given the choice, David would always have preferred going out with friends to writing, especially if he had a chance to go out with my agent, his close friend Maxine Groffsky, to the ballet.

Maxine was a striking redhead who'd served as the model for Brenda Potemkin in Philip Roth's *Goodbye, Columbus*, the title novella included in Roth's first published book. She'd been extremely close to several of the leading painters of the day (including Jasper Johns and Robert Rauschenberg) and had the canvases on the wall to prove it. For years, as the Paris editor of the *Paris Review*, she'd lived in France with Harry Mathews and raised the children he had had with the artist Niki de Saint Phalle. She took dance lessons and carried her tall, slim body with the élan of a ballerina. Maxine was fun and flirtatious and could talk as dirty as Marilyn Monroe but ultimately was mysterious. No one knew much about her private life, and she'd never granted interviews or used her connections to serve anyone, least of all herself.

She and David loved the New York City Ballet, attending several times a week together. In those years, throughout the 1970s, the lobby of the New York State Theater, home to the company, was the drawing room of America. Whereas intellectuals and artists seldom attended symphonic or orchestral events, back then the ballet attracted the best minds in the city. Maxine eventually married the president of the ballet board, Winthrop Knowlton, but for a decade David was her constant companion there. Like rock fans they spoke of the dancers (whom they didn't know) in terms of familiarity: "Karen's put on a few pounds, I'd say," or, "God, Patricia seems more and more neurotic—I think she may be on her way to having a total breakdown one of these days." "Suzanne was sublime tonight in Jerry's boring old Ravel piano concerto."

I, too, had been attending the ballet weekly since the mid-sixties, when it was still in the old Fifty-fifth Street theater with its terrible sight lines. In those days a ticket in the top balcony cost just ninety-nine cents, and Stan and I would count out our pennies on the kitchen table and rush uptown just before curtain time. Cheap seats were still to be had now, but even the least expensive had to be budgeted for in advance. Unlike David and Maxine I never took much interest in particular dancers. I disliked stage gossip and didn't want to compare one dancer to another—all too close to acrobatics for my taste. But of course one can swoon with admiration before the choreography of *Concerto Barocco* just so many times. Finally, to stay interested, one has to notice that close call Peter had when he nearly fell coming out of that second spin in *Jewels*.

New York was still obsessed with the hierarchy of the arts and the idea of the Pure. Many of the figures of the international scene, active elsewhere in the world, remained present in the imaginations of cultured New Yorkers—Nabokov, Beckett, Sartre, to name a few. In the 1960s a New York newspaper had asked American writers to identify the most important living writer—they chose Beckett.

The music of Stravinsky, though he'd recently died, was being played every week during the New York City Ballet season. The three great geniuses of the twentieth century, Stravinsky, Nabokov, and Balanchine, had all started off in imperial Russia, passed through France, and known a second (or third) creative flowering in America. Whereas later New Yorkers, and Americans in general, would turn their backs on Europe, in the 1970s we were all still reading Lacan, Deleuze, Foucault, Barthes, Derrida, and Lévi-Strauss. And many distinguished foreigners would live in rough, grimy, stimulating New York for long periods. Many French and Italian artists had studios in Manhattan; the French sculptor Alain Kirili and his photographer wife Ariane Lopez-Huici began to spend longer and longer sojourns in New York in the seventies, Kirili becoming a major collaborator with American jazz musicians.

The American literary avant-garde was very much in business, including such New Yorkers as Donald Barthelme. They were often published in the *New American Review*, and all made frequent appearances at the 92nd Street Y in New York, events that were well attended. A magazine such as *Esquire* in 1963 was able to generate sales by mapping out the "red-hot center" of American literary life—and locating it in New York and among mostly white men. Norman Mailer, Gore Vidal, and Truman Capote, like Hollywood stars, all appeared on national TV, and Mailer's movements or Philip Roth's were carefully charted by their fellow New Yorkers. David's boss Richard Poirier had written a book in the Modern Masters series about Mailer and Vidal and their contrasting chat styles on television (Vidal's was better suited to the medium, Poirier argued, since it consisted of sound bites rather than complex, sustained arguments). This was the backdrop of Woody Allen films featuring Jewish psychiatrists, of blue blazers worn over faded jeans, of Saul Steinberg cartoons. I remember seeing Steinberg at a party in the Hamptons in the late sixties, when he would glide up from behind a tree and try to spook my date, a girl from work. We thought it was glamorous to be a writer; a highly visible whiskey ad of the time showed a writer pounding his chic little Olivetti and asking his girlfriend, "While you're up, would you get me a Grant's?" We didn't pay much attention to television personalities (there were only three channels in those days); our celebrities were all writers and painters.

Of the various institutions that aided these encounters, this sense of community, almost all of them have subsequently disappeared.

Susan Sontag once remarked that maybe "we" wouldn't have staged such vigorous assaults on cultural institutions if we'd known how fragile they were, how easily they could be swept aside. The New York City Ballet, as David Kalstone observed, appealed to intellectuals because only such a noble and nonverbal vision of a communal utopia as proposed by Balanchine's choreography (or by Jerome Robbins in pieces such as *Dances at a Gathering*) could have attracted and united so many contentious, wordy New Yorkers. The three intermissions each evening meant plenty of time for spontaneous conversations (and drinks) in the lobby. Many New York thinkers and artists—Edward Gorey, Bob Gottlieb, Susan Sontag, Richard Poirier, and the best dance critic, Edwin Denby (by then a nearly catatonic ghost)—attended every night. You could always spot the tall Gorey with his white beard, black jeans, and white sneakers. Denby always arrived in a surrounding cloud of handsome young men; they were full of opinions though he said nothing. These fans recognized the rare privilege of being able to watch Balanchine unveil one masterpiece premiere after another. His famous 1972 eight-day festival devoted to Stravinsky, who'd died the year before, included twenty-two new Balanchine ballets; the two-week Ravel Festival in 1975 featured sixteen premieres by Balanchine and other choreographers.

Fans felt so possessive of Balanchine that no one wanted to admit that he or she shared this passion with others. Fellow fans were seen almost as romantic rivals, but like rivals were drawn to one another in the end since no ordinary person understood their obsession. They wanted to talk about their great love, and who better as an interlocutor than another bewitched swain or maiden? Balanchine proved to New Yorkers that world-class genius had found refuge and expression in their city. His use of Mozart and Bach as well as of the twentieth-century scores of Ives, Stravinsky, and Hindemith pointed toward a way of combining innovation within tradition, just as his classical ballet vocabulary was thrown into relief by eliminating the cumbersome apparatus of nineteenth-century storytelling and replacing tutus with black-and-white practice tights and tops. Balanchine had said that there are no mothers-in-law in ballet, but in almost all his dances even mothers had been eliminated. What was left was a narrative impulse stripped of story, a sense of drama without exposition or denouement, everything in constant crisis. The New York City Ballet was presenting new work every season. It was not a museum, as was the Metropolitan Opera, for instance, or the Philharmonic, the ballet's two neighbors at Lincoln Center.

To watch a genius at work is the highest civilized pleasure, and Balanchine was our resident genius, at the peak of his powers. We saw not only his newest ballets but also the two great works preserved from the 1920s and the Diaghilev years of his past, Prokofiev's *The Prodigal Son* (with sets and costumes by Rouault) and Stravinsky's *Apollo*, not to mention Tchaikovsky's *Serenade* from the 1930s, Balanchine's first ballet composed for an American company. For us something about that ballet was touching as a fossil record of the first rocky rehearsals at Balanchine's brand-new school up in White Plains. As he explained it, "It seemed to me that the best way to make students aware of stage technique was to give them something new to dance, something they had never seen before. I chose Tchaikovsky's *Serenade* to work with. The class contained the first night seventeen girls and no boys. The problem was, how to arrange this odd number of girls so that they would look interesting. I placed them on diagonal lines and decided that the hands should move first to give the girls practice.

"That was how *Serenade* began. The next class contained only nine girls; the third six. I choreographed to the music with the pupils I happened to have at a particular time. Boys began to attend the class and they were worked into the pattern. One day, when all the girls rushed off the floor area we were using as a stage, one of the girls fell and began to cry. I told the pianist to keep on playing and kept this bit in the dance. Another day, one of the girls was late for class, so I left that in too."

Because Balanchine had studied music as well as ballet, he had an uncanny way of "seeing" the deep structure of the music he was setting and of rendering it visible. Whereas lesser choreographers might respond to the ornamentation of the score and set a trill, say, or a clash of cymbals, Balanchine ignored the surface irritation of the music and went right to its unfolding principles of development and contrast. That was the source of the exhilarating beauty of those evenings. On the one side there were the young, superb bodies of men and women entering and running and leaping through strong allées of lighting projected from the wings, all the rush and sparkle of the corps and the dignified, gravity-defying combinations of the soloists, those cantilevered arabesques on point and thrilling female flights into space facilitated by noble, self-effacing male partners. If that component was pulse-quickening, a perilous spectacle, on the other side was the abstract diagramming of great scores, an exploration of music itself, the spiritual alternative to language.

Balanchine knew how to program one "white" ballet and one sublimely simple pas de deux, then a "difficult" modern work and a bang-up Stars and Stripes high-kicking finale. I suppose he was teaching us (without meaning to) the concessions that even the most serious artist (visual or literary) had to make to "show business" and crowd-pleasing if he or she was going to survive and keep an audience's attention. In a quite different way I suppose he was showing us how the supreme manifestations of the mind require sweat and muscles, how the spatial and temporal meditations of an old man can be realized only by willing young bodies with flushed cheeks and taut rumps and long necks and a good turnout. There was nothing charitable about his collaboration with the young; it was a partnership essential to him and to them, especially since he often created a new ballet "on" particular dancers, tailor-made to their limitations and gifts.

And even the most high-minded balletomane such as me had to acknowledge one drama being played out before our very eyes: Balanchine's unrequited love for Suzanne Farrell. She was quite literally his Dulcinea, for he had returned to the stage to mime the role of the besotted, aging Don Quixote in a full-evening ballet that had much more story than anything else we'd seen from Balanchine— his own story, of course. Suzanne, who was too good a Catholic girl to sleep with Balanchine, left the company in 1969 with her dancer husband and went off to Europe to join the company of the vulgar, talentless Maurice Béjart with his vast outdoor spectacles complete with dry-ice fog and wind machines worthy of the Third Reich. Béjart's company was no place for the greatest ballerina of the day— or even for a woman. In his works the hunky men were stripped down to their loincloths and the women bundled away in burkas; everything was as tackily homoerotic as a bad Cocteau porn drawing.

Only six years later did Suzanne Farrell come back to the New York City Ballet. Her return, full of wisdom and tenderness but still sexless, crowned Balanchine's last days with an unexpected but entirely deserved happiness. This love story, unrequited and, paradoxically, fertile, was a breathtaking drama unfolding for us, his greedy audience.

David had a new lady to squire about and to invite to the ballet—Lillian Hellman. She was then at the height of her fame, since decades after her most successful plays she had begun to write short, punchy memoirs in which she played *le beau rôle* of quiet heroism. After her death we would all discover that Mary McCarthy had been right—Lillian was a liar. She hadn't taken money into Central Europe to save Jews in the late 1930s. The person who'd done that was a psychiatrist in Princeton. The two women hadn't known each other but they did have the same lawyer—who must have told Hellman the story of these brave exploits. Hellman had simply appropriated them. That story, joined to her well-known and well-publicized defiance of the House Un-American Activities Committee—"I will not cut my conscience to fit this year's fashions"—had elevated her to the dubious distinction of becoming the Pasionaria of the American Left, though in fact she was an old-fashioned Stalinist without scruples. Obeying Stalin's party line, she had opposed the U.S. government's granting of asylum to Trotsky. She admitted to being a Stalinist to her biographer Joan Mellen.

In everyday life she was an appalling person. She would pick a fight with other customers in a store. The New York State Theater had no central aisle, and to get to the best seats one had to slide past a line of seated people. One night, with David accompanying her, Hellman had deliberately aimed her high heel and stabbed the foot of a seated woman, a complete stranger, then cursed her out for howling in pain.

I met her at David's apartment, where she was extremely nice to me. Strangely enough, she shared one virtue with her greatest enemy, Mary McCarthy. Both women by habit were elaborately polite to the youngest, least known person in the room—me, in both cases. Lillian made a point of asking me questions about my writing and life and provenance; of course I was charmed. She had terrible emphysema and never stopped smoking. She was as lean as an old Indian brave and her face was deeply burined with lines.

David had met her through a Venetian pal, Peter Feibleman, who would leave messages for her at the hotel in the name of "Rabbi Hellman." Now David struck up the acquaintance again through one of her closest friends, Richard Poirier, who at about this same time was persuaded to invite me to lunch. He was then living just off lower Fifth Avenue, near Howard Moss. (Eventually he had to move because the house next door, at 18 West Eleventh

Street, where James Merrill had been born, was accidentally blown up by a Weatherman woman while she was constructing a bomb.) At the start of the lunch, Poirier was cordial enough but soon began to tongue-lash me for the duration of the meal, furious because I'd said I thought there was such a thing as gay fiction, even gay poetry—worse, a gay sensibility!—and that at the very least works by gay people could be read in a special light, to illuminate them. Richard was enraged that I would even propose to isolate gay writers from the literary mainstream. He had a rough, gravelly voice, a strong, virile face, and one eye that wandered, and he relentlessly pursued his thought without ever smiling. I felt as unprovided with arguments as I had when I'd told Maitland Edey about feminism.

Frankly, I couldn't see what the big deal was with the idea of "gay literature." I said, "Well, there's no reason the same text can't be read from several different perspectives. It's just that for us gay writers now, it's fun to—"

"Gay writers!" Richard thundered. "I've never heard of anything so absurd. It's obscene!"

I wanted to concede the whole dispute just to end it, but I knew that David would be ashamed of me if I gave in too quickly. I knew how much he admired Richard's "fierceness," his "bearish strength." In their world Richard was "famous" for his intransigence. Of course I didn't have their training, having studied Chinese at Michigan and not humanities and English at Harvard. Nor had I ever taught literature. I'd only written a few unpopular book reviews, out of step with the critical opinion of the times.

I couldn't help noticing, at least to myself, that all these writers I was meeting who were gay—Ashbery, Howard Moss, David Kalstone, Elizabeth Bishop, Richard Poirier—might be open about their sexuality in their private lives, but no one in the general public knew about it. Richard Howard and James Merrill were the only ones who were out in their poetry as well as in their lives.

"But things do change," I said confusedly. "There are always new movements in fiction, aren't there? The word *novelty* is contained in the word *novel*. Why not have a gay school of fiction? Is there any harm in that? At least it's exciting and new."

"Exciting! But it's a betrayal of every humane idea of literature. Have you never heard of universalism?"

Now, all these years later, when "gay literature" has come and gone as a commercial fad and a serious movement, I can see his point. It's true that as a movement it did isolate us—to our advantage initially, though ultimately to our disadvantage. At first it drew the attention of critics and editors to our writing, but in the end (after our books didn't sell) it served to quarantine us into a small, confined space. Before the category of "gay writing" was invented, books with gay content (Vidal's *City and the Pillar*, Baldwin's *Giovanni's Room*, Isherwood's *A Single Man*) were widely reviewed and often became bestsellers. After a label was applied to them they were dismissed as being of special interest only to gay people. They could only preach to the converted. The truth, however, was that gay literature was every bit as interesting and varied as straight literature.

Something similar happened to gay people themselves. Before they were "liberated" and given an "identity," they were everywhere and nowhere. As long as the word *homosexual* was never pronounced, many boys and men slipped across the border of convention and had homosexual flings and then hurried guiltily back into heterosexuality under cover of obscurity and anonymity. The past saw many more casual experiments in same-sex love than later, when the category was finally clearly labeled and surrounded with the barbed wire of notoriety. It became easier in certain milieus to come out, but at the same time the stakes were higher (especially after the advent of AIDS in the early 1980s). In places like contemporary Greece fewer and fewer men and boys were willing to have sex with another male. Only the highly motivated made it across that barbed-wire fence. I sometimes regret the invention of the category "gay."

Yet I'm grateful for gay liberation and for gay literature. The depression and guilt that beset me in my teens and twenties subsided after Stonewall, just as the rejection as a writer I experienced in the 1960s slowly gave way to literary acceptance in the 1970s. I'd always wanted to write about being gay, even when I was fifteen and in prep school. My first novel, written just then, was called *Dark Currents* or alternately *The Tower Window* and was a coming-out story. I wrote this gay novel before ever reading one (except *Death in Venice* and Gide's *The Immoralist*, and they were far from contemporary—or cheerful). I wrote about my sexual and romantic feelings because they plagued me. I sometimes thought I was desperately bailing water in a sinking boat, and that if I stopped writing, I'd drown. As a result, I felt that the new visibility of gays gave me a chance to be seen, or rather heard. Now I was allowed to publish, which made all the difference to me.

Nevertheless, thirty-five years later, in 2009, I can see what Richard Poirier meant. I'd still say that even if he was right ultimately, we were very much living in the urgent short run. After centuries of oppression we had a sense of community we wanted to celebrate in novels that would create our identity while also exploring it. In the early days of gay liberation writers had an unprecedented importance (that quickly faded) in their own community; for a short while we were virtually the only visible or audible spokesmen for a whole movement, in those years before AIDS forced political leaders, actors, and athletes to come out.

In the late 1970s I became friends with Michel Foucault, and he and I disagreed about gay identity as well. I never quite understood his position, which struck me as ambiguous. He'd given an early interview to the French gay magazine *Gai Pied* (which Foucault had named) without letting his name be cited in the article. He was fascinated by gay life, especially sadomasochistic scenes in San Francisco, and never was there a more self-conscious and highly organized subculture than that one. Yet Foucault was very much against identity politics and "the culture of avowal," by which he meant a culture that thought every individual had a secret, that that secret was sexual, and that by confessing it one had come to terms with one's essence. He traced the need to avow to the early Christian church, which had been obsessed by evil thoughts even more than evil deeds (the pagan world had worried only about the deeds). I could understand his objections to the *Oprah*-like emotionality and the revival-meeting "change of heart" so appealing to Americans, but it did seem to me undeniable that "coming out" was still a liberating moment, especially since most gays could "pass" as straight and still did, to their own harm. Yes, it might be wrong to consider one's sexuality to be the key to one's identity—and in the ultimate scheme of things perhaps gay identity politics have led to the easy packaging and commodification of our experience, a trivialization of the bacchic rites ("Yeah, I'm a power bottom into domination but not pain, highly verbal, into role-playing of the coach-athlete sort but no scat or blood, please, though water sports are fine"). Nevertheless, what we desire is crucial to who we are. I agree with Nietzsche, who said, "For what does one at present believe in more firmly than one's body?" To be fair, Foucault was combating all general ideas, all categories, and what he clung to as a good positivist were particular facts, tiny clusters of verifiable events. I wouldn't dare to defend gay identity against such a convincing argument, but I would still say that people who are oppressed by an entire society can free themselves only by taking on that entire society and redefining the terms that were imposed on them, switching all the minuses to pluses.

# Chapter 13

In 1978 I met William Burroughs, who'd lived abroad (in Morocco, mostly) so long that he seemed more a myth from the past than a living writer. His pulseless, saurian persona as a smack addict— and in his work his Sade-like mechanical repetition of erotic hangings for everyone, of shiny faces for lesbians made out of penis transplants, of his predatory insectlike characters coolly sipping spinal fluid through straws—all enhanced his status as someone already dead, too cold and totemic to be alive.

I was invited to a dinner at the apartment of Ted Morgan on the East Side. Later, in 1982, I would write a positive review of his biography of Somerset Maugham, in which he gave a horrifying portrait of the aging writer as having lost his mind to Alzheimer's though he was pumped full of youth-enhancing monkey glands. Virile and hyperactive but incapable of thinking, the once witty and ironic author would greet guests at the gates of his Riviera compound by presenting them with a welcoming handful of his own shit. Ted Morgan had known Burroughs in Tangier and eventually wrote his biography in 1990. Morgan was a tall, loping, edgy man, famous for his travels through Africa, who had once been French and a duke, born Sanche de Gramont. His father, people said, had married once for position, once for money, and once for love. Ted was the son of the love marriage with a beautiful Italian woman. Sanche had disliked his name and title so much that he'd changed his nationality, thoroughly expunged his French accent, and redubbed himself Ted Morgan (an anagram of "de Gramont").

That first evening over dinner Burroughs spoke little except to say that he was able to manipulate his mood as a writer through obvious techniques. "For instance," he said, "if I want to write about sex, I don't jerk off for several days, then I'm sure to be horny and ready to describe it in lots of detail and a state of excitation." We were all fascinated by every word the sphinx pronounced. Burroughs had a way of muttering that, as the evening wore on and joints were brought out, became completely incomprehensible. He produced none of the usual little social smiles or encouraging nods. He seemed remote and indifferent though cordial in a ghostly way. He had on the worn suit and thin, uninteresting tie that comprised his uniform—the look of an unsuccessful Kansas undertaker.

Burroughs had a new minder, James Grauerholz, a tall, sexy, slightly spooky youngster from Kansas. The story was that Grauerholz had never read much literature until the day he fell upon the poems of Allen Ginsberg. He'd tackled Ginsberg after a reading and offered his services. Ginsberg turned him down, saying, "But I do have a friend who does need someone to look after him. He's just come back from years abroad and is rather lost."

James immediately became Burroughs's manager. He decided to present Burroughs at readings in New York at the Mudd Club, a punk redoubt, where his mixture of literary violence, drugginess, and avant-garde credibility joined up with his look of a "clean old man" to make him famous to a whole new generation.

Grauerholz renegotiated Burroughs's contracts and set up something called William Burroughs Enterprises, which brought his backlist into paperback reprint and engineered some media coups. Suddenly this half-dead but brilliant man was fully alive again in the public imagination. Grauerholz also edited all of Burroughs's last books. Whereas Balanchine as an old man had lived through the young Suzanne Farrell, the young Grauerholz realized himself through this venerable, hollowed-out figure.

Usually I felt some connection with another gay man. Not necessarily a vital link, but a real one, such as one might feel with another American in Berlin, say, neither more nor less. With Burroughs, however, there was no conspiratorial wink and his sexuality seemed like something that might take place only once every hundred years, like the midnight blooming of a century plant. What amazed me was that so many young straight guys revered Ginsberg and Burroughs despite their homosexuality. I guess for those young guys Ginsberg was primarily a hippie guru and Buddhist chanter and wild poet freak, and Burroughs was a reactivated drugged-out zombie, both cool in their ways. Legendary. I knew a young straight guy who put out for Ginsberg and bragged about it. When I asked him how he could do that, he said, "Man, he was Allen Ginsberg, man . . ."

William Burroughs eventually went off to live near Grauerholz in Lawrence, Kansas, where he dabbled in art by shooting at cans full of paint that spattered blank canvases. These were the "shotgun" paintings.

*The Joy of Gay Sex* had come out and was something of a success, selling all over the country as a mainstream book in ordinary bookstores with a minimum of fuss. Since Mitchell Beazley had contracted the book and Charles Silverstein and I were hired guns, our contract was a good deal less favorable than it would have been had we originated the project. No matter. People thought I was making money and I didn't disabuse them. I discovered that making money is what publishing really cares about and that once again I was bankable.

I was able to sell to Michael Denneny, the first and foremost openly gay editor, a new novel, *Nocturnes for the King of Naples*. Michael, who had a strong Rhode Island accent and who'd studied under Hannah Arendt at the University of Chicago, had a deeply curious and skeptical mind, with equal emphasis on both adjectives. He wanted to know about everything (an invaluable characteristic for an editor), but was quick to contest anything that struck him as dubious or factitious. He refused to rush in an industry that demanded speed, and this leisureliness would eventually be his downfall. That, and that he embraced and launched gay fiction in a way no one else before him and few after him dared to do. When gay lit didn't make big bucks, he was fired. But in the meantime Michael had a run of many years in the offices of St. Martin's Press. In that time he was able at least partially to fulfill his dream of putting gay content into all the genres—gay romantic novels, gay cowboy novels, gay gangster books, etc. He would bring out just a few thousand copies of any title and let it sink or swim on its own. There was a moment, before the market became saturated, when an ordinary straight first literary novel could be expected to sell five thousand copies—and a gay literary title would sell seven thousand. For a long while gay readers had a greater hunger for books than did the ten-times-larger straight public for heterosexual literature.

In the seventies some fifty gay bookstores opened all across the country. This was the era before the big chains such as Barnes & Noble. Suddenly, in the bars in every small town lots of small, free gay publications were being handed out that would reprint syndicated book reviews. It was all pretty tacky, but it was undeniably grassroots. Some publications, such as *Christopher Street* and later the *James White Review* and the *Harvard Gay & Lesbian Review*, gave a dignified and intelligent forum to gay art and thought.

*Nocturnes for the King of Naples* was once again a book that I'd written for myself alone. Not that I didn't have a reader in mind, but that reader was much like myself—as demanding, as romantic, as besotted with poetic language. Buried into the book were many bits of poetry written out as prose. Jimmy Merrill was the only reader who ever detected on his own those buried poems. Early on, in a scene that described an evening at Peggy's without any recognizable details or anecdotes, I composed a sestina, just to keep myself awake. Later there was a sonnet, an imitation of a French poem, "Aux yeux de Madame de Beaufort." In the last chapter I buried some couplets. This story of lost gay love and a Gothic childhood alluded throughout to saints and Sufis and to St. Gregory of Nyssa and to Solomon's Song of Songs. I suppose I had learned from Nabokov to make literary allusions unobtrusive so that they might delight the initiated and not disturb anyone else. I subscribed to the baroque confusion between the spiritual and the sensual, though I believed in the spirit only as a word, just as Melville caressed (and didn't believe in) the word *mystic* and Henry James spoke reverentially when he used the word *moral*, though one scarcely knew what he meant by it.

Readers (my few readers!) had spoken of *Forgetting Elena* as a "baroque" novel, although I now realize that it's quite unornamented and syntactically modest. *Baroque*, I guess, was just a vogue word of that period for anything offbeat (and gay?). I took the description seriously, however, and wrote *Nocturnes* according to a genuine baroque aesthetic that stresses movement, above all, that proceeds through constant metamorphoses, that employs unusually rich materials and is designed to produce a single overwhelming theatrical effect—and expresses religious feelings through the erotic (Bernini's St. Michael stabbing a writhing St. Theresa in the side, for example) or vice versa (all those old poems comparing the beloved to the Madonna or God).

Under all this elaborate theatrical machinery (one chapter had my characters actually living onstage), I was reenacting my thwarted passion for Keith McDermott and my intense, prolonged suffering over him. In the true baroque style of transformation, everything was converted into other terms. In real life I had spent a memorable night having sex with Keith, one of the half-dozen times that that occurred. Ever the formalist aesthete, he'd set everything up as a ritual by candlelight. I metamorphosed that experience into my chapter in the theater where the lover, me, was dressed as Bottom and the beloved, Keith, as Titania. Nor was it just any theater. It was a baroque theater, full of the machinery of the past, all of which I carefully researched.

I had decided that exposition "bored" me and looked for a form that would skip it—the letter! Yes, in letters people don't spell out to the beloved the key moments of their affair but rather allude to them in shorthand. My novel would be addressed to a mysterious "you," who might by turns seem to be Frank O'Hara or God—in any event, someone dead. Whereas countless gay poets had used the "you strategy" to avoid designating the sex of the beloved (it only works in English and Chinese, where adjectives have no gender), I would be quite clear that I was addressing a man. The "I" in my book, however, wasn't me but rather Keith McDermott many years from now when he would mourn his lost lover—who resembled me, in a few ways. This was a sort of "Cry me a river/'cuz I cried a river over you" novel. Now that thirty years have gone by, Keith and I are best friends and all this spleen has withered away.

*Nocturnes for the King of Naples* came out in 1978, the same year as several other gay novels: Andrew Holleran's lyrical Fire Island book, *Dancer from the Dance*; Larry Kramer's clumsy, pleasure-phobic *Faggots*; and Armistead Maupin's *Tales of the City*. My book was the least noticed of the lot, though a certain kind of romantic lad still reads it from time to time. For some people it's much of a muchness. I remember in the mid-1980s Italo Calvino's wife, Chichita, read it in French and said to me dismissively, "It's sentimental, Edmund, and you're not." My novel did have some nice blurbs from Gore Vidal and Cynthia Ozick, and it received few reviews but positive ones—except in the *New York Times Book Review*, where the critic said that I had been talented when I was still in the closet but that I'd lost my gift by coming out.

A tall, blond biologist named Doug Gruenau, four years younger than I but like me a graduate from the University of Michigan, was living with the novelist Harold Brodkey on West Eighty-eighth Street. Harold had—which sounds like a contradiction in terms— an immense underground reputation. Everyone in New York was curious about him, but few people outside the city had ever heard of him. Long ago, in 1958, he'd published *First Love and Other Sorrows*, a book of stories that had been well reviewed, but they weren't what all the buzz was about. Now he'd bring out a story occasionally in the *New Yorker* or *New American Review* or even *Esquire*. The one in *New American Review* (a quarterly, edited by Ted Solotaroff) was highly sexual but not dirty—a fifty-page chapter, published in 1973, about a Radcliffe girl's first orgasm. The prose in "Innocence" could be strained if striking: "To see her in sunlight was to see Marxism die." It seemed the longest sex scene in history, rivaled only by the gay sex scene in David Plante's *Catholic*—and reminiscent of the sex scene "The Time of Her Time" in Norman Mailer's *Advertisements for Myself* (except that one had been anal!).

Then there had been troubled, labyrinthine stories about Brodkey's mother in the *New Yorker* of a length and complexity no one else would have been allowed to get away with. This was obviously a writer, we thought, who must, above all, be extremely convincing. The mother stories nagged and tore at their subject with a Lawrentian exasperation, a relentless drive to get it right, repeatedly correcting the small assertions just made in previous lines. Everyone was used to confessional writing of some sort (though the heyday for that would come later), and everyone knew all about the family drama, but no one had ever gone this far with sex, with mother, and with childhood. We were stunned with a new sort of realism that made slides of every millimeter of the past and put them under the writer's microscope. In *Esquire* in 1975 a short, extremely lyrical story, "His Son, in His Arms, in Light, Aloft," appeared, about a baby boy being carried in his father's arms. Mother might get the niggling, Freudian treatment, but Daddy deserved only light-drenched, William Blake–like mysticism.

All these "stories," apparently, were only furtive glimpses of the massive novel that Brodkey had been working on for years and that would be the American answer to Marcel Proust. Brodkey's fans (and there were many of them) photocopied and stapled into little booklets every story he'd published so far in recent years and circulated them among their friends, a sort of New York samizdat press. His supporters made wide fervent claims for him. Harold was our Mann, our James Joyce. That no one outside New York knew who he was only vouchsafed his seriousness, his cult stature, too serious for the unwashed (or rather the washed, a more appropriate synecdoche for Midwesterners).

He and Doug lived in a big, rambling West Side apartment with a third man, named Charlie Yordy, whom I met just once but who reeked of a hoofed and hairy-shanked sexuality. He was a friendly, smiling man but seemed burdened, as are all people possessed by a powerful sexuality.

Harold was as bearded and hooded-eyed as Nebuchadrezzar but tall and slim and athletic as well. He must have been in his forties. His constant swimming and exercising at the Sixty-third Street Y (the one I'd lived in when I first came to New York) kept him as fit as a much younger man. His moods and thoughts were restless, rolling about like ship passengers in a storm. Sometimes he looked as if a migraine had just drawn its gray, heavy wing across his eyes. The next moment he'd be calculating something silently, feverishly to himself—then he'd say out loud, "Forget it." Cryptic smiles flitted across his face. He seldom paid attention to what the people around him were saying because he was concocting his next outrage—for most of his remarks were outrageous, and he could not be cajoled out of them.

Harold had lived with Doug for some eight or nine years. Doug was so polite and respectful that even when Harold would say something absurdly far-fetched, Doug would cock his head to one side and up a bit, as if he were a bird trying to make sense of a new, higher, quicker call. Doug was a big man with a bass laugh, but around Harold he didn't take up much space. I think he'd decided that Harold was both cracked and a genius and that even his insults were, ultimately, harmless, but Doug taught biology in a private school and had endless hours of grading and preparation and counseling and teaching to do, whereas Harold appeared to have enough money to be idle—and to meddle. When I told David Kalstone about Harold, David sang, "Time on my hands . . ."

I wasn't quite sure what Charlie did, though I must have been told. (Americans are never reluctant to ask strangers what they do.) I think he was a math teacher and then he manufactured clothes in the Adirondacks. He wasn't around often and seemed to be more Harold's boyfriend than Doug's, though I'm sure Harold told me they were all three lovers. The apartment was big enough to accommodate them all and even give each of them privacy. Harold was on the prowl. Not all the considerable time he spent at the Y was devoted to swimming. People who knew him said he was a tireless, overt cruiser.

Harold seldom talked about his own work but loved to deliver pronouncements about literature and how to make it. He particularly enjoyed giving other writers—even older, more successful writers—advice. As the years went by, I kept hearing strange and then stranger stories about him. One of his great defenders was Gordon Lish, a top editor at Knopf and the man who had virtually invented minimalism. Gordon apparently walked into the office of his boss, Bob Gottlieb (who'd started his own career as the editor of *Catch-22* and had even been the one to persuade Joseph Heller to change the title from *Catch-18*), and said something like "You've published a few good books, Bob, but nothing that will make people remember you after you're gone. Now you have the chance to publish Proust—but you must write a check for a million dollars and not ask to see even a single page."

At that point Harold had been signed up with Farrar, Straus for years, but they'd paid him a considerably smaller sum—and they weren't willing to give him the full attention he demanded. Harold needed not one editor but several to go over with him the thousands of pages he'd already written. As far as anyone could tell, he was years away from delivering. But Farrar, Straus's reluctance to put the full resources of their staff at his disposal ate away at Harold. Responding to the challenge, Gottlieb wrote the check.

In a slow groundswell of media attention leading up to publication, various magazine articles appeared about Harold, all wildly laudatory. I remember one in *Esquire* in 1977 by the religious novelist D. Keith Mano ("Harold Brodkey: The First Rave"), who confessed he'd set out to debunk Harold and his myth but who'd stayed to be conquered. Mano even told Brodkey about some of his personal problems—a minor betrayal by a friend. The passage is worth quoting because it reveals one of Harold's seduction techniques:

> In passing I mention a personal misfortune, a betrayal—none of your business what—that had shocked and demoralized me the day before. Harold listens, advises; he parses it out. I hang up feeling both presumptuous and stupid. What am I to Harold

Brodkey, he to me, that I should lay my tsuris on him? Yet, one hour later, Harold calls back. My distress, a stranger's distress, has alarmed him. We talk for thirty minutes on Harold's long-distance dime. The man cares. I am moved: such concern is unlooked-for. Subsequently, we talk several times. In fact I became, well, jealous; his stamina, his integrity, his grasp of circumstances is better than mine and these, dammit, are my circumstances. After a while I'd prefer to forget; it's human enough. But Harold won't sanction that; his moral enthusiasm is dynamic; he knows I'm copping out. And I feel understood, seen through, swept into the rational and oceanic meter of his fiction. A Brodkey character. Me. Imagine.

Denis Donoghue and Harold Bloom had both compared Harold to Proust. Bloom, after reading some of Harold's new novel in manuscript, added that he was "unparalleled in American prose fiction since the death of William Faulkner." Cynthia Ozick declared him to be a true artist. Harold concurred: "I'm not sure that I'm not a coward. If some of the people who talk to me are right, well, to be possibly not only the best living writer in English, but someone who could be the rough equivalent of a Wordsworth or a Milton, is not a role that a halfway educated Jew from St. Louis with two sets of parents and a junkman father is prepared to play." The press response (always by straight men) was so extreme that I developed a theory about what was behind it. I figured that gay men were not competitive in the way straights were; it was no accident that gays played individual not group sports. Nor were gay men awed and half in love with their fathers. Most gays I knew had rejected their fathers and despised them. Finally, gays were thoroughly disabused and especially suspicious of flattery—more likely to hand it out than to take it in. As a result, Harold's methods didn't work on them (on me), but they instantly seduced straights. Harold would suddenly announce to a straight admirer (or adversary), "You know, Tom, you could be the greatest writer of your generation. There's no doubt about it. And by the way I'm not the only one to think that." Long pause. "But you won't be— wanna know why?" Strong eye contact. "Because you're too damn lazy. And too damn modest. You don't work hard enough or aim high enough."

His interlocutor, after having his rank raised as high as it was in his most secret dreams, suddenly saw his hopes dashed, unless . . . unless . . .

He suddenly needed Harold to help him, to inspire him, finally to judge him. Harold was his father/coach, while the challenger was the son/rookie. With any luck he might yet emerge as the world-class genius he dreamed of being.

Bitchy and disagreeable as gays are sometimes thought to be, they don't usually play lethal games like these. They don't try to mold behavior—perhaps they (we) aren't confident enough to challenge another man in his heart of hearts, the private interior place where he lives. We gays don't want to belong, we don't want to play ball—we're not team players, so how could we bow before someone evaluating us? We'd rather lose, quit the playing field— be a quitter. How can our father or father's brother bully us when we're all too ready to cry uncle? That sort of ducking out is our way of winning.

Of course it probably helped that Harold went to almost every literary party and spent hours on the phone every day with Don DeLillo, Harold Bloom, Denis Donoghue. DeLillo told him the way to stop worrying about death was to watch a lot of television.

The funny thing is that no one ever mentioned that Harold lived with not one but two men and that he was notorious in the YMCA steam room. Harold was not known to be gay—and he was far from a cool, impersonal writer. His whole life's work was based on his childhood and adolescent experiences. He had turned himself into a tall, complicated, handsome, athletic, brilliant Jewish lad, and that's how everyone who didn't know him personally perceived him.

Harold had raised expectations so high—after all, he wasn't just trying to "get a second book out," he was writing the great American novel—that of course he had to introduce roadblocks in his path. He bought a computer. But this was still the era when a computer filled a whole room, when only industries and spies owned them, when one had to master a whole new method of writing, of programming. Harold invited me to see the machines humming and buzzing in one room, which someone from IBM was teaching him, day after day, week after week, how to operate. The entire long, sprawling manuscript would have to be transferred to the computer. Only then could it be properly analyzed for content, repetitions, inner consistency, and flow.

My heart sank, I who still scribbled with a ballpoint in student notebooks. I rewrote but quickly, only once; it was the least demanding part of composition and by far the most pleasant. Much of my rewriting was cutting. What was hard for me was composing, writing. I had so little confidence or stamina that a single paragraph could send me into a paroxysm of self-doubt. Sometimes I felt I was blasting my way through a sheer wall of granite, forcing a small path through vast, thick ramparts of low self-esteem. At other times I felt I was racing through the woods but that the trail had given out, was overgrown—or had broken into two paths or three. I had no idea where to go, no momentum, no sense of direction.

Harold appeared to have none of these doubts. He sometimes spoke of writing in a way that reminded me of the methods discussed by French writers. A French author might say that he'd worked the whole book out in his mind, done his research, constructed the whole intrigue—and now all he had to do was the "redaction," by which he would mean the actual writing, as if that were a detail, the way some composers refer to the orchestration. I was never shown any segment of the manuscript in all its voluminousness, but I would get vague, haggard battle reports about how the organization was going.

I think you could have called Harold a phenomenologist. He once said to me (apropos of some of my own writing), "When someone writes, 'She went down on him,' it's always a lie." His idea was that shorthand expressions (going down on someone) were smug and false because the real experience (of sucking or being sucked) is so profound, so unrepeatable, so thick with emotions and half thoughts and fears and tremblings that the only expression adequate to it is minute, precise, original, and exhaustive. In print Harold wrote, "I distrust summaries, any kind of gliding through time, any too great a claim that one is in control of what one recounts."

I learned something from him—perhaps because it suited my own artistic temperament to "defamiliarize" the world and to render it in the freshest, most Martian way possible. Where I disagreed with him was that I thought not everything could be treated so thoroughly. There had to be background and foreground, and what was in the background necessarily should be sketched in—not with clichés but with some familiar shorthand, even facility.

If that was the most sensible and useful part of Harold's advice, he was also capable of strange little obsessions. In reading a description of mine of a skylight above a library (installed in a nineteenth-century opera house), Harold insisted that I describe the overhead windows as an eye. I didn't think it made much difference in a book of 220 pages whether I used that metaphor or not, but I quickly acceded to his demand to humor him and to show him that I was flattered that he had had a concrete suggestion of any sort. Presumably he had read the rest of the book (*A Boy's Own Story*) but he made no comment on the other 219 pages.

When my book was in the proof stages, he called my editor, Bill Whitehead, and said, "Stop the presses! White has stolen my style." Bill, who could be firm, said, "That's nonsense—he wouldn't want your style and anyway a style can't be patented," and hung up on him. Harold kept calling back, threatening legal action, but he seldom contacted me and Bill never again took his calls. Harold also accused John Updike of stealing his personality. "I am the Devil in *The Witches of Eastwick*," Harold announced.

The years went by and Harold threatened to publish his book. Sometimes it was said to be two thousand pages long and sometimes it was said he'd written between three thousand and six thousand pages. The most famous fashion photographer in the world, Richard Avedon, told me that he was collaborating with Harold since Avedon was convinced he was America's greatest author. Harold wrote the introduction to a book of Avedon's photos taken between 1947 and 1977, an essay that had the distinction of being both laborious and stylish. The title of his novel changed from *Party of Animals* to *The Runaway Soul*, i.e., from a striking title to a forgettable one. It was reported he'd gone from Knopf back to Farrar, Straus. As the new high priest of heterosexuality and the female orgasm, he had no need of the embarrassing evidence to the contrary that Doug Gruenau and Charlie represented. Charlie had already moved out with a new lover in 1975, and Doug left the apartment in 1980. Harold moved a woman in—Ellen Schwamm, a writer he'd met jogging in the park. (There are other versions of how they'd met. In one, Ellen asked Gordon Lish who was the greatest living writer, and when she found out it was Harold, she set her cap for him. In another they met at a bookstore, the then fashionable Books & Co. next to the Whitney.) Ellen and Harold cut their hair so that they would resemble each other, like the couple in Hemingway's posthumous and thrillingly good *The Garden of Eden*. She had left her rich husband for Harold. Charlie was an early victim of AIDS and died. Doug found a new lover and remained friendly with Harold and Ellen, though he must never be mentioned in the press. I tried to date Doug but he was too sweet, too genuine for me—and besides he didn't smoke, took long hikes in the desert to photograph bison, and got up every morning at six to go jogging around the Reservoir. With any luck I was just rolling into bed at that hour, putting out my seventy-second cigarette of the day. I felt sooty and superficial next to Doug—and soon he found a serious lover he's still with after these many years.

I kept hearing nutty reports about Harold. He'd accepted a job teaching a semester occasionally at Cornell. Alison Lurie, who taught there, told me that Harold had accused a sweet elderly novelist, James McConkey, of climbing across several roofs and slipping like a cat burglar into Harold's room in Ithaca in order to copy out long passages of Harold's novel and to publish them as his own. This tremendous row would in a more sensible century have ended in a simplifying duel instead of the mess that went on for years.

Susan Sontag told me about her evening with Harold. He had said to her, "You and I, Susan, are the greatest writers of the twentieth century." She had replied, "Oh, really, Harold? Aren't there a few others? What about Nabokov, for instance?"

"Oh, he's nothing," Harold said, "but at least he had the decency to acknowledge his debt to me."

"Really, Harold? Where did he do that?"

As though slowing down and simplifying things for a child, Harold took a breath and smiled and said, "You remember that at the beginning of *Lolita* that Lolita has a father who's already died?"

"Yes . . ."

"And do you remember his first name?"

"Yes, his name is Harold."

Harold shrugged—case closed. Harold seemed seriously to

believe that his stories in *First Love and Other Sorrows* had inspired Nabokov—another instance of his style being stolen.

The writer Sheila Kohler told me that when she had dinner with Harold, she told him that she was happy to meet him since Gordon Lish had said he was the greatest living writer. "Why, he compares you to Shakespeare," she told Harold.

Harold looked at her balefully and said, "I bet he wouldn't put Shakespeare on hold." Harold suggested that for this grievous insult he was considering changing publishers yet again.

C. K. Williams, the Pulitzer Prize–winning poet, the sweetest and one of the most talented men of Harold's generation, was introduced to him by Avedon, but rather quickly Harold fought with him. Harold accused him of pilfering some of his pages to put into a poem—though later Harold realized that Williams could never have seen those pages since they hadn't yet been published. For once in his life Harold apologized.

And then *The Runaway Soul* came out and it was a terrible flop. James Wood, even though he was defending it, called it "microscopically narcissistic." Pages we'd once admired in the *New Yorker* were now so bent out of shape through rewriting as to be incomprehensible. No one could follow the action. Hundreds of pages went by and we were still mired in earliest childhood—and Harold's insights and observations seemed utterly implausible. No one had that kind of detailed recall about what had happened when he was two or three. Piaget had demonstrated that even if we were given complete access to our infant memories, they would make no sense to us since they were inscribed in a different, earlier language than the one we think in now. And, anyway, who cared? It was all the fault, I thought, of that infernal computer and Harold's infinitely expanded opportunities to rewrite. The book was no longer a performance but a smudged palimpsest.

Once his masterpiece went belly-up in such a conspicuous

and unresounding way, Harold filled his days more usefully by writing bits and pieces for "The Talk of the Town." He was a good journalist, good at getting the story and willing to curb his eccentric style enough to communicate with the average educated reader. Reputedly he wrote TV pilots for money as well.

Then one day Harold wrote a short piece in the *New Yorker* announcing he had AIDS and was dying. Apparently—or so Harold claimed—he'd been infected in the 1960s, since that was the last time he'd fooled around with a man. I wondered how Doug reacted to this denial of all their many years together. I thought, only Harold could write a page and a half about his imminent death from AIDS and manage to irritate the reader.

He published a strangely homophobic book about his AIDS, *This Wild Darkness: The Story of My Death.* He claimed that the book was born of a decision to be honest, not to lie, but he obscured many facts. He never mentioned Doug Gruenau or his countless tricks. He acted as if his major contact with Charlie Yordy was based on their both being orphans (Harold's parents died when he was very young). He claimed that his affair with Charlie (which in the book sounds like his only gay relationship) was a way of reliving the childhood trauma of being sexually abused by his stepfather. As an adult, he said, he had "experimented with homosexuality to break my pride, to open myself to the story" of being abused as a child. This experience may have helped Harold to come to terms with being repeatedly raped, but, Harold suggests, "I think he was the one who gave it to me," i.e., AIDS. In the gay community it had been decided early on that it wasn't kosher to try to pinpoint the one who'd infected us. Hurling accusations of that sort was a waste of breath—especially since Harold, like the rest of us, had had not one but hundreds of male partners.

When Harold died, it felt anticlimactic. He was obviously a brilliant if underemployed and meddling man. He had great natural gifts and more than a touch of madness. His wife Ellen had written a novel (the ironically titled *How He Saved Her*) in which Harold appeared as the devil, destroying everyone around him. He died nearly the same day as the more famous Russian poet Joseph Brodsky and had the misfortune of being confused with him in many people's minds. Now he's practically been forgotten—and the loss of this large, ambitious talent seems tragic. We all wanted him to be a success. It's more fun to have a genius in our midst.

# Chapter 14

J. D. McClatchy ("Sandy" to his friends) arranged my first teaching gig, in the mid-seventies. I wasn't working and supported myself badly with occasional freelance magazine pieces. In those days Yale did not have creative writing as part of its regular English Department curriculum. Princeton had had a distinguished creative writing program since 1939, when it was started by R. P. Blackmur (Allen Tate had taught there and so had Elizabeth Bowen and Kingsley Amis and Philip Roth), but Yale and Harvard had been a bit sniffy about anything so louche in which mere writers without degrees were allowed to shape young minds. When Nabokov wanted a job teaching Russian literature at Harvard, the man who turned him down said, "Would you ask an elephant to teach a course in elephant science?" To which Nabokov replied, "Yes, if he were a highly articulate elephant."

The most Yale could do by way of creative writing courses was to have house seminars. Each dormitory or college offered some electives to students. I was hired at Jonathan Edwards College. Once a week I took a train up to New Haven (a two-and-a-half-hour trip each way) to teach my twelve undergrads. I kept imagining that the students would be much better educated than I and would unmask me as a sham; after all, I thought, I've never read *The Faerie Queene*!

Of course few nineteen-year-olds, even at an Ivy League university, have read widely and deeply. They simply haven't had enough time, especially when the admissions departments at such schools insist they be "well-rounded." In high school they have to do some sort of community outreach, sing in the glee club, play lacrosse, work as a volunteer for their state senator in the summer, hold down a part-time job to learn the value of a dollar—and study with a tutor the rudiments of Mandarin Chinese twice a week after school. When would they find time to read Spenser or Flannery O'Connor?

Europeans often ask what is actually taught in a creative writing class. Funny, I think, they don't ask the same question of drawing or musical composition instructors. Literature is at once more banal and more sacralized than the other arts—or, better, since everyone can write a letter or a theme paper, it's assumed that what separates great "authors" from mere writers is some magical and unteachable talent.

The really popular creative writing teachers (I'm not one of them) talk a lot about "creativity" and "awakening the imagination" and "loosening up" the writer from his inner "inhibitions" and letting him express himself. They have exercises for doing all that and for putting the student in touch with his or her "unconscious."

That approach would make me feel like an impostor, since I've never subjected myself to such exercises and have never once discussed "creativity" with a real writer. Writing as therapy was something I had done in my teens and twenties, but after thirty, as I began to get control of my problems, I had to find a more professional reason to write. I'd always been interested in technique and devoured all the *Paris Review* interviews of established writers, especially for their hints on how to write. Elizabeth Bowen once wrote nine or ten useful pages on technique, but it's amazing how few writers have anything to say on that subject. Perhaps they're afraid to bore the general reader with "shoptalk."

At Yale every week I gave a minilecture on something technical, such as when to use dialogue, how to establish character, the care and feeding of figurative language, creating suspense—and setting up constant dynamic tension, sentence by sentence, paragraph by paragraph. I discovered an invaluable little text by the Russian psychologist Lev Vygotsky, an analysis of Bunin's story "Gentle Breath." In *The Psychology of Art*, Vygotsky speaks of the disconnect in every successful literary work between the figurative language and the direction of the plot. He discovered that the greatness of a novel requires an antagonism between the style and the story. Bunin, for instance, tells a dreary tale in "Gentle Breath," but the final effect of the story is exhilarating. Why? Because all the similes and metaphors, all the descriptions, even the rhythm of the paragraphs, are excited, light, uplifting. This dynamic tension is the real secret of prose, Vygotsky argued—the opposite of what every aesthetician from Aristotle on down through history has averred. Whereas they all believed in redoubling their effects, in reinforcing the general impression of the "anecdote," in truth the great playwrights and novelists undermine the drift of the plot through the "ornaments" of their prose. The melancholy of *Don Quixote*'s plot is undercut by the buffoonery of the writing.

New, insecure teachers usually say all they know in their first class and are afraid to call on the students. As teachers leave the classroom after the first session, they panic and can think of no way of filling up all the hours and hours during the coming weeks. Of course in creative writing the classes are small enough and the students eager enough that soon general discussion takes off. Once the students' stories start coming in, they can be analyzed and argued about: "What do you think of Marjorie's story, Helen?" Most creative writing courses soon enough become classes in applied morality or situational ethics. Although purists laugh at the idea of treating characters as if they were real people responsible for their actions, everyone does in fact respond to fiction in exactly that way. Stories generate interest precisely to the degree they manipulate readers' sympathies. Chekhov's stories, for instance, are endlessly rewarding because it's so hard to figure out who's bad and who's good in them. This ambiguity doesn't lead the reader to abandon his or her judgmental instincts but to refine them and to broaden his or her sympathies. Expecting readers to put aside their good-guy/ bad-guy criteria is absurd. As David Hume says, the mind of man when confronted with anything "immediately feels the sentiment of approbation or blame; nor are there any emotions more essential to its frame and constitution."

I was afraid that I looked so young the students would laugh at me when I announced I was their teacher. Charles Silverstein, to whom I confided this fear, said, "Usually you're complaining that you're aging too quickly. Now you're afraid you look too young." In truth I had a highly unstable "body image." I didn't *know* what I looked like. If I managed to pick up one man (or seven of them) in an evening, then I was certain I was handsome, though I did worry why the eighth one had turned me down. Most of the time, when I was less successful, my confidence in my looks plunged. People don't usually pay each other compliments—maybe lovers do, but I chose lovers who rejected me. I can remember that once Brandy Alexander, a famous drag queen, said to me at a party, "Ed White, everyone wants you, you're the universal ball." I hugged those chance words to my chest. I was twenty-four and I still remember them. I can also recall the one time a bartender sent me a free drink. I can remember a mad Southern seamster—is that the male version of seamstress?—who wrote a whole novel about me, which I was too bored to read. Years later, after my looks had faded and I'd become paunchy, a few men and women told me how attractive I'd been and how much they'd desired me. Harry Mathews got angry and said once in Key West, "Why don't you lose all that weight? You used to be so cute!"

Later, when I began to teach at Johns Hopkins as an assistant professor (twelve thousand dollars a year), I spent two days a week in Baltimore. There no one ever looked at me and I felt gray and invisible. I commuted on the Metroliner and the moment I stepped off the train in New York the swiveling eyes were all around me again, reassuringly. New York was the only place in America where everyone—young and old, straight and gay—cruised. People in big cities cruise; it's no accident that in French the word *cruise* (*draguer*) is applied to straights and gays alike, since both groups do it. *To put the make on* someone (*mater*, literally "to subdue") is also polysexual in French. In New York people check each other out to find out who they are, whereas in other cities there's no reason to bother since no one is ever anyone. As Stan used to say, "Half the people in New York if they were anywhere else would be either interviewed or arrested."

In the 1970s New York was so shoddy, so dangerous, so black and Puerto Rican, that the rest of white America pulled up its skirts and ran off in the opposite direction. Tourism was way down, and guests on talk shows would quite regularly laugh when New York was mentioned, as if that querulous, bankrupt cesspool should be pushed out to sea and sunk. My Texas relatives would call me and wonder how I dared to live there; my cousin Dorothy Jean, a militant Baptist, located and contacted the Baptist minister nearest me, then called me to say he was waiting for my visit. "The Big Apple" campaign and the slogan "I Love New York" (with the icon of a heart standing in for the word *love*) were invented to take the curse off the city. The opposite was true. No one loved New York except us, the gay and artsy misfits from the Midwest. Native New Yorkers hated their own city and were saving up to move to California. Corporate officers who were transferred to New York demanded hardship allowances and barricaded themselves in expensive suburbs such as Greenwich, Connecticut, and forbade their children to go into the city. Sometimes at the chemical company I met pink-collar workers from Staten Island who took the subway and the ferry back and forth to work. They were extruded from the subway directly into the building and had never dared to wander the Manhattan streets around them. Columbia students were advised never to walk south of 110th Street, and of course never above 125th into Harlem. Schoolchildren from the other boroughs were brought in virtually under guard in buses to the Metropolitan Museum, quickly herded through the vast collections, then driven straight back home to the Five Towns on Long Island. Darryl Pinckney, the great black novelist and critic, describes how when he walked down the street, in order to reassure a lone white woman just ahead of him that he wasn't going to rape or rob her, he would brandish his copy of Heidegger, but to no avail. She still looked back, panicked, and almost ran. Women were advised to take taxis home after dark and have the driver wait until he saw his passenger had actually gone through the front door and closed it safely behind her.

Perversely, we were proud to be New Yorkers, but not Americans. Nevertheless, we expected disaster. Our sleep was filled with doom scenarios. Shots rang out in the neighborhood somewhere. Traffic lights blinked out of sync with each other. Old people on chromium walkers were mugged. Jules Feiffer started a play with a New Yorker undoing six locks to get into her apartment; when she comes onstage, her grocery bag is leaking milk everywhere, riddled by bullets. I wrote a play about a hermaphrodite living in an apartment building where everyone in it was tragic and messed up; it was my vision of New York. Just a block away from me was Central Park, but even I was afraid to go into the Rambles to cruise, ever since a body had been found at the foot of the Gothic weather station behind the stage where Shakespeare in the Park was performed. Audiences watched these great, gory, eloquent plays as if they were battle reports: "That Lady Macbeth? Isn't she that wigged-out chick in 9B? The one who killed her sleepover and then started getting funny and ate him and had to have her ass hauled off to Bellevue?"

We knew nothing about the boroughs or the dense population on the closer half of Long Island—which is 118 miles long. To us they were these Jews and Poles and Ukrainians and Italians and Irish who had humorous substandard accents and who chewed gum and sprayed their hair and wore ankle bracelets. The movie *Saturday Night Fever* symbolized the immense distance between Brooklyn and Manhattan. Now every other apartment on Manhattan is inhabited by a corporate lawyer or private banker, and many of them are young and gay and date our friends, but back then we didn't know any people from Wall Street nor did we want to. New York, the New York we knew south of Fourteenth Street, was loud and leaking—the manholes were leaking steam, the fire hydrants were illegally spraying water in which naked neighborhood kids were dancing, the ambulance and fire-wagon sirens were shrieking around the clock, people's bodies were leaking blood and sperm and the emergency rooms and backrooms were packed, the apartment windows were thrown open to expel the excessive hot air generated by uncontrollable central heating—and the city was hemorrhaging money. And people's milk cartons had been shot through and were leaking.

We talked seriously about New York's declaring its independence from the rest of the United States. If Americans didn't want us, we didn't want them. We'd sacrificed comfort, safety, and respectability to live here, and we wanted to condescend to our landlocked relatives and not permit them to look down on us. We didn't see why our tax money had to support their wars. We wanted to raise the drawbridges and lower the portcullises isolating our island from the horrid mainland. Americans looked at a movie like *Taxi*

*Driver* (1976) as a portrait of lawless New York, but we knew that aside from the ambulatory psychotics there were artists and lovers and beats, hippies and bohemians—in fact, *La Bohème* struck us as a greater likeness, and years later *Rent*, our own New York AIDS version of the opera, predictably became a hit musical. We were radicals politically, and radical causes packed our streets with demonstrators, whose hair was too long, whose tempers were too short, whose speeches were wild-eyed. The rest of America didn't know whether to laugh in derision or channel-surf away from our images out of fear. From 1970 on, the Christopher Street parades, celebrating gay liberation, got longer and longer and more and more freakish, with drag queens and motorcycle lesbians (Dykes on Bikes) and leather boys leading the human tidal wave, which invariably stopped for a special anti-Catholic moment outside St. Patrick's. When I look at old newsreels of those parades and many others, I am always surprised that these hordes of stoned, starved, shaggy kids with their long sideburns were marching in 1980 and not 1965. The sixties had cast a long shadow.

# Chapter 15

In the fall of 1977 Jasper Johns had a retrospective show at the Whitney Museum and I was sent by *Horizon* one afternoon out to Stony Point, New York. The house had the sort of simplicity that only money can buy—a large living room with high windows looking out on woods and a narrow river. I was fascinated by Johns—and disconcerted. He had read my books or at least *Forgetting Elena* and he treated me with respect. But he had a Noh mask for a face and seldom smiled and spoke even less often. As Vivian Raynor had said in *Artnews*, "He has a remoteness that, while very amiable, makes all questions sound vaguely coarse and irrelevant."

I had my list of prepared questions and we worked through them. If the question was too invasive or stupid, his eyes would just bug and he'd say, "I'm not sure what to say," and laugh his gallery-of-horrors laugh. He told me that his favorite television show was *The Gong Show*, and I could just imagine Johns laughing with that mad roar as the shamed contestants were hauled off the stage. Raynor had noted that Johns had laughed uproariously after he'd said, "The problem with influences is that the thing or person you say is an influence has to accept some of the blame for what you've done." He was quick to see the absurdities and futilities of life, and even its minor moments of quirkiness could make him guffaw.

We were drinking whiskey on the rocks and I felt like putting my head down on my desk (yes, it seemed like being in school) and napping. Or possibly on his lap—I found him sexy in a daunting way. I could get him to make only one remark about Robert Rauschenberg, who was said to have been his lover in the 1950s, and that remark was slighting. Or rather he was quick to distance himself from Rauschenberg and to say that he was happy that I detected no resemblance in their work. And in fact they no longer saw each other. Nor did Johns ever discuss being gay, if indeed he really was. Years later I spent a night at a new house he'd just bought and he went out late and picked up a woman; at the very least he was bisexual. I thought a bit resentfully that all these "blue-chip" artists—Jasper Johns, Cy Twombly, John Ashbery, Elizabeth Bishop, Susan Sontag, Robert Wilson—never came out. We openly gay artists had to deal with the dismissive or condescending judgments all around us—"Of course since I'm not gay myself your work seems so exotic to me"—while the Blue Chips sailed serenely on, universal and eternal. It paid to stay in the closet, obviously. Of course they'd all eventually be outed after their death, but that would only add to their posthumous reputations and generate another shelf of theses by suggesting a whole new set of affiliations. During their lives they were secure and would never be marginalized. Well, more power to them, I thought. They definitely knew how to shape their careers.

I'd always admired Johns. Although the targets and numbers and flags were considered the seminal works behind Pop Art, they didn't feel like Pop Art to me. First of all, they were too beautifully painted, even juicily painted, to make the flat, strong statement of the sort Warhol or Rosenquist or Tom Wesselmann was making. In fact Johns seemed to have chosen his flags, for instance, not because they were ironic (like Lichtenstein's comic strips) or iconic (like Warhol's Campbell's soup cans) but precisely because the flags were exhausted images, so banal (if beautiful) that no one could focus on them for long. Once when Johns was asked to list his favorite contemporary painters, all but one turned out to be an abstract expressionist (with de Kooning heading the list). It seemed no accident that though Johns was considered to have rebelled against abstract expressionism, he dismissed just such claims as mere "sociology." And he prized the expressionists' beautiful brushwork.

To be sure, in keeping with his reserved, even guarded personality, he was not a splashy painter nor did his brushwork suggest speed and spontaneity. On the contrary—he'd executed the flags in encaustic (pigment suspended in hot wax), a slow, cumbersome technique that he liked precisely because it inhibited improvisation. Initially he'd painted the flags in enamel, but, as he said, "Although I wanted the strokes to remain separate, the enamel wouldn't dry fast enough to allow this. But encaustic allowed me to keep my strokes separate but to paint over them very soon after." Years later, during another interview assignment, he showed me the little electric appliance that heated up the encaustic.

Johns has always recycled his imagery, as if invention were a rude intrusion—or an unwelcome demand on the imagination. Working was not something he did gladly. He remarked to Raynor that he'd "never taken any pleasure in compulsive work," and "I do what I do without any strong sense of its importance." He told me that he'd met Samuel Beckett in Paris and mentioned to him that he wanted to illustrate something new. "He looked horrified. 'A new work?' he asked me. 'You mean you want me to write another book?'" This sort of dandified fastidiousness and stylized "laziness" was very much in Johns's mode. He said that when he looked at a retrospective of his own work, he was distressed by how much work he'd already done. Targets, flags, numbers have reappeared again and again, along with beer cans and flashlights—always the objects that you can't remember whether you just saw them or not.

This repetitiveness, he claimed, also distressed him. "I've always thought my work was too much of a piece. One wants one's mind to be agile and not overly repetitive, yet any painter has unavoidably formed unconscious habits." He seemed proud of this.

The first time I wrote about Johns I didn't dare mention even a word about homosexuality. By the time I did an article about the 1996 MOMA retrospective, I thought I didn't want to alienate Johns altogether by bringing up the subject of his sexuality, but at the same time I didn't want to appear cowardly by not broaching it at all. I ended up by mentioning a very personal book about Johns and his homosexuality by his old friend Jill Johnston, *Jasper Johns: Privileged Information*, which was a memoir about their relationship and an effort to decode his work by seeing in it personal and sexual references. Another art critic, Jonathan D. Katz, has worked on the concealed gay content in Johns's work, certainly against the explicit purpose of Johns. Johns once remarked to Vivian Raynor, who turned it into a title, "I Have Attempted to Develop My Thinking in Such a Way That the Work I've Done Is Not Me." Even Katz admits that after the breakup, "It is as if, without one another, Johns and Rauschenberg have lost the ability to represent themselves."

After we'd finished our first interview, Johns told me a couple of funny anecdotes. He said that when he was young, he'd gone out in a truck with a dealer to Utopia Parkway in Queens to help pick up some boxes made by Joseph Cornell, the American surrealist, for a new exhibit. Cornell was apparently quite fussed and ran out to the truck to say, "You didn't tell me what you wanted—a few masterpieces and the rest minor works or what—so I just did all masterpieces." Johns also told me about a trip to Buffalo where he did the sets for Merce Cunningham. Duchamp came along and insisted everyone go to see Niagara Falls. Duchamp worked out their itinerary down to the last detail, but when the time came for them to leave, Duchamp refused to join them. "But I haven't the least interest in Niagara Falls," he said. I was sure that Johns remembered these stories because Cornell's simple, almost simpleminded, vanity was the exact contrary to his own complicated diffidence, whereas Duchamp's elegant *désinvolture* was obviously an ideal, a beacon, for Johns.

The nicest moment of the afternoon came when Johns showed me Picasso's 1971 series of etchings to illustrate *La Celestina*, a fifteenth-century Spanish play about a procuress. I was so drunk I don't remember what Johns said about the process, but I remember Picasso had used sugar—and indeed the lines were granular and "crumbling." I can still picture the old procuress with her thin lips and big nose and the pure, spotless virgin she was selling—a girl whose firm young breasts were kept constantly on display. Johns pointed out dozens of small details in the etchings—it felt like a rare privilege to be shown by Johns this superb book by Picasso.

Now when I chance upon a Johns in a museum collection, I'm always struck by how sober his work looks, how dark and dignified. It's hard to imagine that it ever looked flashy or shocking. Now it's become cerebral and aloof—almost invisible in a crowded room in which other brighter, easier works are competing for attention.

# Chapter 16

I got my job teaching at Johns Hopkins through Stephen Orgel, David's first lover, the same man who had lent me his house in the Berkeley Hills. He had moved from California to Baltimore and recommended me. I had an interview with John Barth, the well-known novelist, then at the height of his fame, having published in 1960 a long, serious eighteenth-century pastiche, *The Sot-Weed Factor*, and more recently metafictional short stories in the collection *Lost in the Funhouse*. I guess I passed muster; he told Stephen that I was the first homosexual he'd ever knowingly met and that, strangely enough, he liked me. Stephen merely smiled and made a clicking noise and closed his eyes. He had a quietly insolent and wildly appealing way of shutting his eyes for a second and then reopening them, as if he couldn't quite trust them, and then chuckling steadily. He acted as if the victim of his subtle satire should share in his delight.

Stephen never lied. I overheard John Irwin, the head of the department, ask Stephen if he'd read his book on Faulkner, in which he proved that Faulkner, after the death of Alabama, his nine-day-old daughter, developed an incestuous relationship to his fiction. It was called *Doubling and Incest/Repetition and Revenge: A Speculative Reading of Faulkner*. Stephen's eyes got very round and closed, then switched back on. He stared at Irwin for a moment, then said, "I don't see why I would have read your book since I've never read Faulkner."

I taught one literature course for writers and one fiction workshop. In the literature course we read *One Hundred Years of Solitude*, *The Tin Drum*, *Blood Oranges*, *The Sound of the Mountain*, and *Gravity's Rainbow*, among others. I doubt if I would ever have read the García Márquez, the Grass, or the Pynchon if I hadn't assigned them, but I learned something by analyzing them. Since it was a course for writers, the main emphasis was on technique, not symbolism, influences, or sociological import, the usual stuff of English Department contemporary-fiction courses. Louise Erdrich, who went on to become the author of *The Beet Queen* and many other bestselling literary books, studied with me. When I look back at my twenty-odd years of teaching, I have to admit I've had only five or six students who became known writers. Among the ones who spring to mind are Stephen McCauley, Mona Simpson, Louise Erdrich, Christopher Beha, and Andrew Sean Greer. Two or three brilliant students, from whom I expected great things, could never finish a book. Not one of them, with the possible exception of Greer, writes in any way similar to me.

I had become friendly in New York with Manuel Puig, the Argentine author of *Kiss of the Spider Woman* (1976). I'd suggested he be put on the cover of *Christopher Street*, not long after the gay literary magazine had started up. I'd had lunch with Puig, who'd won me over with his strange mixture of seriousness and campiness. "I spent the whole day yesterday at the baths, Edmund, looking for a husband." Long, sad look. "I didn't find one."

I invited him down for the day to Johns Hopkins, where he'd be lunching with John Barth, addressing Barth's grad students, then giving a reading. As we were walking around campus, Barth said to Puig, "Tell me, Manuel, when you turned to the epistolary novel, were you trying to return to the very roots of fiction, as I am doing in my epistolary novel *Letters*?"

To Barth's astonishment, Puig said in his Latin-queen cantileña, "Oh, no, you see I was living in America and France so long I forget my Spanish, so I thought I have them write letters and if they make mistakes in Spanish, it's their fault."

No matter how bleak I felt on campus, I cheered up the minute I arrived at Stephen's house. I knew I was in for a long, delicious evening of far-ranging talk and good food, though it began with an English sort of anchovy paste called Gentleman's Relish. We had wonderful evenings with the poet Cynthia Macdonald and various young beaux Stephen was trying out—one nearly hysterical concert pianist was all big white hands and wasp waist who went on to write a biography of Horowitz edited by Jackie Kennedy. Young Elizabethan scholars were always around—but Stephen's interests were broad. He was a major and discerning and greedy collector of rare editions, especially anything related to Shakespeare and his spiritual descendants. He was already embarked on reading all of Trollope and Wharton, whose best books he would introduce in new editions. I first read Mavis Gallant in his spare room. She became one of my favorite writers and eventually a friend when I lived in Paris. Stephen kept a journal in which all our lives were recorded moment by moment—he will end up being the Pepys of our generation. He liked to think of himself as the country mouse and David as the city mouse, but of course he recorded all of David's gossip, too. Like David he had an unparalleled gift for friendship, domesticity, and loyalty. Stephen was always tender and sustaining to his "dear hearts" and coldly arrogant to the hordes of people who didn't interest him.

Anne Freedgood, my old editor at Random House, had published John Gardner and launched his career by bringing out *The Sunlight Dialogues* in January, when no new books of importance are published. The novel was favorably reviewed on the front page of the *New York Times Book Review*, which then had the power to make or break a book. Other hefty tomes by Gardner were subsequently published (*Nickel Mountain* and the only good one, *Grendel*, Gardner's retelling of Beowulf, which had come out the year before *The Sunlight Dialogues* but drawn little attention initially). Yet nothing created such a furor as his attack on all his contemporaries, *On Moral Fiction* (1978). His polemic was obviously indebted to Tolstoy's *What Is Art?* and took other writers to task for anything opaque or experimental. Gardner wanted the style of a book to be totally transparent so that the action could unfold behind it like a constantly moving, panoramic dream.

A strange man in his forties, Gardner had long, straight hair on the sides but was going bald on top, reputedly had had a colostomy, drove a motorcycle. He had a girlfriend, Liz Rosenberg, who was a grad student in poetry at Johns Hopkins. Later she became a professor at Binghamton University. I think Gardner was jealous of John Barth's influence over her. He'd attacked Barth's writing in *On Moral Fiction*, which had just recently come out, after Gardner had been invited to speak at Johns Hopkins. Barth announced to his staff that he would not be host of the luncheon for Gardner (I had to do the honors), but that he would attend. Barth lay down only one rule—Gardner could not discuss Barth's writing before Barth's own students. During the lunch Gardner told me that my own writing was "immoral." I assumed he meant because it was homosexual. Not at all, Gardner assured me. What was immoral is that the father in *Nocturnes for the King of Naples* is not angry when he discovers his son's homosexuality but rather pleased, since that means more women for himself and no competition from a younger man. In the novel the father is represented as a total roué who shoots heroin, drinks to excess, stages orgies in a rented villa in Spain . . .

Gardner: "You know your own father would never have reacted that way."

Me: "That's true. In real life he was very upset. But the father in my book is a character—"

Gardner: "Who never existed, who never would exist. No father would react that way. That's why your book is immoral."

I was amazed that he'd bothered to read that far in my book (which was virtually unknown), and his objections to it were less impressive to me than the seriousness with which he took it. I did, however, point out that not all fathers were middle-class Americans and that my character was an invention, someone I'd imagined—

But no, Gardner didn't want to hear that. I was immoral, but I was of course in good company, along with most other American novelists of the day, especially the reprehensible Barth and Updike, though I hadn't rated a mention in his version of Who's Who in Hell. What was fascinating to me in later years was how this one book, *On Moral Fiction*, remained something serious people read long after they'd forgotten Gardner's fiction. Despite its Puritanism and narrow, hectoring tone, it nevertheless took a firm stand and pursued its point. My theory is that readers, especially serious young students of literature, are so at a loss as to how to evaluate fiction that they will respond to any critic (F. R. Leavis, Harold Bloom, John Gardner) who tells them what to think, has a simple principle for determining quality, and uses often and forcefully the word *great*.

Although Gardner had promised not to mention Barth's fiction, the very first thing he did in front of Barth's students was to attack John Barth. Barth, who was sitting toward the front of the crowded room, objected, but Gardner plowed on. Angry words were exchanged between the two great men. A reporter from the *Baltimore Sun* was sitting in the back and furiously scribbling notes—and soon the story had gone national.

A confrontation of this sort was especially dramatic in Baltimore. In crowded, pedestrian New York where everyone was a loudmouth and defended his or her turf with a ferocity unknown to mild auslander, verbal fights occurred daily. The leader of the New York teachers' union would attack a black educator who'd proposed that Ebonics be taught in the public schools. In the spring of 1970 Earth Day was celebrated, one of the first mass demonstrations in favor of the environment. Gay Day, anti–Vietnam War protests—every month brought another huge march.

But in the rest of the country (this melancholy, lonely country) the streets were empty, people were sealed off in their offices or cars or houses, no one saw anyone outside his or her circle or had any contact with strangers. Suburbia, television, and the automobile had isolated everyone—perhaps a good thing in such a potentially violent country. Even in gated communities, miles and miles away from the nearest ghetto, the frightened golden-agers were all buying weapons or taking karate classes. It was precisely in those places that were the safest that the sheltered populations most often expected imminent violence. Armageddon was both a religious and a looming social reality for nearly a third of Americans. In Utah, houses for sale were advertised as having "fully furnished" basements, meaning set up as bunkers for survivalists when the Final Days began, when the Rapture started separating the sheep from the goats. Which would be tomorrow. Or the next day.

I'd lived through both of the blackouts in New York. The first one, in 1965, went more or less peacefully by since it happened when it was getting cold, but the second one occurred on July 13 and 14, 1977, and led to two days of rioting and looting. Some 1,616 stores were looted, and at certain points the looters were looting the other looters. Altogether 3,776 people were arrested—the largest mass arrest in the city's history—and 1,037 fires were reported.

New York was a mess by the late 1970s. The city had lost hundreds of thousands of jobs. It was from time to time incapable of paying teachers their salaries. Graffiti covered every square inch of the interiors of subway cars, which were awash with garbage. Passengers were subjected to the intolerably loud music coming out of boom boxes. Crime had risen faster in the sixties (and was continuing to rise in the seventies) than in any other American city since the 1930s. In 1975 Mayor Beame had furloughed thousands of city workers, including cops and garbagemen. When Beame asked President Ford for federal assistance to meet the payroll, Ford told New York to drop dead. New York had been called Fun City. Now it had become Fear City and Stink City. Garbage left on the streets would go weeks without being collected.

I remember I had a boyfriend at the time, Ken, who sold sappy greeting cards and was a determined masochist. He was from Kentucky and talked all the time—in such an irritating, constant motormouth way that it was easy to whip his butt from time to time out of sheer frustration. We were sitting in his apartment—him talking, me smoldering with boredom—when the 1977 blackout started. He thought it was a lark, a sort of "trend," and he was always alert to trends. He lived in the Village on West Fourth Street around the corner from Pizzeria Uno, where within an hour or two the hundreds of frozen pizzas were quickly thawing and were being handed out to passersby completely free. Ken grabbed several and "we had a ball," as he put it. "This is fabulous," he said. He wanted me to get "into" it more, but there was a limit as to how much cheery excitement a sadist could exhibit to his slave. I was self-conscious about my role because it wasn't my usual one. We sat on his fire escape. The earlier blackout had been reassuring because it had shown how good-natured and ultimately how disciplined New Yorkers were. The new blackout showed how racially divided we were, how much anger seethed just below the surface, how rapacious and every-man-for-himself we'd all become.

In 1978 I moved back downtown. Keith McDermott was living

mostly on the West Coast, my nephew had decided to return to the Midwest and was enrolled in the University of Chicago—and I found the West Side depressing. I had a part-time beau, Norm Rathweg, who found me a studio apartment in the Colonnades on Lafayette Street, a series of scruffy Greek Revival buildings from the 1830s—the most elegant address of the period, filled with Astors, but by the late 1970s in a picturesque state of decay worthy of the French Quarter of New Orleans. My big studio apartment had twenty-foot ceilings, parquet floors, a small white-marble fireplace, and tall windows outfitted with wood shutters that folded back into the deep window frames. My windows looked down on a garden restaurant, and in the evening in summertime I could hear the friendly murmur of voices and the rattle of silverware on dishes. In the winter I usually had a fire on the grate, or a hibachi on which I grilled swordfish or lamb for guests. Norm put in a new kitchen and bathroom and loft bed and painted the whole thing gray-blue with white woodwork. When my nephew visited with a school friend, Richard Kaye, they were shocked by how humbly a writer could live. They were invited to dinner and were impressed and confused that I, an out homosexual, was trying to fix up the literary critic Richard Gilman with a single woman I knew. What business did I have, they wondered, meddling with the lives of straights?

I had met Norm Rathweg at the Sheridan Square Gym, where I'd been working out since the mid-1960s. When I started lifting weights, it was still an unusual activity for a gay man. In the fifties and sixties gays wanted to be as thin as possible but it never occurred to them to be—well, not boys but *men*. In the seventies, however, we stayed thin but began to add muscles—a well-defined chest, a firm, prominent butt, massive legs, baby biceps, more muscled shoulders. I was one of the first in this metamorphosis from boy to man.

A more dramatic example of the transformation was Norm. When he arrived at the gym, he was a tall, skinny boy, pale with nearly invisible blond eyelashes and a blancmange complexion. He was timid and never spoke to anyone except his lover, Louis Keith Nelson. They were at the gym every day but kept to themselves. Norm wouldn't even meet my eyes or anyone else's. The only assertive thing he did was to burp loudly, which seemed to be unconscious.

But slowly he changed. He began to fill out and muscle up. He became more confident. I started to go out with him though it was understood that he and Louis Keith Nelson were a couple and would stay together. Back then, in the 1970s, these questions of fidelity and couplehood didn't come up and we wouldn't exactly have known how to respond to them. Introducing the issue now slightly falsifies the quiet, natural way in which we assumed everyone would have multiple sex partners, that jealousy was definitely not cool, and that new people could be regular fuck buddies or part-time lovers, that the molecule could always annex a new atom. Of course everyone tacitly feared that a new dalliance might take a lover away forever, but this seldom happened. It was as if the three elements (love, sex, friendship) that straight people centered on one other person we gays distributed over several people and this distribution was a more solid form than companionate marriage.

While I lived in that apartment in the Colonnades, I had lots of group sex—there was a beefy, slightly crazy American Indian from Colorado who'd been "discovered" at sixteen by Allen Ginsberg at the Naropa Institute in Boulder. He had a smooth body like pillows stuffed tightly inside a silk parachute. There was a handsome Norwegian flight attendant from St. Paul with a cool, bemused manner, though he was open to almost any suggestion. There were lots of other guys and we lay around in my loft bed talking and kissing and listening to music and getting high. I was in my late thirties and gay men of my generation had earlier always assumed that sex would come to a screeching halt at age thirty, but now that we'd long before reached that landmark age, it seemed just to go on and on, as did one's youth. People of my parents' generation had been married at twenty-two, had had children two years later, and were worn-out and paunchy by forty, but we kept working out and staying up late and falling in and out of love, "immature" but weirdly youthful.

We wondered where we were all heading. We assumed that gay life had branched off from normal family experience, sort of like *Homo sapiens* evolving in a separate direction from *Homo erectus*. We thought that gays had a separate destiny, that we were meant to point the way to more elegant and comprehensive models of adhesiveness. We were hostile to the idea of assimilation since we knew that would mean resembling straights, whereas we felt we had something better to offer.

Norm was emblematic of many of the young gay men who came up in the 1970s. He was from Florida, where he'd been a bookish nerd. His father had been a famous college athlete who'd had a devastating motorcycle accident and lost his legs and as an invalid would lie in bed drinking and insulting his big, fearful, skulking son, calling him a creep and a faggot.

Norm was turning himself into someone new. Bruce Mailman, who owned our building in the Colonnades, hired Norm to design and build the St. Marks Baths on St. Marks Place. I had gone to these baths years before when they'd been dirty and Ukrainian with a masseur in the basement rumored to be the cannibalistic original from Tennessee Williams's story "Desire and the Black Masseur." Norm put in lots of "wet areas" and solid primary colors and spotlights and warm terra-cotta tiles. He who'd been scared of his own shadow was now wearing a hard hat and climbing on steel beams several stories high and pulling girders into place and making hundreds of small decisions every day—and they all worked. Then Bruce asked him to build the ultimate disco—what I called "the *Hindenburg* of discos," little realizing that it would indeed be the biggest and one of the last giant gay dance halls. The Saint opened in 1980 in the old Fillmore East, a rock-concert hall on Second Avenue. A mesh-enclosed ramp led up and up to the immense dance floor of nearly five thousand square feet inserted under a dome in the building with robotic arms shuffling and pinpointing whole phalanxes of lights. In the center was a stage where Madonna or Whitney Houston would perform. Late, late at night (in reality toward noon the following day) the dome would turn into a planetarium and thousands of stars would slowly drift through space. Above and outside the dome on one side were the remaining seats of what had once been the top balcony. There stoned young men would sit in confused isolation in the dark and look down at the illuminated antics of the dancers. If you were properly stoned, they would look like miniature Santa's helpers manufacturing mountains of invisible toys. Since I lived just five blocks away, I'd sometimes set the alarm and show up at five in the morning and head right to the balcony, where many of those lonely men were ready for sex.

Norm turned himself into a big man among men. He and Louis built the Chelsea Gym, which epitomized gay Chelsea for nearly a decade. I'd see Norm marching down the street with four other young men all in their thirties, wearing jeans and leather jackets, their hair cropped short, their voices loud. They weren't bullies or pigs. They read books. They listened to classical music. They fell in love. Their politics were progressive. They talked about ideas. But Norm could command a team of straight workingmen on a building site and hide his emotions under a gruff exterior. He was the New Gay Man. A straight journalist would devote a chapter to him in a book on contemporary men.

At Norm and Lewis's apartment a lot of these big, hearty sensitive men would sit around and eat good food buffet-style and drink white wine and talk about their feelings or their wider interests. I can remember marching in a gay pride parade with all of them, our arms around each other's shoulders. We were with the leather boys, all of them smelling of hide and beer.

One of the stars of that group was Thom Gunn, the great English poet who'd lived most of his life in San Francisco. Thom was tall, bearded, lean, a serious leather guy and a decade older than all of us (though he looked our age). He was fascinated by Norm and maybe was just a bit in love, even if his "type" was younger and frailer. But when Norm died early on of AIDS, Thom wrote a beautiful elegy to him, "Courtesies of the Interregnum." If you google Norm you'll find nothing about the astonishing buildings he designed. You'll find him only as a link to Gunn's elegy.

I visited Thom two or three times in San Francisco, and once in a great while I'd phone him from New York out of the blue. He lived in a small commune of gay men and with a lifelong lover, Mike Kitay, an American he'd met at Trinity when he was a student. Each of the five or six men in the commune had his cooking night, and Thom took the meals and the shared responsibilities seriously. The commune was comfortable and calm up on the Haight off the Castro on the other side of Market. I brought Thom out to Princeton once to give a reading, but he seemed uncomfortable and failed to convince the audience of his true qualities. He'd lost his confidence and mumbled. He'd retired from teaching poetry at Berkeley and stopped writing; this silence was painful for him. He was also doing a lot of drugs toward the end of his life, mostly connected with sex.

He'd always been fascinated with America. His mother had committed suicide when he was fifteen, and after Trinity he came to the States. Donald Hall, the poet, told me that he'd seen Thom even at that time in full leathers and on a motorcycle, and a great photo shows him looking like a Hells Angel on a bike (it's a 1963 picture by Mike Kelly). He's in jeans and motorcycle boots and a tight-fitting black leather jacket and a hood, the only incongruous element his broad smile. One of his early books, *My Sad Captains*, has a Shakespearian title that seems suitable to all those leather men he liked, though Thom wrote chiseled, formal, rather impersonal poems early on—the influence of Yvor Winters, his teacher at Stanford. Winters, a critic and poet born in the Midwest at the turn of the century, preached an austere, imagistic ideal of formalist poetry, and Gunn responded to it. Fortunately, in the 1980s, AIDS—and the death of many friends—made Gunn a warmer, more expressive poet, especially in his best collection, *The Man with Night Sweats* (1992). AIDS gave us all a subject and a seriousness that our work had never before possessed. Thom brought to bear on this subject a rigorous technique and quiet control he'd acquired over the years.

Typical of Gunn's late strong work are these lines, with their beautifully subtle enjambment, written to Mike Kitay:

> Nothing is, or will ever be,
> Mine, I suppose. No one can hold a heart
> But what we hold in trust
> We do hold, even apart.

As the seventies progressed, gay sexual tastes became more and more outré. Gunn celebrated those extremes. He quoted with approval an article in the *Village Voice* by Ellen Willis in which she said that the lesbian movement of the seventies was not about liberating desire but about extending female solidarity. "For the gay male community," on the other hand, "solidarity was, at its core, about desire." I suppose another way of putting that was, lesbianism was to feminism as male homosexuality was . . . to nothing. There was no fourth term in the equation. Gay men had never suffered as men but had been stripped of male privilege by the straight community. They wanted back what they considered to be their birthright.

Gunn saw gay men in the seventies—the ones who were out there, sexually active—as heirs to the drug-taking hippies. Gays at the saunas were "drug-visionaries." "At the baths," Gunn wrote, "or in less organized activity, there was a shared sense of adventure, thrilling, hilarious, experimental." Gunn saw gays as crossing dramatic, enormous gulfs "on the huge pinions of our sexual momentum." Referring to a San Francisco baths, Gunn wrote:

> This was the Barracks, this the divine rage
> In 1975, that time is gone.
> All here, of any looks, of any age,
> Will get what they are looking for,
> Or something close, the rapture they engage
> Renewable each night . . .

I can remember that in the midsixties New York had just one leather bar, and it was inconspicuous and customers would wear their normal clothes and carry a change of costume in a bag, then switch to their chaps and black leather vest in the taxi. They were terrified a friend, even a gay friend, might see them going out in this freaky rig. Sadomasochism still sounded perverted and ever so slightly tacky—sort of New Jersey. And elderly. As if working-class, old gay men who couldn't compete in the real bars could look appealing in leather, or at least threatening.

By the seventies all that was changing. In 1972 *L.A. Plays Itself*, a hard-core porn film starring the charismatic director Fred Halstead, opened at the Fifty-fifth Street Playhouse and ran briefly before the cops closed it down. It had a notorious fisting scene, and the whole atmosphere of the second half of the movie was in complete grim contrast to the plucked pretty-boy look of the new East Coast porn such as *The Boys in the Sand*. The Anvil, a bar with go-go boys, opened in 1974 just south of Fourteenth Street. Boys danced on the bar on the ground floor while men had sex downstairs in the darkened bowels of the building. I never saw it, but people claimed uptown customers—even elegant women—fisted the go-go boys after carefully removing their rings.

In 1975 a hard-core S&M monthly magazine, *Drummer*, started publishing. It had fairly technical information about how to torture and submit to it—we read it with avidity. The whole look and smell of gay New York culture was changing toward beefier bodies, beards, and the odor of brew, harness, sweat, and Crisco. Keith McDermott said that New Yorkers were so pale and unhealthy looking that black leather was the only look that suited them.

The leather bars kept pushing farther and farther uptown until they reached Twenty-first Street and Eleventh Avenue with the Eagle's Nest. There all the men seemed older and bearded and muscular and over six feet tall. At five foot ten I'd never felt short before except in Amsterdam. Now I was a shorty in my own city. To get from the West Village up to the Spike and the Eagle, gay men had to go past three blocks of projects on Ninth Avenue starting at Sixteenth Street. Gangs who lived in the projects would attack single gay men. We started wearing whistles around our necks to summon other gay men to our defense—a fairly effective system. I thought back to the fifties when everyone was a sissy boy with straightened hair, cologne, and a baby-blue cashmere sweater and penny loafers. Back then we would have been terrified of gangs. Not anymore. Now many of us were taking judo classes.

And now the dress code was strict:

*Edmund White*

# N.Y. EAGLE DRESS CODE ANNOUNCED or REVISED?

SHIRTS: **No** patterned, dress, sports or baggy pants, or shorts.

SHOES: **No** sandals, sneakers, track shoes, tennis, or gym shoes, any multi-colored, white or brightly-colored shoes, or open front-, back-, or side-shoes, or clogs or stack heels.

BELTS: **No** skinny, plastic, or white belts, or suspenders.

SHIRTS: STRETCH OR KNIT.: **No** buttoned, colored, patterned, second-color trim, multi-colored, lettered ( unless for bar, club, or the "scene" ), V-neck, or "designer shirts".

SHIRTS: COLLARED AND CUFFED: **No** pattern (except for plaid or western-cut shirts) dress shirts or extremely flamboyant western shirts.

HATS: **No** hat other than leather cycle caps, western hats, construction hats or uniform hats.

JACKETS AND COATS: **No** jackets or coats other than leather or western style.

Ed Note: For those of our Leather/Western/Biking readers that prefer to maintain their individuality (pea-caps/coats, warm jackets, winter riding gear/sweaters or whatever) may we suggest patronizing the **SPIKE BAR** whose advertisement appears elsewhere in THE BOLT. Located one block from the Eagle, their courteous and "friendly" atmosphere is more than condusive to the scene.

At one time, the Mineshaft was New York's most notorious "members only" club. Membership was granted on the spot if one passed muster—no designer clothes, no sneakers, no cologne. Located on Washington Street at Little West Twelfth Street in the heart of the meatpacking district, it was open around the clock from Wednesday night through Monday morning, featuring a clothes check, dungeons, and other amenities. Yes, one was allowed to check all one's clothes and stroll about naked or in a jockstrap—

undress was encouraged. The Mineshaft opened in 1977 before the AIDS era and was finally closed by the city's Department of Health in 1985, four years after AIDS was first diagnosed.

People from out of town were astonished by the club and the neighborhood. All night long in the neighboring blocks, butchers in streaked aprons were unloading skinned and dressed calves and lambs onto overhead hooks traveling from the refrigerated trucks parked on the sidewalk (slick and smelly and black as varnish with blood) into the huge refrigerated warehouses. The butchers' voices were loud and their faces lurid as they bent over oil drums containing warm-up fires.

Within the nondescript street-level door of the Mineshaft were stairs leading straight up to the doorkeeper sitting on a barstool, no longer the stogie-smoking Mafia guy of yore in a porkpie hat but rather a bearded and equally heavyset gay man in jeans and workboots. Inside was the big bar area with its low lights and pool tables. Behind a partition was the "action" part of the club on two floors. There was an entire wall of glory holes with people kneeling in front of crotch-high holes and servicing disembodied erections. A fist-fucking sling was suspended on heavy chains from the ceiling, and a small crowd of men stood around looking at the nearly gynecological examinations. A whole rabbit warren of small rooms was downstairs and in one was a bathtub where men would take turns being pissed on.

In 1979 I wrote an essay in the left-wing *New Times* justifying gay S&M. I acknowledged, "As for gay S and M, it is as disturbing for heterosexuals to contemplate as was the thought of fair Celia on the potty for Jonathan Swift." I was alert to the drama and romanticism of glimpsed scenes at the Mineshaft: "In the basement two stoned men are kissing under black light. Absurdly, touchingly, anachronistically romantic, they are unaware of everyone around them, their fluorescent white shirts gleaming eerily like Baudelaire's swan bathing its wings in the dust."

My main argument was that S&M was a scaled-down way of enacting and exorcising the brutality of our class society. As I put it, "Whereas ordinary social interactions are characterized by the joke, humor has always been inimical to sadism, just as light is to vampires. This humor that defuses outrage, no matter how justified, and dampens indignation, no matter how righteous, is just another name for surrender. Sadomasochism rejects the laugh that paralyzes social conscience. Within the charged space surrounding the master and his slave, true deeds are performed. One man does submit to another. One man does humiliate another. The same relief we experience in watching a Shakespeare play, the relief of participating in action devoid of irony and freighted with clear values, is the release offered to the sadist and masochist. The couple perform the mysteries of domination, of might, that obsess our culture. As Gilles Deleuze and Félix Guatarri have said in the *Anti-Oedipus*, 'Class struggle goes to the heart of desire.' "

I'm not sure I would subscribe to such a penitential view of S&M today, nor do I believe now in such an un-nuanced Shakespeare. Moments of intellectual "breakthrough" are always difficult to recapture, and embarrassing to mention, since later they seem so obvious—or wrong. But I remember distinctly that when I wrote "Sado-Machismo" for *New Times* a young straight writer from the *Village Voice* and I were fired up by the notion that sex need not be Freudian or Darwinian but could be "artistic" or "expressive" or possibly "Marxist." We were so thoroughly part of a puritanical society that it seemed daring to claim that sex might be as "useless" as art or that, alternately, it might be as dramatic as class conflict. We sat on the couch in Richard Sennett's Washington Mews town house, egging each other on in this strange new direction.

In the early eighties the Mineshaft scene turned sour. Not only was the specter of AIDS dogging everyone's steps, but there was also a ghastly ritualistic murder. Apparently a coke-snorting art dealer, Andrew Crispo, while sitting in his apartment, kept dialing the number of the public phone booth just outside the Mineshaft. A handsome Norwegian model answered and agreed to be picked up by Crispo's passing car and to submit to a night of torture. The fun and games got out of hand, however, and the model, after hours of being tortured, was shot twice through the head by Crispo's assistant and bodyguard, a renegade rich boy. The body was dumped in a smokehouse on the estate of the bodyguard's parents' estate on Long Island. When the victim was found much later, the leather mask had burned into his face but most of the body had become unrecognizable.

A new friend was Robert Mapplethorpe. I don't think anyone before him in the art world had ever courted me. But Mapplethorpe, who was just becoming prominent, had spotted me as someone who could write about him. I don't remember where we met—maybe on the street through a third person or at a party. He made it clear that he wasn't interested in sex; no, he wanted me to write about him.

He certainly wasn't afraid of being considered gay—on the contrary. He was interested in leather, S&M, scat, pain, blood—all those things that most gay men are careful to exclude in their list of desired activities when they write a personal ad (or now an online profile). He had had a famous affair with the punk singer Patti Smith, but now he was famously in love with the tall, much older, aristocratic Sam Wagstaff. Sam had launched Robert's career by buying and exhibiting the greatest private collection of photographs ever put together, going back to Fox Talbot, then placing Robert at the end of this magnificent tradition. Sam showed all these photographs together, then had a big party for Robert at what was then the chic watering spot, One Fifth Avenue, and inviting all the press and all the important critics and collectors (Sam lived upstairs in the penthouse).

Mapplethorpe was the high priest of virilization, that moment in the 1970s when gay men rejected other people's definitions of homosexuality and embraced a new vision of themselves as "hypermasculine"—the famous "clone" look. Soldier, cop, construction worker, these were the looks celebrated and parodied by the disco band the Village People. But Mapplethorpe rejected the conformism and anodyne masculinity of the look and made it transgressive by pushing it toward pain, torture, sacrifice. His pictures weren't erotic and were seldom arousing except to fetishists. Nor were they of unnamed subjects by an unnamed photographer, one of the usual prerequisites of pornography in the past. No, Mapplethorpe, like the good Catholic boy he was, believed in the devil. When he would have sex, he would whisper in his lover's ear, "Do it for Satan." Perhaps Pasolini, the Italian film director, was one ahead of him, since in his scandalous movie *Salo* he honored the two greatest sins or crimes in the gay world: satanism and pedophilia. Although Mapplethorpe was uninterested in children, he had his biggest scandal in England when he showed at the Tate a little girl exposing her crotch. That the child did this innocently, and that her mother had attended the shoot, meant nothing to the dirty-minded.

When I knew him, Mapplethorpe went nearly every night to the foot of Christopher Street across from the trucks and the Hudson River piers. There he was one of the few white men to be found in a gay black bar called Keller's. Robert would sometimes wear his leathers, but they weren't clunky Marlon Brando, *The Wild One* leathers with chains and buckles but rather elegant formfitting Dutch leathers seamed in blue or red. There he would stare with rapture and a single purpose at the person he most desired that evening.

I never understood Mapplethorpe's sexuality. He would explain it to me and keep correcting with a little smile the wrong conclusion I'd jumped to. He'd say, "No, it has nothing to do with fantasy." Or he'd say, "No, it's not a matter of role-playing. Nothing could be realer than what I like. That's why I like it—it's real."

He was soft-spoken and polite. He was completely unpretentious and talked freely but without too much interest about his poor Catholic family on Long Island. He'd lived with Patti Smith at the Chelsea Hotel, but he seldom talked about her. Maybe I didn't ask enough questions, but, no, I think the reality of being young and on the make in the seventies in New York was so absorbing that people didn't dwell much on the past. People who talk a lot about the past believe it was better, but for us the present was the golden age.

One day he called me and told me he was sending over an interesting new writer—Bruce Chatwin. We had an instant sexual response to each other, possibly because we were meeting through Mapplethorpe. Bruce with his bright, hard eyes and his odorless WASP body and flickering, ironic smile and his general derring-do instantly groped me while we were still standing just inside the door, and a minute later we'd shed our clothes and were still standing. We had sex in the most efficient way, we put our clothes back on, and we never repeated the experience with each other though we continued to see each other up until months before Bruce's early death from AIDS. Bruce wrote a wonderful essay about Mapplethorpe, but so did Susan Sontag. Robert was good in finding the best writers to talk about his work, though he himself was anything but a reader.

Robert lived alone in a gloomy loft on Bond Street, not too far from my place on Lafayette. It was filled with dark Stickley furniture from the beginning of the century and big Arts and Crafts pots, beautiful pieces all, but heavy. In the long, skinny sitting room, a curious tray swung out from the bathroom. I never understood its functions, but Robert told me that he'd been "into shit before it got too dangerous when everyone started having amoebas." It was because he gave up shit, he told me, that he got "into niggers."

Several times we had lunch together at a restaurant called Binibon on Second Avenue. My friend John Purcell and I called the restaurant Twisty-Tables because of the way the tables were set at strange angles to each other. A famous murder was committed at the Binibon in 1981 by Jack Abbott, the author of *In the Belly of the Beast*. Abbott had been released from prison, where he'd been confined for forgery and bank robbery; his sentence had been increased by twenty-one years when he'd stabbed a fellow inmate. Abbott was given early parole due to Norman Mailer's vouching for his character, but the day before his book was published in July, he killed a Binibon waiter. The whole sorry episode coincided with the end of the Leftish idealism of the seventies. Reagan was just about to be elected.

I wrote the catalog for *Black Males*, an early Mapplethorpe exhibit, this one in Amsterdam in 1980 at the Galerie Jurka. I argued that whenever a white man in America looks at a black man, it is a complex and guilty act and that Mapplethorpe went through the repertory of possible responses (art deco figurine, sex object, etc.). Later the black poet Essex Hemphill attacked me (and Mapplethorpe, who was dead by then) for objectifying blacks. He singled out the picture of Mapplethorpe's lover Milton Moore in *Man in a Polyester Suit* in which the model's penis is shown emerging from his fly but his head is cut off. In a debate in a gay magazine I pointed out that Milton had made Mapplethorpe sign a contract promising he would never show his penis and his face in the same frame because he, Milton, didn't want his family to know he was gay. One could also have argued that the French word for a camera lens is *objectif*, and that there is no way of not objectifying someone in a photo.

When Robert had to go to Amsterdam for the opening of his show, he asked me to babysit Milton, who was pretty crazy (eventually he tried to swim the Hudson to New Jersey). He seemed a sweet man, Milton, though he was overwhelmed by Robert's New York life and would take a dictionary with him to dinner parties to keep up with the big words the others were saying. Before he died of AIDS in 1989 at age forty-two, Robert received a letter from Milton, who'd been convicted of murdering a man with a lead pipe and was serving time in an Alabama prison. He asked if he could borrow three thousand dollars. I don't know whether Robert sent the money.

When Robert and I were friends, he didn't have much money. Sam Wagstaff had undoubtedly bought him his loft, as later he would buy him a bigger one on Twenty-third Street. Robert didn't seem to have much spending money. In 1980 we did a story on Truman Capote together for the glossy, semi-gay theater magazine *After Dark*, and another article for *SoHo News* on William Burroughs in 1981. I doubt if Robert had ever read either writer (or my books for that matter), but that didn't seem a requirement. At the United Nations Plaza, where we arrived on a June day, the air-conditioning was on the blink and Capote met us at the elevator in bare feet and with a palmetto fan in hand. All through the interview Capote kept dashing out of the room to sniff more cocaine. He went through phases of being sharp-witted and nearly nagging and other moments of mumbling incoherence, as if someone were alternately pumping air into the balloon and deflating it. Robert was accompanied by his handsome assistant, a James Dean lookalike, Marcus Leatherdale, who later became a well-known photographer in his own right. Capote seemed quite uninterested in any of us, though at the very end he told me he'd read some of my stuff and been impressed with it. "You'll probably write some good books," he said. "But remember, it's a horrible life." Mapplethorpe insisted on taking a picture of Capote and me together. I asked him why. He smiled in his riddling way and said, "You'll be happy someday that I did so."

Burroughs received us in the Bunker, his name for his apartment on the Bowery. He lived in the same building as the poet John Giorno, who at the time was writing poems on sugar, alcohol, and meat.

Burroughs lived in the old locker rooms of the former YMCA and proudly showed us the ancient graffiti on the toilet walls. So often in Burroughs's fiction a gray wind is blowing through half-remembered scenes of adolescent loneliness, and these nearly obliterated obscene drawings seemed to be the perfect emblems of that vision.

As the evening wore on, Burroughs became more and more stoned. Though technically homosexual, he seemed as sexless as Capote, though in a different way. I called my piece "This Is Not a Mammal," using a remark that Susan Sontag had made to me about Burroughs.

In the late 1970s, a glory-hole venue suddenly appeared next to the other leather bars. You paid an entrance fee and then suddenly were in a large room full of little booths with doors that latched. The booths had waist-high holes through which you could suck the cock of your neighbor. It was a bit like a confessional booth in that no one could see what you looked like, though sometimes things became romantic and people kissed through the hole and even stuck their hands and arms in and caressed each other's body and face. I remember that in the center of the room was a big booth with maybe eight glory holes, two on each side. Once I saw a man roaming that room sticking his big, hard dick in one hole after another, a restless minotaur. As I looked from my hole across the room at the other holes, they all seemed to be disconcertingly alive—protruding hands waving him over, mouths gaping, or liquid eyes pivoting and blinking. The minotaur was so angry and passionate, stabbing himself into each living desperate orifice.

One night when I was there, the boy on the door got me high because he was hoping to slow me down so that I would wait till he got off at two in the morning. That sounded like a good plan and I was chatting with him at the cash register when all of a sudden a hot young man with a dancer's butt and turnout but none of the effeminacy stormed in. I was so high that I followed him closely, almost walking on his heels, and just as he was about to drop the latch on a cubicle, I pushed the door and entered his booth. That was against the rules but no one was monitoring the room.

I went home with him. His name was Chris Cox. He and I were lovers for the next three years off and on. He was on acid that night and couldn't get it up, but he was basically a top and I a bottom, so he gave me precise orders about how to fuck him, and that was the last time I ever did that in our relationship. Even then as I was fucking him, I was completely under his spell. I looked at the stacks of books beside the bed and was surprised how many of the titles were the same as those in my room. He was so ardent—even crazy passionate—that I thought if he was this hot and also had all the same books, then we should be lovers.

The next morning he took pictures of me as I awakened. I look dazed and vulnerable and happy in the photos, a lot younger than my thirty-seven years, well fucked though I'd done the fucking, an anomaly that he immediately set to rights. He lived in a big, empty loft on Twenty-third Street with a skylight overhead and hanging spider plants above the bed, which was just a mattress on the floor. The bathroom was ancient, in a big, separate room. In those days an empty loft was the height of chic, and it was hard to know if a loft-dweller was really poor or just an artist pretending to be a minimalist. Chris's loft had what seemed like acres of hardwood floors and windows without shades and a phone on the floor next to a metal folding chair and an ashtray. The space was large enough to be a dance studio and sometimes Chris did rehearse there, though he'd given up the theater by and large by the time I knew him. Lofts were often only semilegal as residences and usually went for a low rent.

Chris hung on my every word and started booking me for every evening. He loved to take pictures of me and shot an author photo for my novel *Nocturnes for the King of Naples* in which by mistake he used an expensive red filter that brought out the circles under my eyes and turned my hair a shade darker and my skin a shade paler. When he took the picture in Key West for *States of Desire* two years later, he produced the best photo of me anyone ever did, by which of course I mean the most flattering. I was rested and had just lost twenty pounds.

Chris had a demonic energy and suddenly it all seemed lavished on me. He quizzed me endlessly about my family and friends. When he met my mother, he called her by her first name, Delilah, and made her many highballs. He listened to her monologues nodding along and murmuring assent like someone in a Pentecostal church, but his eyes were wandering and he couldn't have repeated a thing beyond the last thing she'd said, still echoing in his ears.

In the middle of all this, my stepmother phoned me to tell me that my father had died, on January 27, 1979. He'd been born on December 18, 1905. She said that she was going to bury him in two days outside Findlay, Ohio, where her family lived. I called my sister and made plans to rendezvous with her in Toledo, where we'd rent a car and drive to the funeral home. I reserved a seat on a plane to Cleveland with a connecting flight to Toledo. My sister would be coming from Chicago, where she lived.

Chris held me all night. He could be warm and loving, when he wasn't subject to jealous rages.

The next morning at six A.M. I staggered out onto the nearly empty street and hailed the first driver. A Haitian who barely spoke English, he didn't know where he was going. He had no idea where the airport was. He was high on something. He wasn't on the highway headed for the airport but rather aimlessly and recklessly roaming the streets of Brooklyn. He looked so crazy that he resembled the devil in a bad Brazilian movie. When I saw another taxi, I leaped out and got into that car.

I missed my plane. All of my complicated feelings about my father's death fed into my anxiety about not missing the funeral. I reached my sister and worked out new plans, and eventually we made it to the funeral parlor. Our father seemed to have shrunk and to have been bathed in a white wax, like an expensive white eggplant that the greengrocer fears will go off.

My father's death had a much more powerful effect on me than my mother's many years later, possibly because I was on good terms with her and had supported her for a decade. My father, however, I'd rejected, just as I'd always felt he'd rejected me. I hadn't seen him for a decade except briefly a few months before he died when I was passing through Cincinnati.

When I saw him in that open coffin in that tawdry little funeral home, it seemed absurd that I'd ever attributed such satanic powers to him. Here he was, this tiny waxen doll, painted and somehow *reconfigured*. No wonder they had so many strong-smelling flowers; a distinct odor of rotting meat permeated the room.

I'd often wondered if I would have had a better understanding with my father if I'd been straight. When in 2003 my nephew wrote a book about my childhood, he interviewed a neighbor boy who said that Mr. White had been a wonderful man who'd introduced him to the Cincinnati Symphony by inviting him to concerts. Perhaps if I'd been straight and played softball with my dad, he would have liked me.

But if I'd been straight, I would have been an entirely different person. I would never have turned toward writing with a burning desire to confess, to understand, to justify myself in the eyes of others. If I'd been straight, I wouldn't have been impelled to live in New York and to choose the hard poverty of bohemia over the soft comfort of the business world. My father was disappointed because I didn't take over his business. He was embarrassed by my homosexuality.

Once he died, I began to see him more as the misanthropic bore he was rather than the sadist I'd conjured up. He was certainly the dullest man who ever lived—and he seemed half-dead even while he was still living. Before his death I had terrible dreams in the late seventies in which I was trapped inside a series of mummiform coffins that perfectly resembled me but that were inert. I feared that like my father I was already dead to the world, alive but contained within a frame that perfectly resembled me but that was larger and lifeless.

Chris had been an actor and was still a photographer, but he wanted to be a writer. During our three months in Key West he wrote the first page of a novella 156 times and never got beyond it. He was always angry and frustrated, balling up each rejected page as soon as he ripped it out of the typewriter. His cat was always escaping and going under the house in the crawl space, and Chris was always down there shouting at it. But Key West being a writers' colony, as soon as important people in the literary world came by, he was all smiles.

He earned his meager, meager living as the administrative assistant to Virgil Thomson, the composer. Born in 1896, Virgil was in his early eighties by then. He was dumpy and crabby and terribly deaf—a horrible sort of deafness for a composer that transposed some but not all notes a few intervals upward. People had to shout to get through to him, and a concert was torture for him. His usual solution to the babble and screech around him was to fall asleep. He'd doze off at the table unless addressed directly. Then he'd open his eyes and say mildly, "Yes, baby?" without missing a beat.

The formative influence in Virgil's life and career had been Gertrude Stein, with whom he'd written two operas. He said that as soon as he and Stein first met in Paris, they got along like two Harvard men. I'd seen *The Mother of Us All*, which is about Susan B. Anthony, not once but twice, first at Hunter College and once years later at the New York City Opera. When I first met him, Virgil was still licking his wounds after the failure of his first new opera in forty years, *Lord Byron*, a big conspicuous flop in 1972 at the Juilliard School in New York directed by John Houseman. The Metropolitan Opera had commissioned the work but never put it on. The *New York Times'* music critic had slammed it, calling it "cutesy" and complaining, "All those waltzes!" (Funny, no one ever made the same objection to *Der Rosenkavalier* or *A Little Night Music.*) The thumbs-down must have been particularly galling since Virgil himself had been the leading critic in New York for many years and had mastered the art of dismissing others, once calling Heifetz's ultraromantic playing of the violin "silk pajama music." Once I saw a staged production of another Stein text Virgil had set, *Capitals, Capitals*, in a small theater on the West Side, where it was teamed up with Erik Satie's *Socrate*. In the Satie, the Princess Yasmin Aga Khan, the daughter of Rita Hayworth, sang with a sweet, small voice.

Chris Cox worshipped Virgil in a nice friendly Southern boy-to-man way. Chris could be deferential without being cringing and was well-informed about every detail of Virgil's life, including the entire dramatis personae he'd accumulated over many years. Chris was anything but a silly chorus boy, but he did have the actor's view of life as essentially glamorous, and for him Virgil was the height of sophistication, genius—even history! Chris was sometimes irritated with me because of my big mouth. Once I said in his and Virgil's company, "Oh, God, that was the era before Balanchine found his way and they were still putting on terrible Americana things like *Filling Station*, this terrible ballet where—" Chris was violently kicking me under the table; Virgil had written the score, though luckily he was too deaf to have heard me. Another time Chris introduced me to Dominique Nabokov, soon after her husband, the composer Nicholas Nabokov (the writer's cousin), had died. I was so impressed with the Nabokov name that I chattered hysterically all evening though my shins were black-and-blue the next day. Chris knew the art of small talk, whereas all my talk was big and ponderous or at least gauche and self-serving.

Virgil was part of history since he'd studied with Nadia Boulanger in Paris, had first befriended Aaron Copland in the 1920s, and had taught orchestration to Ned Rorem, who'd been Virgil's copyist in the 1950s. Virgil was friendly with the French violinist Yvonne de Casa Fuerte and the composer Henri Sauguet and spoke of them often. To Chris, they were all household gods. Especially since he'd traveled to Paris with Virgil and been introduced to them and been invited to dinner by Mary McCarthy, who drew him aside to a window seat and chatted with him for a full twenty minutes (she was a diplomat's wife).

Virgil had a high, nasal voice and could deliver some real zingers with a deadpan expression. He called everyone "baby." When I was working on *A Boy's Own Story* in Key West, Virgil came to stay with Chris and me in a big, old-fashioned house with a porch and swings, a living room and a dining room, three bedrooms, and, in the huge garden, a grapefruit tree, an orange tree, and a plant producing tiny bananas. I gave Virgil the first chapter of my novel to read. He spent a day with it, then came shuffling out of his room and screeched, "As we say back in Missouri, baby, 'a lot of wash and not much hang-out.'" Another Southerner, by then my colleague at Columbia, Elizabeth Hardwick, damned my book by saying with a lilt and a dance step, "Ah don' know, honey, it's awfully 'I did it *myyy* way!'" In Virgil's case, I think his only idea of "gay literature" was pornography, and he was disappointed that my book was low on the peter meter.

I might not have had the courage to work on my novel if I hadn't been supported by my writers' group, the Violet Quill. The six or seven of us only met eight times over a year and a half, but the thought that other gay men of one's age and experience were waiting to read one's latest chapter gave me, at least, the strength to go on. I felt that in *States of Desire* I'd written about dozens of other gay men across the country, but now I wanted to write in depth about one child and adolescent: me. It seems hard to believe now but at the time almost no one had written a coming-out story, the tale that each of us told one another in bed as pillow talk. We'd all been telling that story for years and years and to us it seemed banal, but when written down, it seemed brand-new.

Virgil lived in the Chelsea Hotel in the original wood-paneled manager's suite. On the wall hung a large portrait of Virgil as a young man by Florine Stettheimer (she'd done the original cellophane sets for *Four Saints in Three Acts* in 1934 at the Wadsworth Atheneum in Hartford). Virgil was a simple but excellent cook. Chris would do the shopping and chopping, but Virgil knew how to bring it all together into a delicious dinner—a green salad, a tarragon chicken, a *purée de pommes de terre* (he couldn't just call it mashed potatoes), and a store-bought dessert. Virgil's lover of fifty years, Maurice Grosser, who painted blown-up Cézanne-inspired apples, was often in attendance. Though he was up in his late seventies, he still rode a motorcycle and Virgil said of him, admiringly, "He is the only man of my generation who can still undrape becomingly." Maurice was the oldest person I knew in the 1980s to die of AIDS, which was also a distinction. He was indisputably sexually active. Although Virgil seldom spoke of homosexuality, he had a darting eye and an asp's tongue and a nice sense of humor. Once when he asked me what a certain boy looked like, I said, "He has a charming body," and Virgil cracked up over the *charming* and said, "Not exactly the quality one looks for in a man's body." In Key West he would stay in his bedroom in bed all day long, harrumphing and making terrible sounds of eructation. Then at six thirty he'd emerge perfectly dressed in a seersucker suit and a bright yellow bow tie. He'd be shaking the cocktail shaker within seconds. One night we all three got terribly drunk and at a gay disco we sat in the garden, and Virgil, reeling with drink, told us that as a young man he'd been pursued by many virile men because of his beautiful ass. It was the toad recalling his days as a prince.

Chris was cataloging half a century's worth of saved letters, scores, program notes, reviews, photos, and memorabilia so that Virgil could sell the lot to Yale. The Beinecke Library there must doubly have valued Virgil's papers since it already possessed Gertrude Stein's archives—and even the armchair she mentions in the *Autobiography of Alice B. Toklas*, the very piece of furniture that Ezra Pound broke while hectoring Stein and Toklas with his theories and opinions. The chair was especially dear to the ladies because Alice had done the petit-point upholstery following a design Picasso had drawn directly onto the fabric for her. Pound's bad behavior led Stein to declare that he was a village explainer, which was all very well if one were a village but "if not, not."

Virgil invited Chris and me to dinner with Christopher Isherwood and his lover, the artist Don Bachardy. We were all big drinkers in those days and we were soon screaming with merriment. Isherwood was extremely approachable and unpretentious. I stayed friends with him and Don for years (Don and I are still friends). Chris Isherwood didn't like to receive letters since he had no time or inclination to answer them (he would have liked the e-mail era); he didn't mind if I called him, however. In fact he always picked up the phone eagerly. He had no hesitation about laughing if one became a bit pompous. I remember once calling him from Key West, where I was reading (in English—I hadn't yet learned French) Chateaubriand's *Mémoires*. I read Chris the closing pages over the phone, all about grabbing the Holy Cross and slowly descending into the tomb. I had tears in my eyes at the grandeur of it all, and

Chris burst into uncontrollable laughter. Later when I saw Keith McDermott in the stage adaptation of *A Meeting by the River*, Chris's novel about holy men in Asia, the monks were also laughing all the time, falling about with rocking *fous rires* . . . Laughter was an essential part of Chris's idea of sanctity. Back then I specially liked his exuberant irreverence because I had not yet become indifferent to religion. Now I shrug when the subject comes up, but then I still described myself as a "mystical atheist," as if I were at least impressed by piety—as if I thought it had a place in the world if not in mine. Now I have a Voltairean contempt for it, though Voltaire it seems was actually a pantheist. Isherwood's struggles to meditate and to embrace Vedanta were always amusingly credible. In the story "Paul" from *Down There on a Visit* he wrote in such a droll way about his efforts to sit in his Los Angeles apartment with a beautiful drug addict and meditate—neither of them could ever empty his mind of all thought. I flew out to Los Angeles several times to visit Chris and Don. Don drew me and years later had an intense session with my French lover, Hubert, who was already dying of AIDS. As Don drew Hubert's eyes, Hubert burst into tears. When Don drew the nose, Hubert's nose started running. When Don drew his mouth, Hubert vomited. To be sure, Hubert was already quite ill, but Don's intense scrutiny was like a witch doctor's way of exorcising devils.

Chris Cox and I invited Isherwood and Bachardy to my place for dinner the very next night after we met them that first time at Virgil's. I spent the whole hungover day buying the twelve kinds of fish necessary for Julia Child's recipe of marmite Dieppoise with its complex ivory sauce. It was a triumph and we all screamed with laughter till dawn. Now that I no longer drink, I wonder if I'm capable of such fierce, joyful abandon, such total immersion in the high tides of laughter and forgetting.

*     *     *

Chris Cox became almost pathologically jealous of me. I felt that he was actually envious of my slowly burgeoning and belated "career" (which precisely because it was just beginning, we could still imagine might truly blossom someday). It was easier, however, for him to say he was sexually and romantically jealous and possessive. I would leave his apartment and then walk into mine to hear the phone ringing. "Why did it take you twenty minutes to get home instead of fifteen? What were you doing? Did you duck into a doorway with some tall, dark, and handsome stranger? Come on, you can tell me. That's what happened, right?" I could hear him inhaling on his cigarette and blowing the smoke out of his nose like some condensed form of rage. "Huh? Is that what happened? Don't think I'm naïve. I know what a little slut you are. Just can't pass up a chance of getting fucked, can you?"

When I'd arrive at his loft, he'd embrace me tightly and I'd be flattered and moved until I realized he was sticking a hand down the back of my pants to see if my asshole was wet from just getting fucked. He'd push me away and say, "How many times you been fucked today, huh?" He'd be genuinely angry.

If it had been a sex game once a fortnight, I would have thought it was a turn-on, but as a constant presence in our lives, as if we were in a three-way marriage with his jealousy, it was an intolerable invasion of my sense of freedom. I'd been hopelessly in love with three men and I'd spent all my time suppressing my feelings of jealousy as uncivilized and in any event a fruitless expense of spirit. Now Chris was letting jealousy consume him completely, nor did he question his right to be jealous.

At first, after my years of being rejected by Keith McDermott, I was starved for even this pathological form of devotion. My shrink said that I had such low self-esteem that only a nutcase could send a strong enough signal to get through to me. But soon I resented

Chris's jealous interrogations and shakedowns, especially since I'd always been an apostle of promiscuity.

My new editor was Bill Whitehead at Dutton, a funny, handsome man who would die of AIDS at age forty-four in 1987. He developed a new paperback line and brought Chris to work for him as his assistant. Chris was perfect for the job—his meticulousness, his charm, his energy and devotion to Bill and his authors, his savviness about all the names in New York (that's what New Yorkiness is, primarily: the recognition of a thousand names and faces).

I had a difficult acquaintance, the Southern Gothic writer Coleman Dowell, whom Chris befriended. When gay men say in their personals, "No drama queens, please," they are trying to avoid someone like Coleman. He was from a poor family in Kentucky but lied and said he was rich and that his family owned Heaven Hill bourbon. What he didn't want to admit was that his psychiatrist lover, Bert, was supporting him. Cole wrote elaborately postmodernist novels with Chinese-box narrators, but they were all about spiteful people in positions of power double-dealing one another—or they were rural-Kentucky stories about a farmer cursed with a huge penis, a dick too big for any woman to handle (finally a teenage boy was able to take it all). Ludicrous as these stories were, no one quite saw them in all their pornographic absurdity since they were rendered with such dodgy modernist devices and in an opaque Faulknerian style.

I had first met Cole because the *New York Times Book Review* had asked me to review his *Island People*, probably his best book although it is so consumed with paranoia and spleen about real people (notably Carl Van Vechten, who'd had the ill luck to be Cole's mentor) that it is hard to read to the end. It lacks that key, embarrassing literary quality no one knows how to discuss: charm. I was baffled by such a complicated book, so uneven that it could be called a corduroy road to perdition, but even so I gave it a positive review, while expressing reservations about such highfalutin expressions as "she was an ennuyante of stature."

No matter. My qualified praise got me invited to dinner at Cole and Bert's Fifth Avenue apartment on the fifteenth floor looking down on Central Park and across to the Guggenheim Museum. Cole was a tall, nice-looking man wearing a big, fake-looking wig. Bert's wig was darker and more modest but not on quite right. The main sitting room was large and spacious with mirrors on one end catching the light pouring in through the plate-glass windows. The style was Hollywood Classic with matching upholstered white couches, white rugs, stagily spotlit paintings, a legion of high-backed dining-room chairs flanking a skinny medieval refectory table. It was all a bit theatrical and delightfully comfortable—and so much more luxurious than anything else Chris and I had ever seen that it awed us.

As did the food. Cole was a martyr cook. Since he never left the apartment except to swoop down on homeless black men in Central Park across the street for sex, he had the rest of his time to write, and to construct elaborate dinners that sometimes took three days to prepare. Cole would greet us at the door with dark circles under his eyes and exhaustion pinching his lips. Tammy was our "hostess," or at least that's how Cole conceived of his wienie dog. She was old and lame and an intelligent, seemingly normal dachshund, but Cole was enraptured with her and ascribed to her a whole bewildering range of gracious and malefic emotions. He would hurt her physically when she'd been "bad" (or he drunk and crazy), though she slept every night between Bert and Cole and had a wardrobe of diamonds and tiaras and furs that were contributed to a museum after her death. The writer Walter Abish, author of *How German Is It?*, made a terrible gaffe when in a note to Cole about matters literary he wrote, "P.S. Sorry to hear the dog died." Steam came issuing out of all of Cole's orifices. He trembled with rage when he said to me, "I hope his wife, Cecile, dies soon so I can write, 'P.S. Sorry to hear the woman died.' When I think how many times Tammy graciously received the Abishes here as their hostess!" Cole once told me that all his pleasant female characters had been based on Tammy. The unpleasant ones were based on Susan Sontag, whom he didn't know, though he was convinced that she had personally blocked every positive review he'd failed to receive and had engineered every rejection by every publisher. He knew she was plotting against him day and night because he'd written an attack on her in his novel *Mrs. October Was Here*, though he'd been careful to set it in "Tasmania, Ohio." Of course in real life Susan Sontag, Argus-eyed as she was, had never seen a mention of Coleman Dowell. But Cole needed an enemy, and it helped if he or she was Jewish, as were Sontag, Abish, and Bert, Cole's lover. Cole was wildly and self-defeatingly anti-Semitic, since he was kept by a sweet, patient Jew and all his literary friends were either Jewish or quite conventionally politically correct—and New York had the second-largest concentration of Jews in the world after Israel (two million versus five million). And of course the whole cultural life of New York in which Cole aspired, everything from music to literature to scholarship, was markedly influenced by Jews. Nor was Cole's anti-Semitism actually based on anything other than a desire to shock and to be "interesting," and I suppose it was meant to figure as a declaration of independence from his endlessly indulgent lover.

Most literary writers in the second half of the twentieth century felt wronged, neglected, conspired against, but Cole was one of the few who railed without cease against his Job-like fate. Maybe because his mental literary map starred Tennessee Williams and Truman Capote, he imagined that he, too, should be on the cover of *Time*. Maybe because he'd been on television in his twenties as a performer and was used to big audiences and street-recognition fame, he found sales figures of his books in the hundreds instead of the hundreds of thousands cruel and lamentable. Lament he did, all the time.

When I first met Coleman in 1974, I was still drinking heavily and as a consequence was constantly feeling guilty. I couldn't remember what I'd said or done or shouted the night before—and this made me a receptive friend for Cole and an open ear for his complaints. Because I was timid, I'd written a mostly enthusiastic review of a book I didn't like all that much but that I was afraid to condemn. Why hurt an author who was unknown? And what if it turned out to be an important book? A single review in the Sunday *New York Times* could make or break a reputation. I'd already suffered the consequences of bad reviews in it through low sales, pitying looks from friends, low advances on the next book.

Now if I dislike a book I'm asked to review, I send it back to the newspaper or magazine, but back then I was so thrilled to be asked by anyone to review something that I hesitated to reject the golden offering. None of us was natural in the face of power, of absolute literary power; we were all cringing courtiers, I less than most writers.

But my cowardice that led to overpraising a confused and irritating novel saddled me with a long and painful friendship. Cole would get very drunk late at night (me, too) and he'd bring up the reservations I'd expressed in my review—what's wrong with saying "ennuyante of stature"?—and he'd speak with real venom. There was always a trace of anger and resentment against me—and that kept me so intimidated that I was always eager to prove to him my devotion. Chris Cox and I even agreed to be his agents representing his novel *White on Black on White*. Cole was furious with New Directions for not having sufficiently promoted his earlier works and quit James Laughlin, who was truly devoted to Cole's writing, to search out a new editor. Of course he didn't understand that

Laughlin, mentally unstable himself, was that rarest of things, a loyal and disinterested literary editor. Nor did Cole know how to go about finding a new publisher. Since Chris was by now working in publishing and I had a few contacts, we sent his book around everywhere, with no success. I thought it would be a natural for publication since it dealt with race and sex, the two great American obsessions. But no one wanted it—again the Chinese-box problem and the lack of charm. Finally another friend enlisted the help of the Countryman Press, a tiny house with a minuscule list. The book garnered far less attention than it would have if New Directions had done it—and far less than it deserved.

Dowell jumped to his death on August 3, 1985. We'd all seen it coming. Cole talked about it endlessly, and when Bert visited me in Paris a few weeks before it happened, I asked him if he was prepared for such a gruesome eventuality. We were all horrified and frightened—it seemed something we could all be tempted to do. We wondered if he had AIDS and was too embarrassed to admit it or afraid of the long, slow, painful death. Or we heard that he'd "dropped a dime" on a black prison lover on parole—planted drugs on him and tipped off the police that a man on parole was "holding," as revenge for the guy's infidelity. Or maybe, as he said, he was afraid of aging and losing his "beauty."

If many of the people I knew in New York in the seventies were twisted or paranoid or even evil, we all agreed one was a saint: Joe Brainard. Joe was a writer and visual artist from Oklahoma who stuttered and spelled erratically and was so timid that he danced in place, looking down, if he thought anyone was paying attention to him. Someone had once complimented him on his chest so he always wore his shirt open to the waist, even in subarctic winter weather.

I had a few dates with him and he'd always bring a notepad to dinner. He was too shy to converse normally so he'd write something down and pass the pad and wait for a written answer. It was a bit like being someone who couldn't sign and dining with a deaf person who couldn't read lips. Sometimes he'd look directly at me with a warm regard, but a moment later he'd be looking up at the ceiling, like a bad actor miming innocence and whistling.

He'd grown up middle-class but poor, and when he got to New York, he'd lived in the East Village and eaten out of garbage cans. Kenward Elmslie, the poet and an heir to the Pulitzer fortune, took him up and they were lifelong lovers. More than once I've heard inexperienced people say that the days of being kept are over, that now no one is a Balzacian hero who comes to the capital and finds a protector, but in fact that scenario happens as often as it probably ever did. It's just that only very rich people can afford to do that and one doesn't encounter many of them. And today neither the kept boy nor the older man owns up easily to his role.

No one could have been less on the make than Joe. With the stocks he'd been given he earned extremely large sums every quarter, but he converted everything into cash and put the money in a large drawer. He'd fish out a thousand dollars and ask seriously if that would be enough for dinner. He was usually stoned by dinnertime. He always paid.

He lived in a big loft that was just two huge rooms on Greene Street. In the backroom were hundreds of boxes full of materials he might someday assemble into collages. The front room had a sitting area and a mattress on the floor and a radio tuned day and night to a country-and-western station. Joe worked his way through one mammoth Victorian novel after another. At two in the morning he'd finish *Middlemarch* and start *The Way We Live Now*. He seldom said much about them except that they were good or that he'd liked them. Or he'd say, "What about that Dorothea!" and smile his big goofy smile.

In the late sixties and early seventies he'd been a speed freak, which had enabled him to do hundreds and hundreds of tiny collages. When I knew him, he still did book covers for his friends Ron Padgett and John Ashbery and Kenward Elmslie. He'd also over the years done lots of hilarious variations on the comic-strip character Nancy. Perhaps he was best known for his book *I Remember*, in which he just listed all the things he could remember—the ultimate dandy's book since the method of a dandy is to level all hierarchies and replace all normal value systems with the arbitrariness of taste and personality.

Typically, the book read:

I remember fishnet.
I remember board and brick bookshelves.
I remember driving in cars and doing landscape paintings in my
    head (I still do that).

Joe had long been a friend of Warhol's and had even anticipated Pop Art in an early painting called *7-Up*, abandoning that approach when he saw Andy's work. He collaborated with Jasper Johns on a painting. His favorite work, however, was drawing. He would draw Kenward's beautiful dog Whippoorwill or his own foot, or he would draw a boy's legs in athletic socks or a sleeping nude man. His work was either cool and insouciant Americana or it was funny. He seldom painted, but when he did, the results were highly original and convincing. Once he did a parody of Wyeth's painting by showing Whippoorwill dragging his long white body across the grass toward a house.

Joe would spend every summer in Calais, Vermont, with Kenward. During the summer months we'd all receive letters from Joe in his big, bold script spelling out what he was reading (*Great Expectations*, *Portrait of a Lady*) and gossip about who'd come to stay.

In the midst of this very regular life (reading, dinners out in fancy restaurants, very occasional tricks, constant country-and-western music, summers in Vermont), Joe fell violently in love with my old love Keith McDermott. Keith had moved back to New York after several years away in Los Angeles. I had slept with Joe a few times but it hadn't really worked out in bed. Now Joe was overwhelmed by Keith's looks. Whenever Keith would appear in a play, Joe would deluge him with roses. Joe was a romantic man in the most old-fashioned way, and Keith responded to the lavish treatment. Keith was also very attracted to Joe. Keith had always liked eccentrics and bohemians. With his Armani suits and vast resources of cash and his becalmed, unproductive days and nights after so many years of amphetamine-driven work, Joe appealed to Keith's horror of the middle class and his yearning for the unusual.

Perhaps their affair started because each was the other's ideal. Keith was the small, hairless, perfectly knit young man with a gymnast's body and regular features—someone who'd stepped right out of one of Joe's drawings. Joe was warm and lovable and unlike anyone else.

When the English TV series *Brideshead Revisited* was being shown, we friends took turns hosting for an episode, each cooking his best dish when it came time. Joe had no idea how to cook so he had the most expensive caviar and chocolates catered.

Joe was certainly sweet and disinterested—we called him Prince Myshkin. Later, when he had to die of AIDS at a young age, he became bitter, understandably. I'm glad I didn't have to witness that last phase of his life.

# Chapter 17

I don't remember how I met Richard Sennett, but dozens of roads led to the intellectual and social Rome that he represented. Dick was a professor of sociology at New York University and had written several remarkable books, including *The Hidden Injuries of Class* and *The Fall of Public Man*. He was a well-known professor and sought-after lecturer. He was also an odd combination of schoolboy nerd, flamboyant queen, and Mrs. Astor, in that he loved ideas and intellectuals and enjoyed prancing about in drag, though that was just a phase, and he entertained with charm and tirelessness in his little house on Washington Mews, a brick-paved lane just off Washington Square. The old New York Henry James gentry had lived in the big town houses on the square in the nineteenth century, and the stables and servants' quarters had been lodged behind along the mews, except they'd been converted to artists' studios since at least the early 1900s when cars had replaced carriages. Any sort of gracious, historic, private living space was so unusual in New York that even converted stables seemed to us the height of civilized luxury. Washington Mews and the matching MacDougal Alley across Fifth Avenue were the best addresses in Manhattan. In Philadelphia they would have been just two of dozens and dozens of quiet streets lined with brick town houses, gas lamps, and hundred-year-old trees. In London they would have been beneath notice.

Dick had been married twice before I knew him—and he would later marry a third time, to the lighthearted but formidable Dutch-born economist Saskia Sassen. In the late 1970s and early eighties when we were first friends, however, he was trying to be gay, though without much success. Maybe he was a bit bisexual, but his swooning over beautiful boys seemed more dutiful than instinctual. Dick courted one tall, powerfully built young man with black, curling hair and red, curling lips and thick, muscular legs and huge black eyes, who seemed to love Dick in his anguished way, but I doubt whether their love was satisfying to either of them.

Dick mainly liked to entertain, but not just anyone. At his house on the mews you could meet Isaiah Berlin or Michel Foucault or Susan Sontag or Jürgen Habermas or Alfred Brendel. Like most intellectuals, these men and the occasional woman didn't want to make engagements far in advance—not in the usual busy-busy New York fashion. They never knew when inspiration might strike, and besides, socializing wasn't part of their idea of themselves. They weren't the sort of frivolous (or conventional) creatures who knew what they would be doing a week from Thursday. But since they were apt to get lonely like anyone else, especially after dark on a cold February night, they could always drift over to Dick's house, where it was okay just to ring the bell. Whereas most New Yorkers were barricaded in their apartments and could be seen only by carefully arranged appointment like ministers of state, and then only after two cancellations and three postponements and a change of meeting place, Dick was always available. He was at home downstairs cooking in his modern, roomy kitchen or upstairs entertaining in his atelier-like living room with its skylights and vast airy ceilings and its grand piano. He might be scraping away at his cello while Brendel played the piano part. Or people of every sort, many of them Europeans, might be sitting on the big, deep couch and in the comfy armchairs chatting away. One of his favorites was Diana

Trilling, who was already seventy-five then and a big, lively woman with her hair pulled up in a hennaed bun, her dresses full and plain but her opinions sharp and her interest in everyone around her even more acute.

I can remember sitting beside Janet Hobhouse, the novelist, when Trilling looked up and said, "Who is this young man entering the room like a prince out of a Turgenev novel?" It was Vladimir de Marsano, my pal from Venice. "In fact he is a half-Serb, half-Italian aristocrat," I said, "and he's going to be in one of my novels." Vladimir came over with his wonderful slightly crooked smile and unflinching but kind eyes and the slight asymmetry of his pugilist's nose, as if the head of a classical statue had been copied in wax and then squeezed ever so slightly to one side. Mainly he was a high-spirited but impeccably well-mannered kid, and he did carry himself with the elegance and lightness of a Slavic prince. He had a way of standing close, as if he understood that with every quarter inch of increased proximity he was jacking up his magnetism exponentially. He knew everyone wanted to kiss him. He didn't want to kiss people back, but he did like having that kind of power over us.

He had a tougher, bigger blond man with him, a South African student. It seemed they were devoting most of their time to the disco of the moment, Studio 54. I'd never gone there but apparently the owner, Steve Rubell, let in both beautiful nobodies and celebrities of any sort. In New York Vladimir must have been a beautiful nobody, though to old Venetians such as David and me he was mythical. Vladimir jokingly complained that he and his blond beast of a friend were so inseparable that people imagined they must be lovers. He seemed genuinely proud of the imputation— and perhaps of the reality.

Studio 54 had a giant, smiling man in the moon up above the dancers slowly shoveling a spoon of cocaine toward his nose, over and over. This was still when many acquaintances assured me that cocaine was harmless and not addictive. People joked that it was the perfect yuppie drug since it made your head clearer and inspired you to want to work even more.

Dick Sennett's salon was far from the Studio, though no less exclusive in its way. Dick was an ambitious if hit-and-miss cook, and he could often be found concocting a complicated dish out of the latest cookbook—something he would serve informally.

But no one paid much attention to the food or the liberal lashings of plonk. It was all a plush background for the startling mondaine reality in the frame: the good talk and the promise of even better talk. Dick knew not to quiz the great about their Subjects, their Accomplishments, but rather to tease them about their secret Vices, their hidden Charms, their unheralded powers of Seduction. He was always grabbing the hoary hand of a grizzled Oxford don and saying, "Oh, what a naughty pussycat you are! Aren't you? Aren't you? Such evil, evil naughty thoughts—and Deeds! Yes, Deeds, Mr. Pussy-Boy. Okay, everyone, à table, à table, and remember: Paws up!" No one quite knew what *paws up* meant, but it sounded like a cross between an eating-club slogan and a half-forgotten piece of nursery (or else Masonic) mummery. All these lonely intellectuals, their eyes hollowed out from years of reading microfiches and medieval script, their voices hoarse from gabbling to themselves over tinned beans and Bovril in unheated Rooms, were now being stroked and feted and fed. They were like feral cats being tickled behind the ears for the first time. They were purring, though still looking around anxiously for the next boot in the rear, the next nasty review by a rival in the *Times Literary Supplement*. Nor did Dick invite just the old and famous. He knew they needed young and lovely nobodies to make a fuss over them. Given the average age in the room, anyone under fifty counted as young.

Dick was what the French call a *mythomane*, which involved a flexible and always entertaining approach to the truth, which he never twisted to his advantage. He wasn't trying to impress anyone or get ahead with his tall stories. No, he was just daydreaming out loud, expanding the narrow repertory of the actual, adding a herbaceous border of the imaginary to the dull gravel path of the real. His mythomania could also be a form of nearly oriental politeness. For instance, he met Susan Sontag and Joseph Brodsky at nearly the same moment. To Susan he said that he, like her, had just survived a serious cancer, whereas to Joseph he said that like him he'd just had a nearly fatal heart attack. No one much minded when the truth came out that Dick was in perfect health, both in the past and the present. People just smiled a bit sheepishly and shrugged. No harm done . . .

I heard three versions of his childhood from him. Once he was raised by socialists on Chicago's South Side. Once his parents were a "radical" lesbian pair in Minnesota. And once, when we were strolling through the Île St.-Louis in Paris, I said, "Isn't this the most beautiful perfect place?" and he said, "I'm so glad you like it. I was raised here by my French aunts as a child just after the war," and he vaguely waved toward a darkened *hôtel particulier* along the Quai de Bethune. But why, if he'd grown up there, did he grope for words in French and have such an incomprehensible accent?

Then there were all the different versions of why he was no longer a concert cellist—his paralyzed hand was one. But it wasn't paralyzed. Another was the time he'd vomited into his cello. But why did he play so many wrong notes, even though he had a scarily professional way of freezing his face and breathing through his stiffened nostrils as if he were a Japanese temple-guardian devil or a Dostoyevsky character on the verge of an attack? Dick loved music and he enjoyed concertizing, though it was all pretty hard on the ears. And, hey, does the cello have a hole large enough to vomit into? I think it has just two narrow S-curves on either side of the strings.

But who were we to complain? Dick provided us all with lots of good stories and half our conversation was devoted to his latest inventions and his most notable outrages. Did I tell you about how even though he was nearly bald and the fringe was all gray he tossed back an imaginary braid and exclaimed, "Well, as a blonde . . ."? Or did I tell you about last night at dinner when he came down the stairs in a little pink dress with shoulder straps, though his shoulders are horribly hairy? And then he changed midmeal to the little black dress? He obviously was nostalgic for the eighteenth century when public acts had been expressive, similar to acts of artistic invention. People are still telling Dick Sennett stories. Just recently, some twenty years later, I met someone who claimed he'd advised Dick on his wardrobe during the drag epoch.

He was wonderfully encouraging as a friend. He hired me to be the executive director of the New York Institute for the Humanities even though I was only marginally an academic and had never been an administrator, except briefly at *Saturday Review*. The part-time job paid me just twenty-two thousand dollars a year—and my main duty was getting everyone coffee and telling Dick Sennett stories. In many ways, however, I was a good choice. I liked most people, I wanted to know all about their scholarly pursuits, I was even-tempered, and I had a small reputation as a writer. I was teaching a fiction workshop or two at Columbia and another one at New York University. I had a low rent and few expenses.

Dick did everything to encourage me. When I wrote a play, a fairly tedious one, he decided we should give it a reading at the institute. Val Kilmer, at that point a young, unknown actor, agreed to read the young lover. In real life Kilmer's lover was then reputedly the much older Cher, who would wait for him outside the door in her limo every evening after rehearsals. No fool Cher—she wasn't about to let this treasure (a drool-makingly young, masculine heterosexual beauty) escape from her. The other actors were Bob Gottlieb's wife,

Maria Tucci, and David Warrilow, one of the leading interpreters of Samuel Beckett. Later I would see him perform in French in Paris, and no one there would believe he wasn't born French, so perfect was his accent. He told me that he'd so hated being English that he'd "acted" his way into being a French actor with total conviction. He had a brief movie career in *Barton Fink* and *The Last Days of Immanuel Kant*, but he was too depressed and drank too heavily to be a Hollywood actor. Maria Tucci, whose father was Niccolò Tucci, the Swiss-Italian writer, had had to sacrifice her acting career because of a sick child, but eventually she returned to the stage—and to television in *Law & Order*.

Dick took me seriously at a time when almost no one else did. I'd brought Patrick Merla to the institute and Dick put him in charge of the W. H. Auden festival that lasted for several days. Patrick, who'd never attended a university, knew more about everything than the rest of us put together and was an excellent poet. The institute gave glamorous parties as book launches for its members. But what it mainly did was hold once-a-week lunches in the Deutsches Haus just next door to Dick's own mews house. Visitors from all over the world presented their latest thoughts and findings in an informal, collegial way, and the question-and-answer periods following the brief talks were as stimulating as any I ever attended.

We invited Borges to come to New York. He and his companion, Maria Kodama (later his wife), had to fly first-class, of course, from Buenos Aires, and we arranged for them to stay in a beautiful NYU apartment looking down over Washington Square. The only drawback was lack of room service. Maria Kodama called me on a Sunday afternoon and asked, "Who will wash out Borges's underthings?" I thought to volunteer my own services but I was afraid of embarrassing everyone. Finally I had to hire a maid at a hundred dollars an hour to go over there on Sunday evening and wash out the distinguished panties.

Borges gave a talk, one of the two talks he gave everywhere all the time with no variation. There was an overflow crowd of admiring students, so many that his voice had to be piped out to the sidewalk where hundreds more were gathered and listened reverently. This talk was his one on how the best metaphors are clichés because they're true: Life Is a Dream and Time Is a River, and any effort to invent newer, fresher images is false and misleading. No one paid much attention to what he was saying. He was iconic because he'd written a half-dozen brain-twisting stories of an admirable lightness in the late 1930s and early 1940s, stories that tapped the urbane tone of G. K. Chesterton and other Edwardian writers of his youth, authors his Scottish grandmother had read to him in Argentina so long ago. Now all these years later he was invited everywhere because of these few brilliant stories that few people in the audience would have read, much less understood. Wherever he went, he talked about dead metaphors being the best ones. Right after he left us he went up to Cornell for a Nabokov festival. There he admitted he'd never read Nabokov, but he did have this little speech about dead metaphors he could deliver. I read the clippings from various local papers as he made his way across America. In each city he gave the same lecture about the beauty and rightness of dead metaphors. I suppose I'd never before witnessed up close such a huge career nor noticed how his was based on such a slim oeuvre written four decades previously.

While he was still in New York, a ritzy Hispanic society gave a banquet in his honor on Park Avenue. I was seated next to Borges, and all through the meal he kept asking me to tell him all the latest dirty words in English. Since he was blind, he couldn't see the snowy-haired matrons of the Cervantes Club or whatever it was called bending their heads closer to catch the drift of the great man's conversation ... Luisa Valenzuela, the Argentine novelist, was a member of the institute. She told us that she thought of Borges, with whom she'd collaborated, as a big, unformed baby who'd been coddled by his mother and then married off to a young wife soon after his mother's death—though I thought of Maria Kodama as more a child than a mother substitute.

The institute had one seminar that trailed on for years on sex and consumerism. Broadly speaking, we were all interested in those days in how culture and especially material culture interacted with economic and class pressures and the conflicts generated by the gender divide. Now these connections are familiar and throw off fewer sparks, but back then we were reading Gramsci and members of the Frankfurt School and the Roland Barthes of the *Mythologies* and the Foucault of *Madness and Civilization* because we were no longer Marxists and we no longer believed in the determining role of class warfare, but we still thought that the world around us had hidden patterns to be traced, particularly in the underlying culture, not just economics. The sex and consumerism seminar could become heated and certainly heterodox.

I would dart around making people coffee, printing up programs, fussing over the schedules and budgets and room assignments, but I enjoyed dropping in on the biography seminar of Aileen Ward, the Keats scholar, or chatting with John Guare, the playwright who'd written *Six Degrees of Separation* and was the most tireless culture vulture I'd ever known. Barbara Ehrenreich, who would later become famous for *Nickel and Dimed*, her book about living for a year as a minimum-wage earner, was concerned with social issues in a familiar left-wing way, as was Todd Gitlin, an expert on the New Left during the 1960s. Doug Ireland was the most outspoken Leftist in our midst. He was a big, lumbering man with a broken voice whose body was constantly racked with pain. His parents, Christian Scientists, had not allowed him to be inoculated against polio, and he was one of the last kids to contract the disease in the 1950s. Perhaps not coincidentally, Doug became a militant atheist. He wrote regularly for the *Village Voice*, which back then was still a genuine alternative newspaper of some interest. Doug lived in France for a decade and befriended the charismatic French novelist and gay liberationist Guy Hocquenghem, who wrote the first book ever anywhere of queer theory, *Homosexual Desire* (1972), and codirected with his lover Lionel Soukaz an early film about the history of homosexuality, *Race d'Ep*. I used to sit around in rooms in Paris full of hashish smoke and talk to Doug and Guy with his strange beauty, pale and precise as if carved out of ivory, and the philosopher René Schérer (with whom Guy wrote a last book, *The Atomic Heart*).

Back in the days of the institute Doug was living in his office. He'd hang up underthings to dry in the small room and had a hot plate for cooking eggs. Dick Sennett was always in a bit of a rage against Doug for breaking the rules and posing a fire hazard, but he respected Doug's militancy and was intimidated by his mocking self-assurance. At that time, just at the end of the 1970s, the whole country, and New York along with it, was shifting to the right. In the 1960s and early 1970s anyone who held the most extreme Leftist views automatically won the argument, but now middle-class intellectuals, with their tenure and co-op apartments, were beginning to rebel against this tyranny of firebrand rhetoric. In a sense the potential battle between Doug Ireland and Dick Sennett (a battle that was never openly expressed) was an emblem of this troubled and troubling shift. But don't get me wrong—we all liked Doug, who was generous in a sort of reckless, almost indifferent way, and who laughed at all our sacred cows.

# Chapter 18

The biggest star at the New York Institute for the Humanities was Susan Sontag. I think I must have met her at Dick Sennett's house. At least I imagine I fell into a conversation with her, she who had been my idol for many years. It's strange that I can't remember our first meeting since I can remember in vivid detail reading her essay on pornography when it first came out and agreeing and disagreeing with it in such an intense way. I read it because it addressed thoughts I'd had for years but not known how to formulate. Reading the essay on camp was the same gripping experience. To be sure, Isherwood in one of his novels, *The World in the Evening*, had mentioned camp (high and low), but Sontag thoroughly explored the subject and saw it as a way of rescuing failed glamour—"so bad it's good"—and putting the world in quotation marks, of aestheticizing all experience. Everyone, even *Time* magazine, grabbed on to "Notes on Camp" as a kind of parlor game, the exploitation of a vogue word, the pinpointing of a new sensibility. Sontag, as I learned later, had been influenced by a friend from her Paris days, the American film expert Elliott Stein: a gay man famous for his whip collection. Stein helped her trace the contours of this unfamiliar aesthetic. I'd known about a louder, brasher street version of camp—one drag queen would shriek at another, "Stop camping, bitch!" I hadn't really encountered this other sensibility, which was funny and seemed to have mainly to do with old movies and preposterous divas. What became clear in reading and talking to Sontag was that she wrote best about subjects she was most ambiguous about. Campiness both attracted and repelled her. Indeed her whole personality was based on this same push-pull dynamic. After we became friends I once told her I wanted to write a book about her called *The Dandy and the Rabbi*, since I felt that around aesthetes she became moralistic and around moralists she embraced art and frivolity. With her characteristic anti-Semitism she murmured, "It might be better to call it *The Dandy and the Priest*."

No, it wasn't that she was particularly anti-Semitic, but rather that she was opposed to anything that wasn't "central to our culture," as she would have put it. She was like Proust, who in his novel preferred to present himself in the form of Marcel, his narrative alter ego, as Catholic instead of Jewish. Anything offbeat—homosexuality, Judaism, being African-American—she disapproved of. She was a universalist in the true French sense, believing that Man at his best was an abstract individual in the eyes of the state, the law, humanity itself. To the degree that that abstraction was qualified (female, homosexual, black, Jewish), it was reduced. The French believed fervently in universalism, and Sontag was more passionately a Francophile than she was American.

But then again she was also just a bit anti-Semitic and homophobic. She once told the African-American novelist and essayist Darryl Pinckney that he was "reducing" his stature as a writer by calling himself a black writer. She asked me how I could bear to be considered a gay writer. Her questions were meant to guide the people she cared about, Darryl and me among others, away from our own "narrowing" labels. And it's perfectly true that she maintained world-class status partly by staying in the closet.

Toward the end of her life she told Brendan Lemon, then the editor of *Out* magazine:

I grew up in a time when the modus operandi was the "open secret." I'm used to that, and quite okay with it. Intellectually, I know why I haven't spoken more about my sexuality, but I do wonder if I haven't repressed something there to my detriment. Maybe I could have given comfort to some people if I had dealt with the subject of my private sexuality more, but it's never been my prime mission to give comfort, unless somebody's in drastic need. I'd rather give pleasure, or shake things up.

Soon after I met Susan I started hanging out with her. Other people have described how going out in public with her was like being seen with royalty. By and large New Yorkers were too discreet to bother her, but they did recognize her, especially at cultural events—at the ballet, at movies, at lectures. Phillip Lopate in his *Notes on Sontag* talks about how she'd stroll about in front of a movie audience before the lights went down, supposedly looking for someone but—in his opinion—making sure that everyone was aware of her presence. On the other hand, Susan didn't like people to refer to their friendship with her in print. I remember that the talented, if bitter, writer Gary Indiana, who wrote about heroin in a powerful novel of the period called *Horse Crazy*, remarked in the *Village Voice* that Sontag knew all the best Chinese restaurants in Manhattan—and for that one indiscretion he was banished from court. It was a bit like socializing with Prince Charles, I suppose. I've known writers and actors who've spent weekends with him but they never refer to it in print.

She liked to come to my little one-room apartment for dinner if other amusing people were there. Once I had her with Robert Mapplethorpe and the female bodybuilder Lisa Lyon, the subject of Mapplethorpe's book *Lady*. Lyon wasn't a freak or carnival performer but rather someone who exhibited her remarkable body in the art world, at galleries and museums. She was educated and well-spoken, and when she was wearing a simple black dress with sleeves and a full bodice, she didn't even look muscular. But there at the table (she was a good sport) she pushed her sleeves back and made a muscle. We all had to touch the huge, hard mound—she was impressive. For a while Mapplethorpe wanted to marry her.

Susan felt relaxed around David Kalstone, who was a born courtier without ever being obsequious. Perhaps my best plum was Fran Lebowitz, the comic writer, who kept us sick with laughter with her constant, dry drolleries. Fran, who was wildly famous at the time, had written a blurb for my *States of Desire*. Though she dressed in men's clothes, she, too, almost never spoke about her lesbianism—certainly not in public. Later she became a sort of court jester—no, that's mean, perhaps "funny companion"—to different rich gay or bisexual men such as Malcolm Forbes and Barry Diller and David Geffen. Forbes had a château in Normandy where he had hot-air-balloon races. While the men were swooping around outside competing, their wives were doing their nails inside and responding with various degrees of interest to Fran's advances. When I wrote a magazine article about David Geffen, one of Hollywood's biggest moguls and art collectors, Fran gave me some great quotes about how Geffen and Barry Diller, owner of QVC, the shopping channel, among other things, would quarrel on the yacht over who was first in line to read the one copy of Jack Warner's biography. Perhaps Geffen quietly settled the dispute by being the one who'd bought the Warner house, one of the grandest mansions in Los Angeles.

Susan and Fran started going to fashion shows together, and Susan's appearance at such frivolous events was noteworthy enough to make the gossip columns. America's leading female intellectual checks out the new spring frocks—that was the sort of headlines she was getting. Then suddenly they seemed to have a falling-out. What had happened? Had Fran finally put the make on Susan?

Did Susan refuse to put out? We never knew. Fran herself, though always polite, seemed less friendly around me.

Susan's closest friend was her son, David Rieff. For two years he and I were virtually inseparable and I was very, very fond of him. He had grown up with "gay uncles" such as Richard Howard and Jasper Johns, and I seemed to be falling into the familiar mode of the queer avuncular, though in my mind we were something more like cousins. David could be as contemptuous of other people as his mother was, but for the most part he seemed admiring and vulnerable and just a bit of a puppy dog. He had his mother's strong features and long hair and sometimes was mistaken for her, though he disapproved of being introduced as Susan Sontag's son. He seemed more amazed by my coarseness than to be genuinely reprimanding the one time I made this mistake out of social anxiety. But soon afterward I heard him phone in a reservation at a tony Manhattan restaurant under the name David Sontag instead of David Rieff. I suppose the dependents of famous people always face that dilemma and shift about according to the occasion. Once Jackson Pollock's widow upbraided me for introducing her as Lee Pollock, though when I was presenting her to another celebrity, I was careful to call her Lee Krasner and she chimed in simultaneously with "Pollock."

David attributed more savoir vivre to me than I really possessed and would often greet my innocent remarks with a sly or knowing smile. He had an affair with Mariana Cook, a photographer who became a friend of mine. Then he fell for Sarah, a complex blond beauty who was the daughter of Peter Matthiessen, the American naturalist and novelist. Matthiessen was some sort of Zen master who'd built a meditation pavilion in his garden, but she made him sound cruel and conceited. His uncle had been F. O. Matthiessen, the famous homosexual Harvard professor who wrote *American Renaissance*, about Emerson and Whitman—and who committed suicide by jumping from a window in 1950. Sarah complained that her father wouldn't allow the uncle's name to be mentioned in his presence, but I have no idea if that was true. Sarah seemed high-strung but was so WASP that David doted on her.

Jamaica Kincaid was a friend of ours in those exciting days—a tall black woman with a much smaller husband, the composer Allen Shawn, brother of the actor and playwright Wally Shawn, and they were of course the sons of the longtime *New Yorker* editor William Shawn. When I ran into Jamaica recently after two decades of not seeing her, I asked timidly, "Do you remember me?" and she overwhelmed me by saying, "Of course I remember you—those were some of the happiest days of my life!"

They were happy days for me, too. David was *attachant* and dear. Susan could be impossibly vain and imperious, but she was also protective and generous. She wrote a blurb for my breakthrough novel, *A Boy's Own Story*, which she did in her usual serious, thorough, time-consuming way. Just to write a few lines she felt she had to reread all three of my novels as well as *States of Desire*. She put me up for a seven-thousand-dollar prize at the American Academy of Arts and Letters, which I won, and wrote a letter of recommendation for a twenty-thousand-dollar Guggenheim Fellowship, which I received. After *A Boy's Own Story* came out she said, "You'll never be poor again in your life." And though I've often had to scramble to pay the rent, what she said was true—I was never really desperate again.

I liked to cook for Susan, though I lived so far from the nearest good supermarket, Balducci's, that I wore myself out carrying groceries through the streets. My menus were also so elaborate that I spent too much money buying all those bay scallops and veal cutlets and devoted too many hours to preparing my heavily sauced dishes. Later, after I lived in France, I realized that I could serve much simpler meals—in fact, my heroic dinners of the pre-Paris days were in dubious taste. I'd spend twelve hours preparing a *coulibiac* (salmon with mushrooms and rice in a dill-and-sour-cream sauce inside puff pastry), or *boeuf à la mode,* or a dozen Indian dishes. Like Coleman Dowell, I, too, had become a martyr cook, though on a lesser scale. For me the dinner party was a condensed version of social climbing, intimacy, and commemoration.

For Susan all these themes would coalesce into a lunch at a Chinese restaurant. Years later, after I'd broken with Susan, Marina Warner told me that during a visit to New York she'd met Susan and that I was wrong, she was a delight, no one could be warmer or kinder. I was quick to agree with Marina but I astonished her when I said, "But I'll tell you exactly how you spent your time with her. She invited you to a good Chinese restaurant and ordered for you and paid for it. Then she accompanied you to several bookshops and expressed her scandalized amazement that you'd never read Trelawney's *Adventures of a Younger Son* or Aksakov's *Family Chronicle*. She bought those books for you and gave them to you in a nice little ceremonious moment. During the unrushed afternoon she talked to you about her struggle with cancer and her love affairs—five women and four men." Marina's jaw dropped and I said, "It's perfectly sincere, but that's the day with Susan. Always the same."

I realized from my own experience that buying the meal, visiting the bookshop, offering the "life-changing" books—all of those rituals had originated with Richard Howard. Susan must have learned to do all those things from him. Like Richard, Susan was a nonacademic intellectual, given to pronouncements, alternately tender and imperious, wildly generous. (True academics never buy meals for each other but split every bill down to the last centime.) Like Richard, Susan knew everything about everything, though neither of them owned a television. She, however, true to her adopted French heritage, knew a lot about the movies (French people are always surprised by how shallow my own "film culture" is, not to mention my nearly nonexistent jazz culture). Susan had first made her reputation by talking about movies seriously, and by directing movies. But she never wrote about the Beatles or *The Beverly Hillbillies*. Her taste was more inclined toward Godard and Syberberg. Despite her early notoriety as an iconoclast, she was serious, even reverential, in her respect for high culture.

Although Susan had dedicated *Against Interpretation* to Richard Howard, she seldom saw him during the years that she and I were friends. She seemed to have no old friends. Like all famous people she constantly attracted new people, and she didn't have to cultivate old friendships, resolve disputes, soothe ruffled feathers. She could just move on.

She was a terrible snob. Once I had her to dinner with a beautiful and charming young couple who each eventually went on to write successful novels but who were unknown at the time. Susan said in an embarrassingly loud stage whisper, "Why did you invite them?" I was so vexed that I lied and said, "They're terribly rich." Susan nodded sagely, as if that answered all her doubts. In fact, they weren't rich at all, but later split up and each of them married extremely "well." Oddly enough, when I invited Susan to dinner in Paris in 1981 with Michel Foucault, he whispered, when she left the room for a moment, "Why did you invite her?" I didn't realize that he didn't like to socialize with women, though he was generous and amicable with his female colleagues at work. Foucault and Arlette Farge, for instance, were great friends and did an anthology together of eighteenth-century letters from the Bastille.

Susan was especially close to Elizabeth Hardwick and Barbara Epstein, both from the *New York Review of Books*, and to Peter Hujar, the photographer. She wrote an introduction to a book of his pictures just as later she prefaced a collection of Mapplethorpe's photographs. Old friends were around but they didn't divert her, they didn't promise renewal. Susan was above all a connoisseur, a collector, a sampler. Her son, David, served to bring many new trends and bits of trivia to her attention. Later, after I stopped knowing them, he became an important political critic and thinker, but when we were friends, he had a dandified distaste for politics. In 1981 he wrote a book with Susan's friend Sharon Delano about Texas boots, whereas fifteen years later he'd be writing books on Bosnia.

Sometimes Susan would fight with David. In any event they would go through periods of not speaking to each other. Exactly what was going on between them wasn't spelled out. Here again they seemed a bit like royalty—a dispute was registered throughout the court without anyone knowing the precise terms of estrangement.

Susan was also like a queen in the sense that she had a full life, largely ceremonious. She gave lots of talks and traveled far and wide. Suddenly she'd be directing a Pirandello play in Italy starring her ex-girlfriend Adriana Asti (who'd appeared in Pasolini's *Accattone*, Visconti's *Rocco and His Brothers*, and *Before the Revolution*, by Bertolucci, who'd been Asti's husband). Then she and James Merrill and I along with D. M. Thomas, the author of *The White Hotel*, would be giving a colloquium titled "Tradition" for a university in Virginia.

In February 1981 Susan stunned her world of New York liberals and radicals by saying at Town Hall, during a rally for Solidarity in Poland, that American intellectuals had for decades ignored the horrors of communism in order to take a firm stand against red-baiters in Congress and elsewhere. She added that anyone who'd been reading a conservative magazine for the general public such as *Reader's Digest* was more likely to be better informed about the true nature of communism than if they'd been reading the *Nation* or the *New Statesman*, which consistently hid the truth. In a resounding peroration she declared, "I repeat: not only is Fascism (and overt military rule) the probable destiny of all Communist societies—especially when their populations are moved to revolt—

but Communism is in itself a variant, the most successful variant, of Fascism. Fascism with a human face."

I didn't attend the event but Susan had told me ahead of time what she intended to do, and that it would create quite a fuss, as indeed it did. She was howled off the stage, and for months afterward left-wing thinkers of every stripe relentlessly attacked her. She was giving comfort to the newly elected Reagan. Much to Susan's dismay she was embraced by the Right and asked to speak at their dinners, which of course she refused to do. She was accused of giving comfort to the pope, who was militating against communism everywhere but especially in Poland. Of course these very left-wing intellectuals were themselves of two minds since they'd gathered at Town Hall in support of Solidarity, which was struggling to end communism in Poland.

I admired Susan's bravery. In Europe, where the Left had genuine power still and had had to live out its contradictions, virtually no one remained pro-Soviet. Only in America, where the counterculture had marked a whole generation and where the protest against the Vietnam War had turned so many people against the U.S. government, would she have provoked such know-nothing hatred. She was giving aid and comfort to the enemy, her critics said. She had betrayed the cause—whatever that was at this late date. In fact, Susan was speaking to an isolationist and dated and extremely naïve Left.

Because of her close connections to France, Susan had evolved politically more swiftly and surely than her compatriots in her understanding of the horrors of communism—not just the accidents of history connected to a particular tyrant or a particular national tradition, but also the systemic nightmare of communism wherever it appeared around the world. Inevitably it led to a suppression of human rights, an abrogation of justice, penury for most citizens, a terrifying tyranny, the triumph of military might, not to mention the destruction of the environment. (I remember wandering in the Swiss mountains and seeing all the trees that had been turned brown from the pollution blowing down from Eastern European factories.)

Susan was brave. Just as she had spoken out against the New Age nonsense that had accumulated around cancer treatment, a bad case of Blame the Victim, just as she had—-with her rabbinical/dandified divided mind—condemned the frivolous and morally opaque world of photography, in the same way she was now taking on communism. Nothing she said was startling to the initiated, and I was shocked only that such obvious arguments would be considered so provocative. Her genius was in saying the obvious in a strong and dramatic manner.

Once she read something I'd written where I'd carefully ascribed my thoughts to the sources that had inspired me. She said, "Cross all that out. Claim it for yourself. No one will ever notice who said it originally. It weakens your argument to be so scrupulous." Perhaps she was right, but this kind of recklessness got her into trouble later, when she was caught for plagiarizing, word for word, in a few passages of her novel *In America*. She was always encouraging me to publish papers I'd present at the institute—but I knew they weren't original or thought out enough. And I was sure she wouldn't have made public such half-baked thoughts.

Susan and Richard Howard both came down on me hard in September 1982 when I wrote a prominent review in the *New York Times Book Review* of Roland Barthes's book about Japan, *Empire of Signs*, and *A Barthes Reader* (which Susan had edited and introduced). Richard was mad because I'd referred only parenthetically to him as Barthes's "expert translator." Deeply aggrieved, over the phone he said to me, "Everyone goes on and on about Barthes's beautiful, original style, but I'm the one who invented that style for English-language readers and I never get any credit, not even from you, my dear! When people praise Barthes's style, they're really praising mine."

Susan was even angrier because I had not quoted from her essay sufficiently or praised it enough, though I'd tried to do both of those things, only not "enough." Instead I'd quoted Gérard Genette, whose take on Barthes she found "dated" and "irrelevant." I had been so dutiful in getting in laudatory mentions of my two friends (without seeming toadying, I hoped) that I was surprised by their rancor against me. Suddenly I realized how important the *New York Times Book Review* was to both of them, how much each of them treasured every "mention" that might heighten their fame—and how correspondingly beleaguered and undervalued they must have felt, they who seemed to me at the pinnacle of literary celebrity.

What their attacks on the phone revealed was the extent to which they assumed I was their puppet in the Bunraku theater of their careers. They were supposed to do all the talking, as in Bunraku, while I was busy gesticulating and bowing and striking their enemies with a sword.

I attended a few sessions of a class Susan taught at the New School on Nietzsche. She did no preparation, didn't speak from notes, and seemed incapable of serious or trenchant or original reflection. I suppose she felt a certain contempt for the class, which was full of "nobodies" whose opinion didn't count. I had no doubt that if she wrote an essay on Nietzsche it would be the best imaginable. She once said to me, "Have you ever wondered why my essays are so much more intelligent than I am? That's because I rewrite them five times and each time I ratchet them up a bit higher. I surpass my own limitations."

I appreciated her frankness in discussing in a simple way her limitations and amazing strengths. I also admired her acuity in knowing what constituted an improvement.

I once attended a lecture she gave in Paris. I was amazed by how fluent she was in French. She explained to me that she had never studied or practiced French, that she listened to it for years, then suddenly, one day, she opened her mouth and could speak it. Whether true or not—and she was gifted enough in all sorts of ways for it to be a true story—this fable—for to me that's what it seems like—represents the world according to Susan.

During that lecture I was seated next to a friend of Susan's, with whom I started chatting. She had a similar tale of language learning. She was Italian but spoke idiomatic American English. When I asked her where she'd learned her English, she said, "In Katherine Dunham's attic in East St. Louis." It seemed she'd fallen in love with the great African-American dancer during a performance in Naples. She was just a teen but was completely smitten and followed the Dunham company to Rome. Every night she stood outside the stage door until finally Dunham took pity on her. The girl traveled with them throughout Europe and eventually returned with them to East St. Louis, where Dunham had established a dance center for "ghetto artists" and taught at the nearby University of Southern Illinois in Carbondale. During the summer of 1968, blacks began to riot in a resurgence of an uprising that had started the year before. The Italian girl hid in the attic for weeks with Dunham's white husband, the set designer John Pratt. Both of them were in danger, she said, because of the color of their skin. In that confined space she mastered her perfect American.

The woman was jolly and voluble, and although I never saw her again and hadn't caught her name, I was so riveted by her story that I remembered it in great detail. She was one of Susan's lesbian friends.

Susan could be sweet and melancholy. She was often "out of it" in social settings, never getting the joke and needing everything to be spelled out. Her laugh was mirthless and heavy. She lacked spontaneity. *Elle n'était pas bien dans sa peau*, as the French would say. One of her girlfriends in the 1950s talks in a journal of the period about how maddening the young Susan could be, lecturing her on Hieronymus Bosch, manufacturing enthusiasms at the flea market, throwing her big, awkward body at her. Susan could be little-girlish and tender at times, though normally she was brusque, lordly, dissatisfied. Someone who might have been trying too hard would walk out of the room and Susan would wrinkle her nose and shake her head dismissively.

She should have been given the Nobel Prize. That would have made her nicer. She was friendly with lots of Nobelists, including Nadine Gordimer, Seamus Heaney, Derek Wolcott, Czesław Miłosz, all writers I met through her—not to mention her personal favorite to win, the Yugoslavian novelist Danilo Kiš, who wrote *Garden, Ashes*. Danilo should have won the prize and would indeed probably have if he hadn't died rather young from lung cancer. (Susan would die too young as well.) Around all these people Susan was wonderfully natural, and they perceived her as their equal, even their superior.

She had terrible manners. She picked her teeth after dinner. She yawned and looked almost haggard with boredom when ordinary people bothered her with their defensive chatter. She wanted to be one of the big boys but I don't think she really liked men. That had never occurred to me at the beginning but slowly I came to realize that she was the counterpart to an old-style gay man who didn't feel comfortable with women. She once said late in life that she only liked young, beautiful men, who were unavailable to older women, but I suspect she was deluding herself. She would have preferred an ugly, gifted, aggressive woman to a pretty boy. She did befriend her Italian translator, who was younger than her son, not handsome but wonderfully winning. He was also, of course, very smart.

AIDS first started to be mentioned in 1981. No one had ever heard of it before then. Larry Kramer, a screenwriter and producer

(*Women in Love*) and novelist (*Faggots*), convened a meeting of gay men in his Fifth Avenue apartment overlooking Washington Square. We were addressed by Dr. Alvin Friedman-Kien, who'd studied several cases of Kaposi's sarcoma, a rare skin cancer that usually appeared in old men of Jewish or Mediterranean origin. Suddenly it was showing up in young gay men, as was an unusual and virulent form of pneumonia. Soon this new cluster of diseases was being called gay-related immunodeficiency or GRID.

Larry invited five or six other men, including me, to discuss forming an offensive against GRID (which a year later was renamed AIDS, since we quickly discovered that gays were only one of several "at-risk" groups). We decided to call our group the Gay Men's Health Crisis. We wanted through the name to make it clear that this was not a lesbian condition, since we'd all had so many tussles with lesbians during the culture wars of the 1970s (though later in the 1980s, as many gay male activists were dying, lesbians came to play a larger leadership role in the movement thanks to their generous feelings of solidarity with gay men). We wanted to emphasize that it was a "crisis" and not a permanent condition, since gays were not eager to be equated with yet another medical diagnosis.

We were naïve, but there was no way to be sophisticated about an unprecedented plague. Nothing like this had ever happened to anyone before.

Dr. Friedman-Kien said to us that he thought we should give up sex altogether until researchers understood a little more about how the disease was transmitted. We looked at him as if he were mad. Just as the Crash of 1929 ended the Roaring Twenties, so the AIDS epidemic of 1981 ended the sexy seventies. Sontag once said to me that in all of human history in only one brief period were people free to have sex when and how they wanted—between 1960, with the introduction of the first birth-control pills, and 1981, with the advent of AIDS. For those two decades all sexually transmitted diseases could be treated with antibiotics, unwanted pregnancies were eliminated through the pill and legalized abortion, and AIDS did not yet exist. Religion seemed to be on the wane and promiscuity appeared to be the wave of the future.

In 1981 all that came to an end. Gays of my generation were especially unprepared to accept the new reality since for us, as I've mentioned before, gay liberation had meant sexual liberation and gay culture still meant sexual access and abundance. Now we were being told to limit the number of our partners, to know our partners' names, or to abstain from sex altogether. Later we were told to suck not fuck, but even so the definition of safe sex was highly unstable, and to this day, almost four decades into AIDS, no one seems certain exactly which practices are safe or unsafe.

Sontag followed the developments carefully and soon began to see that the demonizing of the gay population because of AIDS was not unlike the previous blaming of patients with tuberculosis and syphilis in the nineteenth century or cancer in our own day. She thought that she might add an appendix about AIDS to *Illness as Metaphor*, her 1978 study. Charles Silverstein and I thought that our influential *The Joy of Gay Sex* should be revised to include warnings about AIDS, but with still so little information about it, no one knew how to frame that cautionary advice. The revision did not come out until several years later. My own 1980 *States of Desire: Travels in Gay America* read like a period piece just two years after it was published. The cheerful promiscuity and the civil rights struggles I'd described had all been discarded or eclipsed by the sudden, unexplained appearance of a virus.

I was the first president of GMHC, though I quickly retired in favor of Paul Popham, an attractive macho businessman who was far more competent. Almost from the beginning Larry Kramer was sharply critical of the other members, and by 1987 he had founded a much more militant group called ACT UP. Certainly we all made lots of mistakes. Instead of instantly enlisting the help of the federal government, we organized a disco fund-raiser. We thought small. We thought ghetto. We didn't understand that we were watching the beginnings of an epidemic that would soon enough infect forty million people worldwide. To be fair, no one else had that sort of apocalyptic prescience any more than we did. Nor was Ronald Reagan even willing to mention the disease by name until years later.

Because we were moralistic Americans, we thought promiscuity was the enemy and fidelity the solution. We were incapable of understanding that it was safer to have safe sex with ten men at the baths than to be faithful to one lover—and to be unsafe with him.

New York didn't change right away, but a feeling of dread was now in every embrace, the odor of death in every spurt of come. What had seemed innocent revels now felt like the maneuvers of a death squad. What had felt warm and sticky with life was now the cool syrup of mortality. Those gangs of tall men in leather jackets walking joyfully down the street, their engineer boots ringing sparks off the pavement, now broke up, dissipated into the night, melted into furtive individuals. Whereas in the late 1970s everyone wanted to be bisexual, the height of trendiness, now people were starting to deny they'd ever had experiences with members of the same sex. People who'd been fashionably skinny the year before now were beefing up to prove they weren't besieged by a wasting disease.

I didn't want the party to stop. *A Boy's Own Story* came out, with Susan's blurb, and was a success all over the world and was translated into many languages. Thanks to Susan's recommendation, I'd won the Guggenheim Fellowship and I moved to Paris in the summer of 1983. David Rieff gave me some sartorial advice. He told me that every man in Paris wore a coat and tie and that I'd have to get rid of my dirty, torn jeans. David assumed I was leaving New York because I'd become too famous. "You'd never be allowed to write another book if you stayed here, right?" he asked. My concerns were more sybaritic than professional; in any event he exaggerated my success. I wanted to go on having industrial quantities of sex— and I thought I could go on in Paris. New York was turning into a morgue.

Somebody at the New York Institute for the Humanities found me a furnished apartment on the Île St.-Louis. Soon enough I was taking language classes at the Alliance Française in Paris. I got a part-time job with American *Vogue* writing about cultural life in Paris. The dollar bought ten francs and life in France was cheap. My friend John Purcell had moved with me and was taking courses in interior design at the Paris branch of the Parsons School. I had several French friends—Michel Foucault, Gilles Barbedette (my translator), Ivan Nabokov (my editor), Marie-Claude de Brunhoff (who became my best friend).

I learned French by lying on a couch for two years and looking up every word in a dictionary, sometimes as many as five times before I learned it. After all, I was already forty-three. I shaved off my New York mustache, which no one liked in Paris. I bought lots of suits and coats and ties and overcoats and dress shoes. I met rich and titled ladies through my *Vogue* connections. I had sex after midnight in the little park at the foot of the Île St.-Louis. I started to wear cologne, which would have been anathema in New York. I learned how to kiss a lady's hand. (Only at a private gathering, never on the street, and you don't actually touch the hand with your lips.)

I wrote a novel, *Caracole*, that came out in 1985. Although it read like a fable taking place in Venice in the nineteenth century, it could be read as an attack on the institute and on Susan. In all my years of therapy I never got to the bottom of my impulse toward treachery, especially toward people who'd helped me and befriended me. *A Boy's Own Story* ends with the boy (me) betraying his teacher, a man with whom he had sex. I doubt if Susan and her son would have recognized themselves or even have bothered to read the book if they hadn't been warned by an indiscreet mutual friend.

*Caracole* was an accurate picture of Susan, but only to those who knew her. For outsiders there were no identifying signs—the character of Mathilda wasn't a writer nor Jewish nor an intellectual, nor did she have a white streak in her hair. Yet she shared many of Susan's psychological traits. A typical passage reads:

> Mathilda always opposed the people she happened to be among. She would defend whatever was conservative to progressives and argue for liberty on curiously old-fashioned grounds to conservatives: her manner was to challenge, to question. When other people generated enthusiasm while discussing a subject they thought was bound to suit her, she grew restless, squirmed in her chair, looked about with baleful eyes. She picked at something imaginary in her teeth as though she needed this preliminary breach of good manners in order to warm herself up for the real attack she was about to launch. The speaker became nervous, recognizing she wasn't responding to his words with the customary nods and smiles, that in fact she was grooming herself like a lioness; he broke into a verbal run, hurtling over points, scattering notions, hoping something might appeal to her. At last the lioness focused on him with implacable eyes. "What rubbish," she said. "I can't tolerate another word."

Oddly enough, I felt she would appreciate the aptness of my portrait, that she would *learn* from my implied admonitions. Of course on another level I knew I was trashing her and that she'd be angry. When she really was angry, however, I was surprised.

I suffered over our break and for years afterward I'd dream of a reconciliation. Just as I'd dreamed of meeting her before I actually knew her, now I fantasized about a full pardon and a renewed friendship. Because I was bitter and fearful and felt guilty about my "betrayal" (if that's what it was), I joked and said, "The worst thing about a reconciliation would be that then I'd have to see Susan. Ugh!"

But Susan was so angry that she asked Roger Straus, her editor, to contact all my foreign publishers and request as a courtesy to her and to him that they remove her blurb from the next edition of *A Boy's Own Story* in every language. That move was effective. (Years before, Susan had done something similar to the gay American writer Alfred Chester, who'd used her words of praise without her authorization.) Maybe the break was worse because I'd made no effort to stay in touch with her or David. When my editor, Bill Whitehead, gave me a big masked ball in New York, complete with a brass band, David tried to barge in with a bullwhip; I suppose he wanted to beat me as a "cad." He who'd written about Beau Brummell was given to such posturing. Luckily he was turned away by the bodyguards at the door.

Soon after I arrived in Paris I had lunch with George Plimpton's sister, the poet and painter Sarah Plimpton. I told her I was planning on staying just a year in Paris. She said that she'd told herself the same thing but that now she'd been in France for twenty-two years. "You'll see, it's like lotus land," she said.

Indeed that's what it turned out to be, especially in those prosperous Mitterrand years. I didn't really escape from AIDS. Many of my French friends died, including Foucault and Barbedette, just as back in America Bill Whitehead died and so did Norm Rathweg and so did my dearest friend, David Kalstone. Gradually I became more and more somber and my Parisian life became as dark as my New York life. I sat by many bedsides and held many emaciated hands. I didn't feel the famous survivor guilt only because I was positive myself and expected throughout the eighties to die within a few months.

Sixteen years later I moved back to New York, and one day I ran into Susan Sontag in a restaurant. I'd rushed over to her table without recognizing her because I'd spotted a Parisian friend, the Argentine film director Edgardo Cosarinsky. Suddenly I thought, "Oh, dear, this woman with the short white hair must be Susan Sontag after her chemo. And this other woman must be Annie Leibovitz, her girlfriend." I hurriedly slunk back to my table.

But then, in a flash, there was Susan standing by my table. She said, "Ed, I hope you don't think I was ignoring you because of our silly little feud."

I stood and she embraced me. We agreed that we'd get together, that all was forgiven, that we'd patch it up.

But the next day when I saw her at Cosarinsky's screening, she was distant. I realized too much time had gone by. That our reconciliation hadn't really "taken." That was all right. We'd both become different people.

When I look back at the seventies, I remember the decade primarily as one of professional struggle. I started the decade as an unpublished and no longer young writer, fairly driven but susceptible to terrible, almost suicidal despair. By 1983, when I moved to Paris, I was still hustling for money and I was never sure where next month's rent would be coming from, but I was no longer entirely unrecognized and desperate.

What had made the seventies less harrowing than they might have been was that, at least among artists and intellectuals, a tradition of honorable poverty still remained. Writers and painters and composers did not talk all the time (as they do now) of agents, contracts, and movie deals. New York had not yet formed a tight alliance with Los Angeles; rather, New Yorkers defined themselves in contrast to the West Coast.

Recently I consulted a book about the same period, this one by Mikal Gilmore. It was all about rock music and the downtown scene, about drugs and crime—not unexpected since Mikal writes for *Rolling Stone* and is the brother of Gary Gilmore, the convicted murderer studied in such depth by Norman Mailer in his magisterial *The Executioner's Song*. I realized that though we went to many of the same places and probably knew many people in common, our books were entirely different—opposites, really. Although in mine I acknowledge the poverty and violence of a bankrupt New York in the 1970s, I write little about crime and say nothing about punk or rock music. Later I met Patti Smith and came to respect her, but in the seventies I knew no one in her world except Mapplethorpe.

It was only in the eighties that publishers were swallowed one after another by corporations, that the Barnes & Noble superstores pushed out the small neighborhood bookstores, that the multiplex movie theaters chased away the small art-house cinemas. Every time I would come back to New York from Paris in the eighties and nineties, I was shocked by how sleek it had become, how expensive ice cream boutiques had replaced the corner shoe repair shops, how the city neighborhoods were being gentrified as more and more rich young workers in finance moved into town and drove out the older, poorer ethnic minorities. And the bohemians. New York was no longer a dangerous, run-down ghetto; it had become a chromium, spotlit, palm-festooned singles bar.

AIDS killed off most of my circle. Every time I would come back to New York, more and more of my friends would be dying or dead. Chris Cox found a lover, a young curator at the New Museum, and Chris first buried him, then died himself. Chris had become a successful editor at Bantam Books; the last time I visited him (I was right off the plane from France), his hospital room was full of socially inept straight guys, his authors, guys who wrote murder mysteries and were used to hanging out in a sort of collegiate way. I certainly couldn't ask them to leave and Chris was too polite as a good Southern boy to get rid of them. Maybe he preferred their company to mine, their feeble jokes and half-professional deference rather than my seriousness. I've found that people in the terminal ward never want to talk about death.

During the 1970s I moved away from seeing myself as a socialist and even a fellow traveler to recognizing communism for the sustained international nightmare it was and myself as an anarchist (not the bomb-throwing sort but an extreme individualist). I became suspicious of most collective behavior—and of all politics as invariably a form of lying. If novelists attempt to keep all the nuances in, politicians hammer them into extinction under the blows of a deadening rhetoric. Novelists are precise and create scenes; politicians generalize and wallow in warnings and bromides.

As I was slowly moving away from communism, I also stepped back from the avant-garde. My first two novels to be published had been experimental, but by the time I got to *A Boy's Own Story* I'd acknowledged that life had handed me a brand-new subject and that my job was to present it in the clearest, least wavering light. A straight writer, condemned to show nothing but marriage, divorce, and childbirth, might need a new formal approach or an exotic use of language. But a gay writer, free to record for the first time so many vivid and previously uncharted experiences, needed no tricks. Gay writing in the seventies gave a greater depth to autobiographical fiction than had ever before been achieved, a profundity that other writers, straight writers, could benefit from.

In the 1970s, through my agent Maxine Groffsky, I met Marie-Claude de Brunhoff, who almost instantly started writing me from Paris on her sky-blue stationery with her capricious spelling and almost nonexistent punctuation. She would send me French novels to read hot off the press, though I scarcely knew what to do with them at the time. It would be another decade before I could read French easily. In Paris, Marie-Claude became my best friend—as she would remain well into the new century until her death.

She came to fill the void left by David Kalstone's death. He and she were my ideal friends and shared a certain style—a deep pleasure in the delights of every day, a warmth that was never *mièvre* (French for "mawkish"), a fierce loyalty to the inner circle, never the slightest hint of disapproval toward me or other loved ones, though both of them were terrible snobs. Both of them liked to entertain and to go out, to hear the "latest," to meet the current genius. David was always up on intellectual currents and Marie-Claude on literary ones. She was a professional reader who read three or four books a day; she read French books for Knopf and English-language books for Gallimard. David, who was half-blind, was a keen observer and had a novelist's interest in how stories turned out. David was divinely silly—a dimension that Marie-Claude lacked and deeply regretted (she often referred to the much envied "English wit," a phenomenon that exists vividly in the French imagination if not in French manners).

In my twenties I courted people, much as I'd learned to do in high school; only in my thirties and forties was the goal not to make friends but to enjoy them. In the 1970s gay New Yorkers had decided to separate out friendship, love, and sex. The friend, the lover, and the fuck buddy were three different people, not the same one, as they would become in the eighties. This division of labor in the seventies gave the starring role to friendship. We assumed that love affairs would be stormy and temporary and cause more pain than pleasure. We seldom knew or remembered the names of our sex partners; indeed, we were bewildered in the early days of AIDS by the surprising (and pointless) injunction "Know the names of your partners." No, our friends were the ones we cherished and pursued and cultivated. We could say strategic things to lovers and seductive things to tricks, but a friend deserved the truth. With a friend we had to get things right.

At the end of the 1960s I was in despair over my writing. I was going nowhere quick. I had a drawer full of unproduced plays and unpublished novels. By the end of the 1970s I was on my way as a writer. It had taken longer and was less rewarding than I'd anticipated, but like a character in Balzac I'd always been a monomaniac—just one great obsession, to be published. Friends had helped me all along the way. Richard Howard had arranged for my first novel to be published. David Kalstone encouraged me at strategic moments. Marilyn and Stanley would listen over the phone to every word I wrote. Keith McDermott was a constant inspiration through his own unflinching dedication to a bohemian life of art. At times I wrote to amuse my nephew. My editor, Bill Whitehead, became a real friend, though he died young from AIDS. Susan Sontag arranged for me to win awards and gain recognition. The members of my writers' club, the Violet Quill, encouraged one another to explore fearlessly this new gay subject matter.

The Romantic American myth is that the artist works in solitude and that he can create as well on a farm in Vermont as in New York. But I recognized that the artistic climate of a particular city and milieu was crucial to the development of a writer; after he found his way, perhaps he could go off to that barn outside Burlington. I was lucky to live in New York when it was dangerous and edgy and cheap enough to play host to young, penniless artists. That was the era of "coffee shops" as they were defined in New York—cheap restaurants open round the clock where you could eat for less than it would cost to cook at home. That was the era of ripped jeans and dirty T-shirts, when the kind of people who were impressed by material signs of success were not the people you wanted to know.

The seventies saw the last gasp of the old bohemian Greenwich Village, but this time with more of a gay aspect.

I got to know New York better by spending long periods in San Francisco and Venice. In contrast with those more decorous cities I could see how consumed New York was with ambition, how little urbanism or planning of any sort prevailed in New York, how improvised and transient all of New York's arrangements were. All three cities are ports; Venice is many islands, and Manhattan, Long Island, and Staten Island are also islands. Venice, however, is married to the sea, whereas Manhattan turns its back on its rivers and the ocean. Venice and San Francisco glory in their quite different pasts. San Francisco's past is only a hundred years old, whereas Venice's is more than a thousand. New York is a nineteenth-century (and even eighteenth-century) city, but no one notices. Few people are even aware of its history.

I suppose that finally New York is a Broadway theater where one play after another, decade after decade, occupies the stage and the dressing rooms—then clears out. Each play is the biggest possible deal (sets, publicity, opening-night celebrations, stars' names on the marquee), then it vanishes. With every new play the theater itself is just a bit more dilapidated, the walls scarred, the velvet rubbed bald, the gilt tarnished. Because they are plays and not movies, no one remembers them precisely. The actors are forgotten, the plays are just battered scripts showing coffee stains and missing pages. Nothing lasts in New York. The life that is lived there, however, is as intense as it gets.

# Acknowledgments

I would like to thank Nick Trautwein for his expert editing—he's a man with a keen eye and a receptive ear, not to mention impeccable judgment. Michael Fishwick has enthusiastically been behind this book from the beginning and has cheered me along to the finish line. He has proven to be a friend to me and my writing.

Michael Carroll, my partner, did a careful word edit of *City Boy* before I dared to show it to anyone.

I am grateful to my fellow writer David McConnell for reading the manuscript before anyone else and giving me copious notes. Tom Beller, the wonderful writer and editor of *Open City*, has been an enthusiast from the beginning, as has my friend the architect Sam Roche.

Beatrice von Rezzori welcomed me graciously to her writers' retreat in Tuscany, Santa Maddalena. She is also a warm and fascinating friend.

John Logan at Princeton has helped me innumerable times to track down essays and articles I wanted to consult.

My agent, Amanda Urban, has advised me at every point, for which I am deeply grateful.

# A Note on the Author

A novelist and cultural critic, Edmund White is the author of many books, including the autobiographical novel *A Boy's Own Story*; a previous memoir, *My Lives*; and most recently a biography of the poet Arthur Rimbaud. White lives in New York City and teaches writing at Princeton University.